This is my first Chinese book.

全民法力無邊

序

即使你深信自己是一個奉公守法，循規蹈矩的好市民，也有機會不自覺地進行了民事侵權行為；即使你認為只是自己倒霉買了有問題的產品，或遇上了不幸事件，又無從證明責任誰屬，你也有機會可以追討賠償；即使你是業主，對許多事件或傷亡事故也需要負上責任，但責任級別也會是因人而異。

希望了解自己的權益和責任，閱讀這本書「全民法力無邊」會大有幫助。市民要明白自己可能有權追討賠償，才會嘗試尋求法律意見，所以第一步是需要首先豐富自己的法律常識，對

Publisher: Jeffrey Zeldman
Designer: Jason Santa Maria
Executive Director: Katel LeDû
Managing Editor: Tina Lee
Editor: Tina Lee
Technical Editor: Marc Edwards, Gus Mueller
Copyeditor: Caren Litherland
Proofreader: Katel LeDû
Compositor: Rob Weychert
Ebook Producer: Ron Bilodeau

ISBN: 978-1-937557-51-5

A Book Apart
New York, New York
http://abookapart.com

10 9 8 7 6 5 4 3 2 1

TABLE OF CONTENTS: MAKING SENSE OF COLOR MANAGEMENT

FOREWORD

EARLY IN MY CAREER, I worked as a graphic designer dealing mostly with print. Getting color right wasn't easy, but it was completely under my control as a designer, because I could target the output. I'd go to the print shop, examine the first copies off the press, and if they looked good, I'd feel confident that the whole print run would look the same.

Now with digital designs, we have no control over the output platform. Thousands of different displays are in use, and our work might appear on any or all of them.

Getting colors right? Here are a few scenarios: a graphic image and CSS background color should match exactly, but they don't. Or they do match on some devices, but not on others. Or they don't match on *any* devices, and good luck identifying the cause. It's enough to drive one back to vintage Macs that only display black and white.

When I encounter a color mismatch, I deal with it like so (a tactic I suspect many of you take too): fiddle with various color settings in image editing software and source code until it works out, and hope to remember the magic recipe the next time the problem happens. (There is always a next time.)

Craig did something different. In this book, he takes a step back to truly understand how color management actually works. Better yet, he shares that complex knowledge in a clear, immediate way. He tells us not just what to do, but *why*. Craig effortlessly guides us through the principles and practice of color management; as I read, I kept thinking, *Well, that's actually pretty simple*—a big realization given I'd treated the subject as a dark art for fifteen years.

Color computing has never been easy. Our computers are almost unimaginably more powerful than those from years past, but designers and programmers have never stopped pushing the limits of our hardware. The goal has always been the same: to make what appears on screen look as good as it possibly can. Thanks to Craig, it's now a little easier to achieve.

—John Gruber

INTRODUCTION

STEP INTO THE TELEVISION SECTION of any electronics store, and you'll see how widely colors can vary from screen to screen. You'll see how many colors are generated by the exact same red, green, and blue (RGB) values—each TV gets the same digital broadcast, yet there's a huge range in the displayed images. Color management lets us describe those differences, and correct them.

I dug into the guts of color management when I wrote xScope, my development tool for sampling and measuring colors. Back then, I didn't really understand Photoshop's mechanisms for handling color; I went and set some levers, which worked most of the time. But when xScope's colors appeared one way in Safari and another in Chrome, I didn't know which controls were responsible. I *did* know the problem was with color management.

If you've been in the business awhile, this confusion over color probably sounds familiar, and I began this book as a means to share what I've learned in understanding my color issues. In the coming chapters, I'll run through some experiments to show how color works, why colors shift in different environments, and ways to keep those colors consistent.

As conscientious developers, we want to create things that look good anywhere. Just as responsive design lets layouts adapt to variety, color management lets colors and images adjust to their device and presentation.

With knowledge of color management, you'll gain more confidence as you adjust the settings in your image editor, *and* you'll be able to create products that look better for more people. Everyone wins.

COPING WITH COLORS

YOU JUST GOT A GIG to design a website for an optometrist, Dr. Eyeful. Sweet!

The doctor wants you to use his two favorite colors: red and purple. (Bonus points if you include a "site" and "sight" pun in the tagline.)

You've been developing sites since the days of web-safe color palettes. By picking red, green, and blue (RGB) values of (255, 0, 0) and (102, 0, 204), you'll satisfy the doctor's branding requirements while working with tried-and-true colors. Of course, you're careful to use those exact color specifications in both your Photoshop document and CSS styles.

But when you load the page in your browser, you see a weird color shift in the header (FIG 1.1).

Other browsers show a similar color shift, until you look at the page on your tablet—and it's perfect! What the heck?

After a bit of surfing, you find a site that recommends specifying something called sRGB in Photoshop. You don't know *exactly* what that means, but you tweak things and save a new graphic file. It fixes the problem in Safari, but the color is still off in Chrome. No matter what you do, you can't get the CSS and image colors to match.

This inconsistency bugs you. The doctor may have questionable taste in colors, but his eyesight is perfect. He's going to see these shifts and ask what's happening.

Problem is, you really have no clue.

WHAT IS COLOR MANAGEMENT?

At the most basic level, *color management* is a way to specify the range of colors a device can represent.

Many designers and developers, including your author, have found ways to wrangle color without truly understanding the underlying technology. We've leaned on simple standards, choosing three bytes of data for the primary colors of light: red, green, and blue. When we specified R=255, G=0, and B=0, we expected—and could expect—to see red on our displays. We could pretty much ignore anything else about color, whether we were designing for the web or a native app.

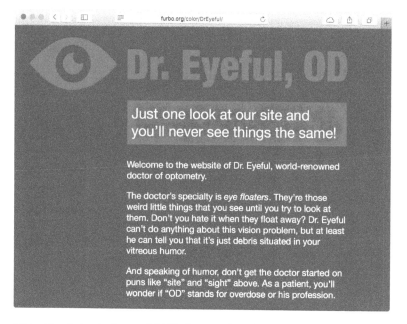

FIG 1.1: The site header is an eyeful. What's worse, the colors are shifting.

This worked for a time, but as you saw with Dr. Eyeful, our basic RGB values don't translate the same way across devices. To find out why, let's take a quick trip through history.

Coping with too many choices

Color management isn't new. Photographers and print designers have dealt with calibrating colors for decades. It all started when people took images captured on film and output them on paper with ink. Sounds straightforward, right? But you had different kinds of film stock, along with paper weight and finish. The variety of inks was astounding; the huge collection of Pantone colors, for instance, got its start in the 1960s as colored liquids.

Such technological diversity made it hard to keep imagery consistent as it made its way from the camera lens to the printed page. Photographers, designers, and printers knew they couldn't rely solely on an RGB or a CMYK color space to get consistent results. Their workflow included another component, which profiled the color capabilities of their equipment—and adjusted colors accordingly. (This component was a complex mathematical model based on the human eye: a color profile. We'll get to this soon.)

We face the same scenario now, the same variety in technology. The digital sensor on a cheap cell phone camera can't capture as many colors as a high-end, pricey DSLR. Similarly, an LCD display from only a few years ago looks absolutely horrible when compared to the Retina display on an iMac. OLED technology on wristwatches is a new animal entirely.

If you want your reds, greens, and blues to look right across browsers or apps, you need to pay attention to how you specify colors in your tools. While you often won't have much choice about how color is processed by a platform, you will get unpredictable results if you ignore the requirements of whatever environment you're working in—which is what happened with Dr. Eyeful's website.

Understanding color management yields dividends. You'll ensure branding and other color elements in your interface look the best they can. And think how many elements are involved in a website—all the interface graphics, hero images, and other bits—wouldn't it be great if you could reuse those assets, without modification, in a mobile app?

You can, once you know how your workflow manages color and your target platforms present the images. As a first step, let's examine how colors got their start on our computers.

Old-fashioned color

In the late 1970s, color began to appear on computer displays. These early machines had little memory—sometimes as small as 4,096 characters total. Processors were also limited, and accessed memory eight bits at a time, giving programmers a minimum value of 0 and a maximum value of 255.

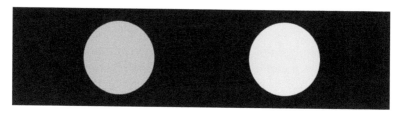

FIG 1.2: Two green bulbs produce different colors.

Although machines have become much more powerful, specifying color with eight bits has stayed with us: three RGB channels together produce 16,777,216 unique colors, a range that closely matches what our eyes can see. Some apps use 16-bit color, but this extended range mostly benefits editing images.

We'll use 8-bit values throughout this book; to get more accurate color, we'll add another type of data.

Green light bulbs

Imagine we have two green light bulbs, made by two manufacturers.

When the bulbs are fully lit, even if you're affected by certain forms of color blindness, you can tell the colors differ slightly (**FIG 1.2**). This is unsurprising, since the manufacturers used separate processes and materials.

But your computer isn't so smart. All it knows is that G=0 means the bulb is off, G=127 is at half brightness, and G=255 is fully on.

Now imagine two displays made with these light bulbs. I have the one on the left, and you have the one on the right. When I specify G=255, I see the color on the left. But when I send you a file with that G=255, you see the color on the right.

Whoops. It might seem minor, but it wouldn't be to a client like Starbucks, Heineken, or John Deere, which takes green very seriously. You could lose hours perfecting the green on your screen and have the CEO see something else. That's just the tip of the iceberg: every customer who visits your client's site can have a completely different light bulb.

As photographers and print designers learned, we can't solely rely on the values for primary colors. We also need information, or a *color profile*, from the manufacturer that explains how they display the color green.

COLOR PROFILES

Anything that can capture or display an image—your camera, your monitor, etc.—has a set of values that describes the range of colors available for use. This set of data is the color profile, and it comes in a format defined by the International Color Consortium (ICC).

Creating a profile involves *a lot* of science. If you're a manufacturer of green light bulbs, you'll take an expensive piece of equipment, a color spectrophotometer, to measure the amount of visible light produced at different color wavelengths. You then use that data to generate a mathematical model—the profile, which is specific to the device: my iMac display profile would look terrible on your MacBook.

Some manufacturers choose to use a standard profile for their bulbs. Two of the most popular are *Adobe RGB* and *standard RGB* (sRGB):

- Adobe introduced its profile in 1998 to represent CMYK printer colors on an RGB display. It's a favorite among photographers, because its wide range of colors produces better images in post-processing.
- Made around the same time, sRGB mimics typical viewing conditions in a home or office, with a smaller range of colors (making it cheaper and easier to produce). Its ubiquity makes it the color space for defining web standards.

Cameras often support Adobe RGB (or ProPhoto, the color space developed by Kodak), while many displays (like that bargain LCD at the electronics store) conform to sRGB.

Let's see what these two standard profiles look like (**FIG 1.3**).

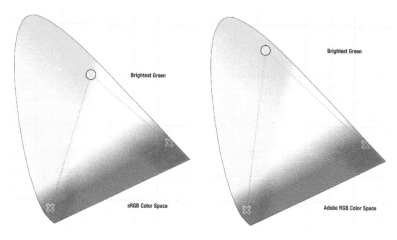

FIG 1.3: The color ranges of two profiles: sRGB (left) and Adobe RGB (right).

The curved shape with a flat side represents all the colors the human eye can see—it never changes. Each triangle represents a color profile; the *X*-corners are fully saturated red, green, and blue.

The black circle marks the brightest green the profile can produce. It's like our green light bulbs: sRGB's green has a yellow tint, while Adobe's is closer to the ideal color our eyes see. (As you'll find out in a moment, the weird shape springs from our physiology!)

The size, or *gamut*, of each triangle reflects the range of possible colors. The larger triangle, Adobe RGB, has a *wider gamut* (which is why the profile is so popular among photographers).

Keen observers will note black isn't present. That's because we cheated a bit and showed only two dimensions. When we add color saturation, the curved shape lies on its side and a fully saturated white appears as a peak, with black as a base (**FIG 1.4**).

That pointy shape is everything our computers need to take the raw numeric values in our files and display them so we all see a similar color.

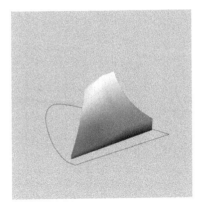

FIG 1.4: sRGB color profile with saturation as a third dimension.

A profile to fit your eye

There's no getting around it: color management is complex. At its core, after all, is a numerical model for the human eye.

It doesn't help that behind this heavy-duty science is a slew of acronyms. Let me take a minute to break down a few names and concepts that led to my first "aha!" moment in learning about color management. First up, the Commission Internationale de l'Eclairage, the global authority on light and color. If you don't speak French, that's International Commission on Illumination—but everyone refers to this group as CIE.

Our retinas contain three types of cone cells that detect light. Each type senses a different part of the color spectrum: blues at short wavelengths, greens in the middle, and reds at longer wavelengths. The curved boundary in the shapes you saw is a plot of chromatic wavelengths visible to our eyes.

Our brains take stimuli from these cells and combine them to give us color perception (and the official term, *tristimulus*.) The scientists at CIE codified this biology into a mathematical model called *CIEXYZ* in 1931.

Over the next 45 years, understanding of the human eye improved. Researchers found that somewhere between the optic nerve and the brain, stimuli are categorized according to degrees of lightness, red/green, and blue/yellow. This led to a second key color model, *CIELAB*.

Don't let the old age of CIELAB and CIEXYZ trick you: both are still the standards to put your eye's behavior into numbers our computers can process:

- Since it takes into account how our brains perceive color, a LAB color space is better at reproducing tones and relative color values. LAB is ideal for color created with inks.
- The XYZ color space is based on the eye's response to stimulation across the visible light spectrum. This works well for specifying an exact color, even though it ignores that our vision isn't completely uniform. XYZ is ideal for devices that emit light, like a computer display.

The eye's color profile makes everything work

Phew: you've dipped your toe into the complicated waters of color science! The important thing to know is both CIE color spaces are device-independent: their only dependence is on our bodies (which thankfully don't change as fast as technology).

The eye's freedom from hardware is crucial to moving colors between profiles.

Converting directly between devices would be painful: every device would need to know about every other device in the world. Your display would need to know about all kinds of cameras before it could work with photos. Same with your printer and editing software. Think about how many models of cameras, printers, and displays exist, and you'll see this situation would soon become unwieldy.

Instead, we base conversion on the eye, so each device only needs to specify how to transform color to and from the eye's color space (FIG 1.5). The raw numeric color values differ depending on the document or device, but they all look the same. Because of their central role, the CIE models are referred to as *profile connection spaces*.

You'll probably never use CIEXYZ or CIELAB directly, but every time a pixel moves from one place to another, one of the eye's color spaces will play a part in making sure that pixel looks its best.

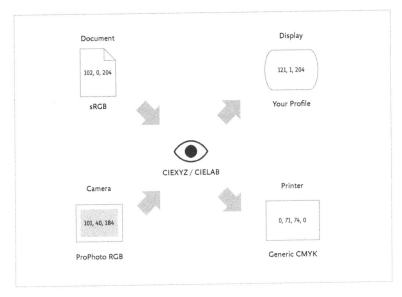

FIG 1.5: Using color profiles, the eye perceives the same color for different raw values.

Profiles are everywhere

Color profiles are relatively small pieces of data, which makes them easy to embed in image files and design documents. A file with this profile information can be handled predictably by any editor or presentation mechanism (including things as diverse as printers and web browsers).

File formats that can embed profiles include popular ones for web images (JPEG, PNG, SVG) and documents (PSD, PDF). Digital negatives (DNG) allow profiles too, and color profiles may even someday become part of your CSS.

The color profile information can also be stored in a separate file. These files typically accompany hardware peripherals like displays, printers, and cameras, where it'd be impractical to embed the data.

Editors and other products that manipulate design use a color profile that describes the range of colors available while you're creating artwork. This profile is often referred to as the *working space.* Some apps, like Photoshop, let you choose the working space. Other apps use a predefined color space, usually a standard one like sRGB.

If you're curious, you can explore all the color profiles installed on your Mac using the ColorSync Utility in the Applications > Utilities folder. Under Profiles, you'll see a long list, sourced from Apple, Adobe, the display manufacturer, and many others. When you select a profile, its graphic representation appears, along with other details.

THE DISPLAYS THEY ARE A-CHANGIN'

While the eye stays steady, let's now peek at the device side. Displays have reached the point where human eyes can't determine individual pixels—increasing the resolution has no benefit. The next frontier lies in color depth, making our images more vibrant. And we're already there, in two ways: pixels that have a wider range of values, and color spaces that boast larger gamuts.

As an example, iMac computers from 2015 onward support ten bits of color per pixel. These new screens can display a gradient with thousands of unique values, versus regular displays with only a couple hundred values. Where you once saw banding and other artifacts, you'll now see smooth transitions between colors.

Along with these superpixels, these displays also show a much wider range of colors (**FIG 1.6**). Instead of the standard sRGB profile from the computer industry, Apple is employing a new profile from the motion picture world: *DCI P3*.

DCI stands for Digital Cinema Initiatives, a collective body of six major film studios. In 2007, DCI created a set of specs to standardize digital cinema systems and ensure uniform quality in theaters. Manufacturers like Apple are now adapting the DCI standard for desktop computers and mobile devices—Apple's Display P3 color space uses the same wide gamut as your local movie theater, but adjusts for the brighter viewing conditions in your home or office.

New profiles mean changes to the way information is displayed; Apple is adding new features to its web browser and

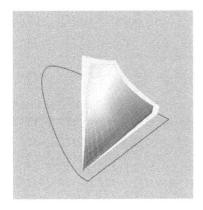

FIG 1.6: The white area depicts the additional colors DCI P3 can display over sRGB.

providing support for color profiles on mobile devices. Other manufacturers will follow suit in the coming years—and as you'll see in later chapters, you'll have more P3 in your life and less sRGB.

When sRGB isn't the only game in town, we may wind up with more goofs like the one on Dr. Eyeful's site. Luckily, with your grasp of color management, you'll be in a solid position to avoid these problems!

UGLY FOR A REASON

Throughout this book, I'll specify colors in the 0-255 range, the 8-bit convention that conveniently fits all tools and documents. While the colors aren't pretty (they might even sear your retinas after prolonged exposure), I've chosen them on purpose:

- Red (255, 0, 0) and purple (102, 0, 204) will push the color gamut of most displays; colors are more likely to shift when they're at the monitor's physical limits. (They're also responsible for a nice paycheck from Dr. Eyeful.)
- The values of brown (123, 45, 67) and blue (12, 34, 56) are consecutive sequences. It'll be easy to spot any color shifts: just look for out-of-place digits.

To that end, you'll need a tool to measure the color values in various color spaces. On macOS, the Digital Color Meter is in the Applications > Utilities folder. Since you'll use it to measure colors in the 0-255 range, make sure to select View > Display Values > as Decimal.

Alternatively, you can use xScope to color-check; the most recent version supports color spaces under the Loupe > Working Color Space menu.

(Those of you working on Windows will have a tougher time with some examples: only Windows 10 supports color management, and it isn't enabled by default. Photoshop for Windows handles color the same as the Mac version, but popular screen-sampling tools like Eyedropper, Pixie, and ColorPix don't support color spaces.)

In some of the screenshots, you'll see "huey D65." That's my monitor, which was calibrated with Pantone's Huey colorimeter. A colorimeter measures the light produced by a display and automatically creates a color profile—this profile is more accurate than the generic one that comes with your display, since it can be tuned to ambient lighting.

You can also manually calibrate your screen on a Mac by using the Color tab of the Display panel in System Preferences. After selecting "Calibrate...," you'll be guided through a process that will likely improve the images on your monitor.

ONWARD

We've zipped through an overview of the past, present, and future of color management, alongside common terms. With this background and vocabulary, we're ready for our first stop: Photoshop.

After learning how an image editor handles color, we'll move onto the web and survey its evolving color needs. We'll end with apps, for both mobile and desktop, and see how wider color gamuts can make your work shine.

PHOTOSHOP

ADOBE HAS BEEN CONCERNED with processing color for a long time—remember when I talked about scanning film and printing with inks? Photoshop (and other desktop publishing apps) needed to manage color as soon as that first pixel came off the scanner on its way to the printer; color management has been part of the editor since version 5.0 for Mac and Windows in 1998.

In this chapter, we'll go deep into the specifics of Photoshop; we'll then take those techniques and close out the chapter with a method you can apply to any other tool.

I've found some people still believe the way to get consistent display of color across development tools is to turn off Photoshop's color management and work directly with the monitor's RGB color profile. While that was once true, the way our apps handle color has changed—for the better. But these improvements aren't universal across platforms, which spells complications.

Apple has recently adopted color management in its desktop apps. Other apps, like web browsers that need to work on platforms outside macOS, don't manage color for all content.

You end up with a situation in which, at this writing, the most recent versions of Safari and Preview support color profiles while Chrome and Firefox don't. As a result, those four apps *can't* display a single color value the same way. Compounding the problem is that *many mobile devices don't manage color*, but many *desktop tools do*.

Given these color disparities, our friend Photoshop needs some attention. Don't worry; you'll create UI graphics as you've always done. But you'll need to set the right levers prior to using "Save for Web" or the new "Export As."

Before we get cranking: this chapter shows screenshots from Photoshop CS6 and CC 2015. Even though Adobe introduced color management many years ago, the terminology and features have not changed much. Some of the controls may look different in your version, but they'll work the same.

WORKING SPACE

Let's open a sample PSD file, **ColorTest.psd.zip**. You can experiment with it as we go through our color settings. (If you get
a "Missing Profile" dialog, select "Leave as is" and press OK.)

To start, you'll want to know which color profile Photoshop
is using. The easiest way to find out is through the menu in
the lower-left corner of the main window (marked with a right
arrow). Select Document Profile (**FIG 2.1**).

You should see "Untagged RGB," which means the ColorTest.
psd file was saved without an embedded profile. Photoshop
automatically displays files without profiles using Photoshop's
working color space. Let's review that setting now.

Hello, Color Settings

Under the Edit menu, open Color Settings... (⇧⌘K). Under
Working Spaces, check RGB. For this exercise, make sure it's
set as "sRGB IEC61966-2.1" (**FIG 2.2**).

(From here on, I'll refer to this color space as *sRGB*. That long
stretch of numbers references the International Electrotechni-
cal Commission 1999 standard, which specifies this profile's
CIEXYZ values.)

Since we're focusing on how to manage color on computer
displays, we can safely ignore CMYK and the other choices.
We'll visit Color Management Policies later on.

Let's return to the document. As you hover over each color,
the Info palette shows the RGB value that's stored in the file:
(255, 0, 0), (102, 0, 204), (123, 45, 67), or (12, 34,
56). Pretty straightforward, right? We'll call those values the
"raw" colors. Next, open your computer's Digital Color Meter
and make sure it's set to "Display native values" (which, as the
name suggests, shows the actual colors displayed on screen).
If you're using xScope, select Loupe › Working Color Space ›
Display RGB.

Hover over the colors again—you'll see the numbers don't
line up with Photoshop's values (**FIG 2.3**). On my display, Digital Color Meter reports the colors as (255, 1, 15), (121, 1,
204), (128, 41, 69), and (21, 38, 59). The values on your

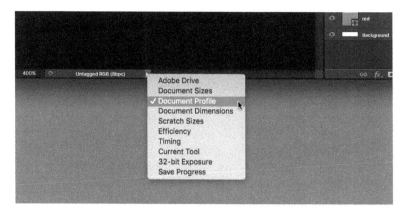

FIG 2.1: Configuring Photoshop to show the current document's color profile.

FIG 2.2: Setting the working space to sRGB.

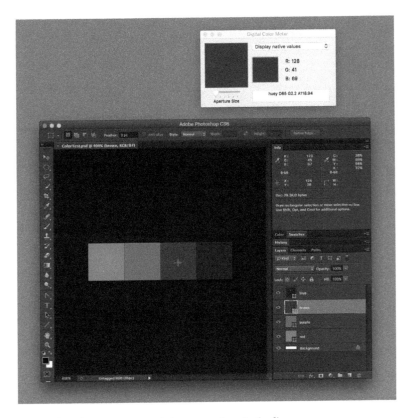

FIG 2.3: The colors on screen aren't the same as those in the file.

display will differ from mine. Why are these reported values so different from the raw ones? And why don't they match across displays?

Remember, we started with RGB values, but our file didn't have a color profile. When that happens, Photoshop translates colors into your specified working space before sending them to your display; in this case, it translated the raw color into sRGB.

To see Photoshop's sRGB colors, set the Digital Color Meter or xScope to "Display in sRGB." Think of this option as "app is set to sRGB"—you're giving the tool a hint about an image

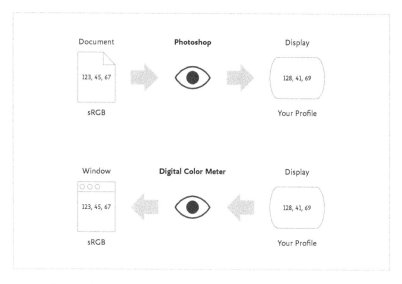

FIG 2.4: The Digital Color Meter reverses the display process in Photoshop.

editor's working space, as the tool has no way to ask Photoshop (or any other app) how it's displaying pixels.

With this hint, the Digital Color Meter converts first your display's native values into a device-independent number (based on the color profile for the eye), and then into sRGB. The process is called an *inverse transformation,* because it's the exact opposite of what Photoshop is doing—converting color from sRGB to the eye to the display (**FIG 2.4**).

When Photoshop and the color sampler both use the same color profiles for your display, eye, and file, the numeric values begin to agree (**FIG 2.5**).

Some reported values will still be slightly off, because you lose a bit of information in the color conversion to and from sRGB for display. It's like clipping in an audio signal: when an amplifier tries to push a sound to the point where the system can't handle it, no amount of attenuation can recover the lost signal. In color management, the biggest limiting factor is the gamut of the color space. sRGB represents a small range; in our

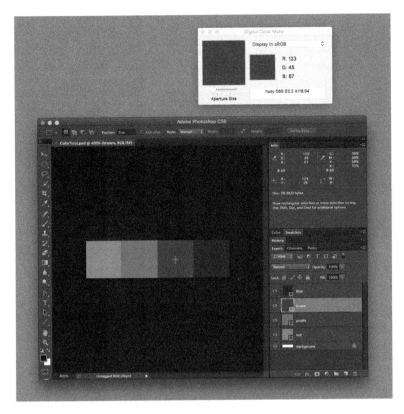

FIG 2.5: Photoshop and Digital Color Meter now match, because they're both using sRGB.

example, the red and purple colors shift the most—these highly saturated colors push the boundaries.

Your working space options

We set Photoshop's color profile to sRGB, but let's see how other profiles look. Go to Edit > *Color Settings...* and check the Preview box. (Have you memorized ⇧⌘K yet? You will have by the end of this book!)

The RGB working space lists:

- Monitor RGB
- Adobe RGB (1998)
- Apple RGB
- ColorMatch RGB
- ProPhoto RGB
- sRGB IEC61966-2.1

And many more. Go ahead and pick a few, to see how the colors change with each setting. You can also adjust the Digital Color Meter to match the raw values, as you did with sRGB.

Now choose Monitor RGB. If you test the native color values with Digital Color Meter, they're the same as the raw values from the file. You might think, *Perfect match!*

Nope.

Problems with Monitor RGB

The key to this not-so-perfect match lies in the name: the *monitor*.

Your monitor differs from mine. Your monitor might differ from someone else's on your team. Your monitor probably differs from your client's.

And these differences can cause color problems that are hard to figure out.

For example, say you use *Monitor RGB* while editing screenshots; you won't get any color shifts since the images are tagged with your display's color profile when they're captured. But this only works as long as you edit the files on *the same monitor*. When someone sends you a new file, it's unlikely your display is exactly like theirs, and you'll wind up with color shifts.

Even Photoshop has trouble with multiple monitors. If you're lucky enough to have more than one display, you might be surprised to learn Monitor RGB only applies to a single display—the primary one. If you're working on a document on a secondary display, a profile mismatch results, which shifts colors (and trying to pinpoint why could waste hours of your day).

Because of Monitor RGB's inherent unpredictability, I strongly recommend choosing sRGB as your working space. Browsers are starting to use it as a default, and sRGB is often the only color space supported by mobile platforms. As you'll see in a bit, choosing sRGB also minimizes your chance of screwing things up when saving files.

EMBEDDED PROFILES

We've looked at how Photoshop displays a file without an embedded profile. But you'll probably come across PSD files with profiles—not every designer or developer uses the same Photoshop color settings as you do. (Weird, right?)

When you open a document with an embedded profile, Photoshop detects the profile, and handles it based on your Color Management Policies under Color Settings. Let's explore those settings.

Default Color Settings

By default, Photoshop sets the RGB working space as sRGB and the color management policy as Preserve Embedded Profiles. The various "Ask When" options are also off. Hit ⇧⌘K and take a moment to make sure your Color Settings match the defaults (FIG 2.6).

Heads up: you might want to take a screenshot of your current settings because we're going to make a lot of changes. Since many of the dialogs that follow have a "Don't show again" option, use Reset All Warning Dialogs in Preferences > General... to make them reappear.

Last, check that you still have Document Profile selected in the lower-left corner of the Photoshop window, as we'll refer to it often.

Preserving embedded profiles

Let's open a sample file with an embedded sRGB color profile, ColorTest-sRGB.psd. Since we enabled Preserve Embedded Profiles, the document retains its profile: you'll see sRGB in the lower-left corner of the main window. That your working space is also set to sRGB isn't a factor here—a saved profile will override Photoshop's default.

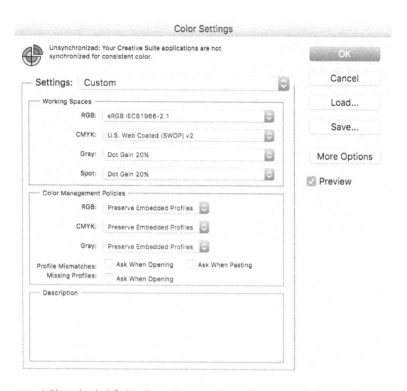

FIG 2.6: Photoshop's default color settings use sRGB and preserve embedded profiles.

To verify this, download another PSD, **ColorTest-Generic-RGB.psd.** Once you open the file, Photoshop will alert you to a profile mismatch; select "use the embedded profile." You'll see Generic RGB Profile in the lower left—compare how Photoshop renders its pixels to the initial sRGB-embedded file: the generic profile is much lighter than its sRGB counterpart.

(The change in brightness happens because the generic profile, from older versions of macOS, uses a different gamma value from sRGB's. It's also the reason many designers complained about the screen being "too dark" when the Mac switched in 2009.)

Embedding a color profile isn't limited to PSD files: here's a PNG, **ColorTest-MonitorRGB.png,** with my monitor profile attached. If you open it in Photoshop, you'll see the document profile in its usual place. Or, if you want to skip Photoshop, you can check profiles with the Preview app: go to the Inspector panel (⌘I) and look at the ColorSync profile field. This trick also works with JPEG and PSD files. Some files—most notably GIF—don't allow embedded color profiles as part of their file format specifications.

Take a look at the three files. All three started with the same raw color values—the red is still (255, 0, 0), which you can verify using Photoshop's Info palette—but each file's embedded profile directs how the pixels are transformed on their way to the screen.

Next, let's visit some other options for Color Management Policies. Time for ⇧⌘K.

Discarding embedded profiles

The color management policy has an Off option. You've likely used this before if you've set Monitor RGB as your working space: Off is the only choice.

The problem with that setting is it throws away important information.

For instance, take ColorTest-GenericRGB.psd. When you open the file and the policy is Off, Photoshop may warn you that the color in the document doesn't match your current working space (FIG 2.7).

As soon as you select OK, Photoshop loses track of the fact that I created the file with a Generic RGB color space. Worse, you may not even realize it—the warning box has an option for "Don't show again," and if you've checked it in the past, you're discarding data by default.

Either way, you end up with "Untagged RGB" as the document profile in the main window, and Photoshop will display the raw color values in the file as sRGB, your current working space.

You've created a situation where our green lights don't agree. My green light used Generic RGB; your green light uses sRGB. On top of that, you threw away the box my green light came in, so you have no way to get back to the color I was looking at.

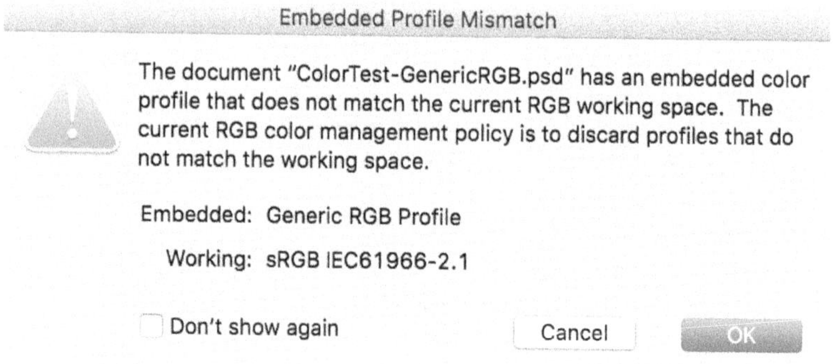

Embedded Profile Mismatch

The document "ColorTest-GenericRGB.psd" has an embedded color profile that does not match the current RGB working space. The current RGB color management policy is to discard profiles that do not match the working space.

Embedded: Generic RGB Profile

Working: sRGB IEC61966-2.1

☐ Don't show again   Cancel   OK

FIG 2.7: Warning: you're about to lose vital information in your image.

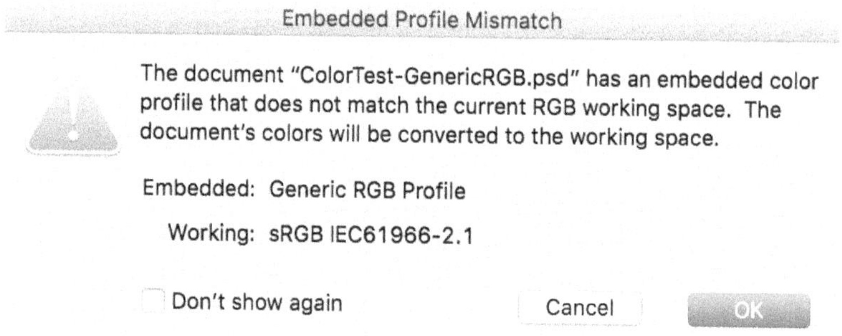

Embedded Profile Mismatch

The document "ColorTest-GenericRGB.psd" has an embedded color profile that does not match the current RGB working space. The document's colors will be converted to the working space.

Embedded: Generic RGB Profile

Working: sRGB IEC61966-2.1

☐ Don't show again   Cancel   OK

FIG 2.8: Photoshop is on the verge of changing every color in your file.

To sum up: don't discard profiles by using Off.

But since your working space is set to sRGB, would it make sense to convert the image? (Trick question!)

Convert to Working RGB

Let's tackle the last RGB policy option in our trusty Color Settings... Select Convert to Working RGB. Now open ColorTest-GenericRGB.psd, and you might see another profile-mismatch message (**FIG 2.8**).

When you click OK, Photoshop converts the file's raw color values from Generic RGB Profile to sRGB. Sounds good!

Until you realize that all the raw color values in your file just got modified. Your (255, 0, 0) is now (255, 38, 0), (102, 0, 204) is (123, 44, 214), etc. Go ahead and verify this with Photoshop's Info palette.

When you're working with user interface graphics and other assets for development, permanently converting pixels is rarely something you want to do.

Why would Adobe provide such a dangerous feature? Again, it's in the name: *Photo*. You're focused on UI work, but other folks are processing pictures. Unlike you, photographers aren't interested in individual pixel values: they're concerned with how the overall image is perceived. Photoshop's conversion process makes an image with a Generic RGB profile look the same when presented in sRGB—note how the lighter colors remain, even though sRGB has a darker color gamut.

This is exactly what a photographer with a high-end DSLR wants when their picture is in a wider gamut (like Adobe RGB or ProPhoto), and they need a predictable presentation in the web's more limited sRGB. The photo will lose some dynamic range, but perceptually it will still hew closer to the original.

You'll want the same thing—like when you're working on a website hero image that has to match colors in CSS. Converting to an sRGB working space lets you preserve the photo's look and prevent color shifts on different screens.

So wouldn't it be great if you could make a choice for every file you open?

"Ask When"

The engineers at Adobe have you covered.

The Color Management Policies section has three check-boxes that cause Photoshop to ask what to do when it detects a profile problem. You'll get a dialog box with options to: use the embedded profile, convert document colors to your working space, or discard the embedded profile (FIG 2.9).

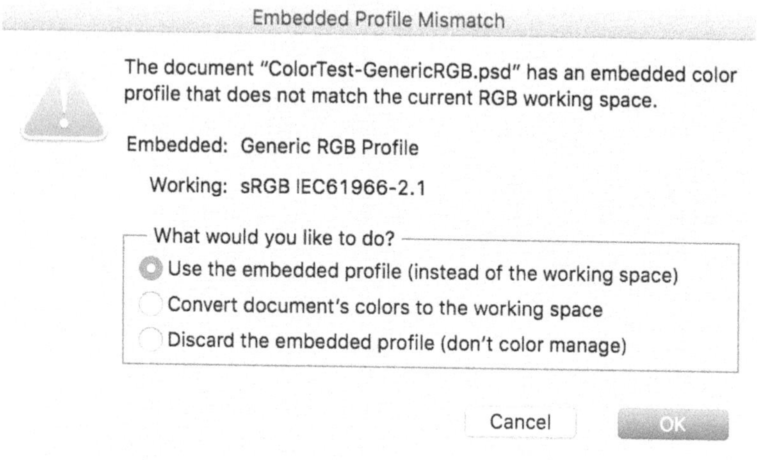

The document "ColorTest-GenericRGB.psd" has an embedded color profile that does not match the current RGB working space.

Embedded: Generic RGB Profile

Working: sRGB IEC61966-2.1

What would you like to do?

◉ Use the embedded profile (instead of the working space)

○ Convert document's colors to the working space

○ Discard the embedded profile (don't color manage)

Cancel   OK

FIG 2.9: Photoshop lets you choose what to do when it detects a file that's not in your working space.

I recommend turning on all of the "Ask When" options for a couple reasons:

- Information in the dialog gives you a better idea of what's happening with each file.
- You can decide case by case how to handle any profile discrepancies.

When the profile-mismatch dialog appears, your choices boil down to:

- "Use the embedded profile" if you want to see what the person who created the file was looking at. Photoshop will adapt the colors to your own display. The color match probably won't be exact, as your display differs from the one where the file originated, but the color will be as close as it can be. This setting is the same as the earlier Preserve Embedded Profile policy—it's likely your safest and best choice.

- "Convert document's colors to the working space" if you're working with a photograph and need it to look right in your sRGB development environment. Don't choose this if you're working with UI graphics. (As you'll see later, altering color values isn't necessary if your target platform can display photos with a profile.)
- "Discard the embedded profile" if you're absolutely sure the person who created the image worked with raw values—and that's all you want from the file. Photoshop will take the raw color values in the file and present them in your working space (which should be set to sRGB). This is the same behavior as when the RGB color management policy is Off. I think of this as expert mode: you're opting to work without a profile at a point when you don't know how color management will affect your results. As we'll learn, it's better to defer this decision until you've opened the file and can see what happens to the image when the profile is removed.

Whatever you choose as the RGB color management policy in Color Settings... will be the default radio button. If you use Preserve Embedded Profile most of the time, all you'll need to do is press Enter in the mismatch dialog.

Finally, have you ever wondered about the octothorp or asterisk that appears after the color space and image depth in Photoshop's window title or tab? Photoshop displays an "#" after "RGB/8" if the current document doesn't have a color profile. When the document profile isn't the same as the working space, you'll see an "*" instead. It's a handy way to remember if you preserved or discarded the original color profile.

Assigning profiles

Wouldn't it be nice if you could see what your raw color values looked like with different profiles? Or how your document would look if you disabled color management? You can do so with Assign Profile... in Photoshop's Edit menu (**FIG 2.10**).

FIG 2.10: Preview color profiles with Photoshop's Assign Profile feature.

When you assign a profile, the raw color values stay the same. You're only specifying how Photoshop should present those values when a profile is selected or removed. Check the box to get a live preview.

Let's open a sample image, **Image-ProPhoto.jpg** (preserve the embedded profile). In the Assign Profile... dialog, you can select any of the current profiles in the dropdown and preview them. If you choose sRGB, you'll get an excellent approximation of how that file will look on a mobile device or in a web browser without color management.

The live preview also demonstrates what happens when you discard the profile, with "Don't Color Manage." (Now you'll know if that's the wisest course, instead of dropping it from the start.)

Converting profiles

Also under Photoshop's Edit menu, Convert to Profile... *does* modify your document's raw pixels (to preserve the appearance of the file). This option can be useful if you're dealing with photography or other types of images where the color values for individual pixels aren't important—say, if you're focused on the overall range of tones in a photo.

But when you're dealing with UI graphics, converting colors from one profile to another does more harm than good: your carefully crafted RGB values will change. For the most part, steer clear of this feature.

SAVE FOR WEB: AND EVERYTHING ELSE

So far, we've looked at how Photoshop handles color while you're editing. It's important to understand how to manage colors as you create graphics, but that work will be for naught if you don't correctly save the file.

Despite its name, Save for Web applies to every kind of file in our web and app work; it'd be more apt to call it Save for Everything. And it brings a whole Swiss Army knife set of options—and as you're about to see, while some are a great help, others can cause confusion or errors in your development workflow. (The color shift in Dr. Eyeful's logo occurred because one checkbox in Save for Web was incorrectly set.)

Let's run through the settings for saving our work.

Keep an eyedropper on things

One of my favorite features of the Save for Web window is the eyedropper.

Hover over any color in the graphic, and see the raw RGB value displayed below the output preview. It's a great way to make a last-minute check that the colors in your user interface are right.

Click on any color, and Photoshop will save it in the well on the left. Clicking the color well will convert the color to a web hex value or any of the other formats supported by Photoshop. You can also add the color to your swatches for later reference.

sRGB color conversion

By default, Photoshop has the Convert to sRGB checkbox ticked.

Like Convert to Profile, Convert to sRGB changes the raw color values in your file. When you leave it on, if your document has a color profile, your colors may be mangled on save, and you'll end up with a file in production that doesn't match your source Photoshop document. (And you wonder why designers and developers fight!)

Of course, if you're working in the sRGB color space, you won't see a difference whether the feature is on or off, since there's nothing to convert. Still, for those times you're not in sRGB—however rare—it's better to be safe than to risk losing profile information.

Turn Convert to sRGB off, and leave it that way (**FIG 2.11**).

(If you really need to convert pixel color values from one space to another, stick with Convert to Profile. You'll have more control over the process, and it'll be easier to compare the image before and after.)

Embedding profiles

Above all else, you need to understand the Embed Color Profile checkbox. When it's checked, the current profile you're using for editing will be added to the file. No color values are changed; the profile tells other software how to process the data for display.

This sounds good on the surface. But remember, there's little consistency to how apps manage color. Safari handles colors differently from Chrome. The same goes for color man-

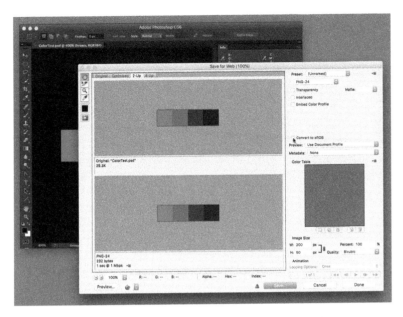

FIG 2.11: Saving the image without sRGB conversion or an embedded profile.

agement on a mobile device (with limited resources) versus a desktop computer.

So when should you embed a profile? Two rules can help:

- If the file is a photograph for a web page or an app, *embed a profile*. The profile gives the system a chance to render an image closer to what you were editing in Photoshop.
- If the file is an image for a user interface, *do not embed a profile*. (We'll examine why when we look at platforms in upcoming chapters. The web browsers in Chapter 3 are full of surprises!)

If you don't embed a profile, you'll also reduce the file size by a couple thousand bytes (the Save for Web preview shows you the exact figure). This is inconsequential for a large photo, but for interface graphics, which tend to multiply like rabbits, these kilobytes can add up to a lot of space.

If you do embed a profile, make sure it makes sense for both the source image and the viewing environment. Here are some guidelines, based on common profiles:

- **sRGB** looks good on a variety of devices, but as the lowest common denominator, it seldom looks awesome. Embedding this profile is also redundant: it's the default when one isn't present in the file. Worse, embedding sRGB in graphics can cause a mismatch with the same color in CSS.
- **Adobe RGB** is ideal when you're working with digital photos, as many cameras capture images in this color space. As with ColorMatch RGB and ProPhoto RGB, this profile can display a wider range of colors (all three have a larger gamut than sRGB). They also produce more vibrant, accurate colors when the images are printed. On the downside, the superior color is lost on many mobile devices.
- **Generic RGB** looks fine on a Mac but feels washed out on a PC. (It's a good idea to do cross-platform testing when embedding profiles.)
- Never embed your **Monitor RGB** profile, unless you plan on shipping your display to everyone who visits your website.

Whether you embed or not, keep the setting consistent on a given type of image or project (e.g., make sure a website's hero images embed the same profile). Use the Inspector panel in Preview to double-check a file's embedded profile. If a profile exists, you'll see it listed as ColorSync profile. If the field is blank, Photoshop (or another app) saved the image without an embedded profile.

For an in-depth discussion on how to get the most out of your digital photos, check out Color Space and Color Profiles from the American Society of Media Photographers. "AdobeRGB vs. sRGB" from Fstoppers lays out the differences between the two profiles.

EXPORT AS: A NEW KID ON THE BLOCK

We've saved the best for last. (Working for Dr. Eyeful has taken its toll in the wordplay department.)

Save for Web was introduced in Photoshop 5.5 in 1999. Sixteen years later, a new way to save graphics arrived in Photoshop CC: Export As.

Why does Photoshop need another way to save images? We've just seen that Save for Web is a perfectly capable tool for outputting files and managing color.

We've also seen a user interface that has a lot of levers, which can be daunting when all you need to do is save a part of your document. And behind that complex interface is code originally written in 1998 for a web that only supported GIF and JPEG images. Many of our needs have changed since those days, but our tools and workflows haven't. The engineers at Adobe are using the new Export As to make a clear break from the past, to give everyone a chance to work more efficiently.

The venerable Save for Web isn't going away—it's still there (for now, and we'll see why in a minute), but it's labeled Legacy and won't get any further love from its developers.

Better? You bet!

Change is hard, and we resist it unless something is in it for us. Luckily, we have a lot to like about the new Export As dialog:

- The biggest improvement is you can now export multiple layers and artboards at once. Anyone who's ever cut up the layers of a Photoshop document to create files for an app or website has known the pain of pressing the ⌥⇧⌘S key combination over and over and over. With Export As, you can select items and save them as a batch. If you have a lot of layers, this saves a ton of time.
- Assets can be scaled as they're saved—letting you quickly create normal and higher-resolution graphics (commonly referred to as @1x, @2x and @3x assets).

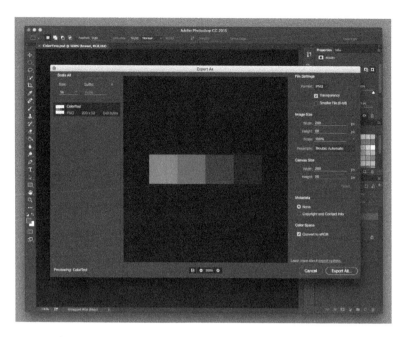

FIG 2.12: The Export As dialog introduced in Photoshop CC 2015.

- Export As supports SVG files. As designs have simplified in recent years, the use of shapes in layers has increased. Saving these types of images in a vector format often decreases their size considerably. As you'd expect, the Export As dialog shows how many bytes each format will use.

The best part is it's all done in a user interface that's much simpler than what we've seen with Save for Web (**FIG 2.12**).

Diving into the specifics of Export As is beyond this book's scope, but Adobe has plenty of terrific documentation to get you up to speed—start with the video tutorial.

But not quite yet

Given these great features, why is Adobe keeping Save for Web?

Writing good software takes time, and Export As is clearly a work in progress. Adobe has been straightforward about missing functionality, and has promised to bring features from Save for Web to this new interface. For example, the initial release of CC in 2015 didn't support scaling all assets, converting between color spaces, or including metadata; it added those features five months later in a .1 release.

For now, as of this writing (late 2016), the key deficiencies to consider are:

- Any preview is presented in the screen's color profile—which makes the preview accurate only for images meant for Chrome or Firefox. As a majority of devices and apps use sRGB, you may see some color shifts.
- Export As has no tools to check your work before saving. Save for Web's eyedropper is a handy way to ensure your raw colors are right; likewise, a 2-Up preview lets you look for color changes. Both of these are currently missing.
- If your source document has a color profile assigned, that information is stripped on export. This is fine if you're working with interface graphics, but if you have a hero image or product photo with a wider gamut (such as Adobe RGB or ProPhoto from a high-end DSLR), the lost information will lead to more muted colors.
- If you've used a Timeline to animate your layers, Export As can't save the result as a GIF. It only saves a single frame.

If these features are important to your work, I suggest sticking with Save for Web until the functionality is brought over.

Convert times two

An unfortunate inclusion in the new export tool is the dreaded Convert to sRGB. Like its predecessor, it's enabled by default and can potentially ruin your work when you save a file.

As before, you need to explicitly turn it off. But Photoshop makes it twice as hard, since the checkbox appears in both

Export As and the Export Preferences panel. In the dialog, each item you're exporting has its own checkbox, and Photoshop keeps track of its state. If you've left the default setting on in the past, you'll need to hunt down each item and turn it off manually. Any new items will get a setting based on the last export. It's convoluted—and another good reason to turn this feature off for good.

The options in Expert Preferences apply when you do a Quick Export—saving files without prompting for settings. If you leave Convert to sRGB on, Photoshop will convert your file on every save.

Instead of removing a dangerous feature, Adobe has made it trickier to permanently disable. Here's hoping they simplify or remove Convert to sRGB in a future release!

WINDING DOWN WITH SETUP

To recap this chapter on Photoshop's color management:

- Set Color Settings to use a Working Space of sRGB IEC61966-2.1.
- Set RGB Color Management Policies to Preserve Embedded Profiles, with all of the Ask When options turned on.
- Turn off Convert to sRGB when saving images.
- Turn off Embed Color Profile (unless you're saving a photo instead of a UI graphic).

As our industry evolves, you may need to deviate from these recommended settings. For instance, a Display P3 working space may make more sense as displays get deeper. Or you'll need to adapt as Photoshop revisits how it exports files.

The crucial thing is you have the knowledge to make the right decisions and adjust your workflows as necessary—I hope you're now comfortable in the parts of the app that used to make you nervous. (I know I am!)

OTHER TOOLS

Photoshop isn't the only image editor in town. Many folks prefer other products in place of, or in addition to, this well-known manipulator of pixels; popular alternatives Pixelmator and Acorn, for example, have excellent color-management support.

Much of our work begins with vectors. Whether it's a simple wireframe or a complex illustration, many visual elements start as shapes in an editor. If you're using Illustrator, you'll have the same color-management controls you've seen in Photoshop, and can sync them via Adobe's cloud. Other drawing tools (like Sketch) output images using the sRGB standard.

The tools we use to craft our web pages also have color management built into their editing and previewing functions. Typically, these tools use the same underlying technologies as our browsers. For example, Macaw uses Google's Blink rendering engine, while Coda uses Apple's WebKit. (We'll explore browsers in Chapter 3.)

Last, it's worth noting that most tools on the Mac will use WebKit to render content. (Apple supplies tools for developers to make it easy to include these capabilities.) When in doubt, it's usually safe to assume your tool will display HTML and CSS as Safari does.

For details on how these apps manage color, I've created a web page with the latest information.

Figure it out

Earlier in this chapter, you used the Digital Color Meter to see how Photoshop displays color. If you encounter an unfamiliar tool and need to know how it manages color, try these simple steps.

Start by creating an area of color with known RGB values, like those we've used throughout this book: (123, 45, 67) for brown or (12, 34, 56) for a dark blue. Then measure what you see on screen with your color meter. If the correct numbers appear when your display is set to sRGB, you'll know the app is using that profile to render your content. Or try different settings to find the closest match.

After you save a file, examine it with the Preview app: the ColorSync profile in the Inspector panel will show you any embedded color information. A dash in this field means no color profile was embedded and sRGB is being used instead. (Remember, this is a good setting for saving web graphics.)

As a final check, make sure the color values you expect are in the previewed file. Set your color meter to the same profile shown in the Preview Inspector, and verify the values match.

WEB BROWSERS

WHILE PHOTOSHOP is a formidable tool for managing the color of your graphics, it's only half of the equation: another app will present your artwork. It's nearly impossible to create an image without thinking about how it will be parsed by HTML and CSS; even native apps use the web in creative ways (including showcasing products in Apple's App Store).

When we talk about color on the web, we're talking about browsers—they turn markup like #ff0000 into a red that people see on the page, and they process our images and any embedded color profiles.

(To be clear, we aren't talking about the rendering framework that puts elements on the page. Something like WebKit isn't responsible for processing color, and as you'll see, framework behavior varies wildly depending on where it's used.)

Commercial browsers—which surfaced in the early 1990s— predate the color-management systems we use now. As such, the web began with a pretty simple view on color. For instance, the #00 to #ff hex representation is a way to specify the 0-255 range we've used throughout this book. But when you drop #00ff00 into your code, there's no mention of a color profile. Will that green hex value match my light bulb? Or yours?

Or take web images, which can have embedded profiles. How will browsers handle those? How can you predict what color your visitor will land on?

To answer these questions, let's start with some guidance from the World Wide Web Consortium (W3C).

SRGB, MAYBE

Here's what the web standards body has to say about color values:

All RGB colors are specified in the sRGB color space.

It's our friend sRGB! But pay careful attention—the W3C says "specified," which doesn't necessarily cover how colors are *presented*:

User agents may vary in the fidelity with which they represent these colors, but using sRGB provides an unambiguous and objectively measurable definition of what the color should be, which can be related to international standards.

When the W3C says that user agents "may vary the fidelity," they're letting browser makers bend the rules. When we use colors in CSS stylesheets and image elements, everyone agrees they're sRGB. When those same colors are displayed on a *web page*, results vary, depending on what you're trying to draw. Let's explore the forms that color can take in your browser.

Good old images

Images have been an integral part of the web from its inception. Since the late '90s, browsers have treated raster graphics without embedded profiles as sRGB—a de facto standard established before the official W3C spec.

In 2005, Safari 2.0 was the first browser to support images with embedded profiles. Safari did something similar to what you saw in Photoshop: it transformed the pixels from the embedded color profile to the screen's color space. After seven years, all desktop browsers had the same capability.

This sounds great until you realize we're talking just the desktop. We'll see very different behavior from mobile browsers in a bit.

Exciting new graphics

Scalable vector graphics (SVG) are increasingly common assets in our web interfaces. According to the W3C specification for SVG 1.1, all colors default to the sRGB color space and use the same formatting as CSS2. Yay!

But then:

Additionally, SVG content can specify an alternate color specification using an ICC profile as described in Specifying paint. If ICC-based colors are provided and the SVG user agent supports

ICC color, then the ICC-based color takes precedence over the sRGB color specification...

Currently, no user agents support these embedded color profiles, but it's clear the standards folks see SVG as a color-managed vector file format, with the same stature as JPEG and PNG for raster images. Don't assume SVG will always be sRGB.

Drawing on the canvas

The specification for the canvas element states that drawing should use the same color management as img elements and CSS. In practice, that means canvas correctly handles embedded profiles and anything you draw into the 2D context will render in sRGB. A test page, Canvas Test, shows several examples of how color varies with a canvas element.

As other elements on the page adapt to color management, canvas likely will as well. At this writing, members of the WHATWG are discussing adding a color space parameter when you create a context.

Evolving CSS color

You're still most likely to specify a color via CSS. Yet as you saw, the W3C isn't strict on how that color appears on the page. Since browser-makers have their own goals, developers now face a situation where Apple and Google interpret the standard differently.

This is not the first time browser-makers have disagreed on what is best! Let's check out the nuances to this discord—and potential headaches in our workflow.

BROWSER COLOR ENTANGLEMENT

A picture's worth a thousand words, so let's open a test page in both Safari and Chrome on macOS (**FIG 3.1**).

The images on the page come from the ColorTest.psd file in Chapter 2. The groups of color on the right are PNG images

FIG 3.1: The same page, two browsers: Safari (front) and Chrome (back) on macOS.

(the square sets) and inline SVG (the round set). The background colors are generated with CSS.

Each image file was created from the Photoshop document with assigned Monitor RGB, sRGB, and Generic RGB profiles. Two images were saved with each profile: one with and one without Embed Color Profile. The background CSS colors use the same values entered in Photoshop.

You may not see as pronounced a difference between the two browsers; the exact results depend on your computer's display.

When you open the page on a mobile device, the colors in the images change depending on your operating system (**FIG 3.2**).

All browsers share the same markup, yet colors vary in both the CSS and images (some slight, some more obvious). This is a big deal—let's zoom in.

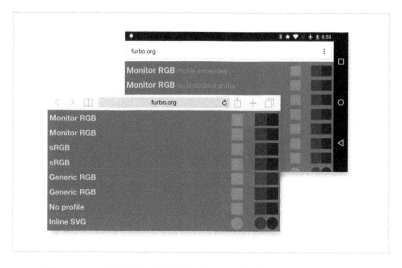

FIG 3.2: The test page in Safari on iOS (left) and Android (right).

MANAGING COLORS IN CSS

In **FIG 3.1**, you'll notice that the background colors on the pages aren't quite the same. The reason is simple: Safari and Chrome use different display color spaces to render CSS. Apple started diverging years ago with the 10.9 Mavericks release, and continued more recently with the iOS 9.3 release. The changes, sparked by better display technology, have been a long time coming—we'll probably see more as computer hardware improves.

Let's take a look at why color management differs across browsers and how it affects your development environment.

Safari pushes forward

Apple found itself in a tough situation: it wanted to improve displays *and* support standard web colors. The WebKit developers have wanted to make their browser "color smart" for years but were stymied by Flash. The decline of that technology and the introduction of new DCI-P3 displays gave developers an opportunity to use color management and have the best of both worlds.

Now, when you specify a color in CSS, Safari takes the raw color values and puts them in an sRGB color space. That color is then transformed using color management to the display's profile. If you type #6600cc in your CSS, it produces something like #7900cf on screen.

You can check for yourself: on our Colorful test page, compare the sRGB (Profile embedded) sample against the background colors. Since the image and CSS colors match, they must use the same profile. Note also images *without* profiles match the sRGB image: Safari uses the same default color space for both types of content.

Safari's new behavior means you need to make sure your tools can take a display color space and convert it back to sRGB—otherwise, you'll sample #7900cf on screen and wonder why it doesn't appear in your code. (Both Digital Color Meter and xScope do this conversion, so you're set.)

You'll also need to pay attention when using Photoshop's eyedropper, which samples color using the display's color profile. When you specify a CSS color as (255, 0, 0) and then grab it from a page in Safari, you'll end up with something like (250, 20, 27) in Photoshop's color well. You won't see this color shift when you sample the same page in Chrome. (I'll explain why in the next section.)

Apple isn't out to make everyone's life more difficult with these changes: again, it wants to give us better displays and follow web standards. Think of Safari's sRGB as a compatibility mode for a DCI-P3 screen that has a lot more color than its peers.

Colors everywhere else

All other browsers, including Chrome, don't touch your CSS colors. Anything you specify in your code goes directly to the screen and adopts its color profile. See this in play in FIG 3.1 by comparing the CSS background and the embedded profiles: the color *does* match my Mac's Monitor RGB and *does not* match sRGB.

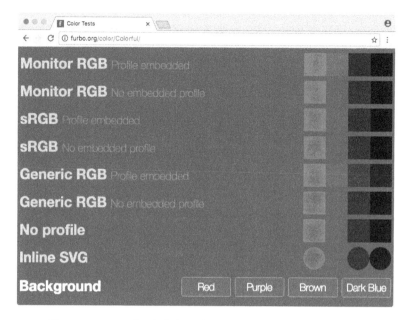

FIG 3.3: The test page on a Thunderbolt Display.

Don't forget: unless you have my Dell monitor and the calibration tool I used to create the profile, you won't see that perfect match when *you* view Monitor RGB. Instead you might see something similar to what Apple's Thunderbolt Display produces (FIG 3.3).

Now Monitor RGB looks completely wrong and sRGB is close but still a little off. Here are a couple lessons about these color shifts:

- Never embed your display's color profile in an image. Everyone but you will see the wrong color.
- Many displays have gamuts that are very close to the sRGB standard, but not exact. If you embed the sRGB profile in a graphic, you're at the browser's mercy when it comes to

matching the colors. While it's obvious in **FIG 3.1**, it's subtle enough in **FIG 3.3** to drive a perfectionist up a wall.

Chrome's use of the display's color space may seem a bit counterintuitive, especially when the W3C recommends using sRGB. But if you assume most displays will be close to this color space, no color compensation is required. For a product that must work on different platforms and devices—many of which don't support color management—this is a pragmatic engineering decision. Firefox does the same thing, for the same reason.

You can use this behavior to your advantage during development. If you want to check CSS colors from the display with no color space conversions, use Chrome, Firefox, or Internet Explorer to display the page. Tools like Photoshop's eyedropper will pick the exact color that was in your code.

Working with Windows

Many folks will still view your work on Windows, especially if you're targeting things like corporate intranets—you may even use this OS as your primary development platform.

Though it only needs to support a personal computer, the last version of Internet Explorer displays color much like what we've seen with Chrome (**FIG 3.4**).

But you'll see one small difference: the sRGB image matches the background exactly, because Windows uses sRGB as a system-wide default. Until recently, if you wanted to run an app in another color space, you needed to install extra software. But Windows 10 lets you calibrate a display and replace its profile.

You can configure your Mac to behave like Windows, which is helpful if you're working on a site that will net lots of visits from a PC. Open System Preferences > Displays, and in the Color panel, select "sRGB IEC61966-2.1." After you relaunch your browsers, they'll mimic what would happen on Windows; as a bonus, all your browsers will use the same colors when rendering CSS. You might miss the beauty of your Mac's built-in color profile, but you'll have a better idea of what others are seeing.

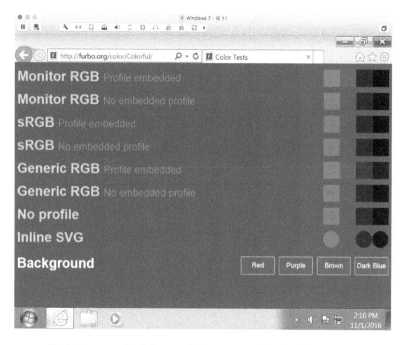

FIG 3.4: The test page running in Internet Explorer 11 on a virtual machine: yet another variation.

CSS changes ahead

To sum up, Safari is the oddball in rendering CSS colors. But we could've said the same in 2005 when Safari was the only browser to correctly render embedded color profiles. Seven years later, all browsers did. As display hardware continues to improve, other browser makers will likely follow the WebKit team's lead. Time will tell.

It's clear the W3C wants to improve color management on the web. The days of sRGB as the lone color space for CSS may be numbered: the original proposal for the CSS3 color module included a color-profile property. Although it was dropped in the current implementations, the standards folks would still like to see it in the future. If and when this happens, CSS will be able to embed profiles, just like images.

Further, another proposal suggests adding a new color() function that extends the familiar rgb() with a color space name. To get a fully saturated red in DCI-P3, you'd be able to specify something like color(p3 1.0 0.0 0.0) instead of rgb(100%, 0%, 0%).

MOBILE COLOR ADVANCES

While browsers on a PC or your laptop all render images as expected, results when you're away from the desk are mixed.

The capabilities of early mobile devices were meager. Processing an image eats a lot of power and memory, and photos—the assets most likely to have color profiles—can have millions of pixels. But in recent years, the devices we carry in our pockets and bags have become a lot more powerful, sometimes even more capable than what we have on our desktops. As a result, color management on mobile is catching up.

Color in your pocket

It might surprise you to learn that Microsoft's new Edge browser (Project Spartan) for Windows 10 was the first mobile browser to correctly handle embedded color profiles (**FIG 3.5**). But it makes sense: since Windows 10 is a unified system that works on both mobile and desktop, consistent handling of color between the two is crucial. As a company, Microsoft also has a long history of maintaining backward compatibility—compare the screenshot of IE 11 in **FIG 3.4** with Edge's in **FIG 3.5**.

Like Microsoft, Apple is a company with a browser that works on both platforms. But Apple has another factor that makes color management essential: it's beginning to produce better displays for both desktop (iMac) and mobile (iPad Pro). The new DCI-P3 display standard has "a color standard big enough for Hollywood."

FIG 3.5: Microsoft's latest browser showing the test page on Windows 10 Mobile.

DCI-P3 gives the iPad Pro 25% greater color saturation. To display sRGB (which has a narrower color gamut) on this device, the WebKit developers needed color management. So they brought Safari's desktop capabilities to mobile in the iOS 9.3 release. In Figs **3.1** and **3.2**, you'll see the browser render the CSS and image content identically.

Be aware that Safari's ability to use color profiles depends on the device's age; older phones and tablets don't have the processing power to convert colors, and that can lead to surprising shifts (**FIG 3.6**). The first chip to boast this new capability was the A8, which first appeared in the iPhone 6.

The last key piece of the mobile ecosystem is Android. The sad news is this platform doesn't support color management. In **FIG 3.2**, you'll see all images render the same, whether or not they have an embedded profile. You'll also get the left-hand results of **FIG 3.6**, even on the latest devices.

It's always difficult to predict the future, but given the intense competition in the mobile industry, it's easy to imagine that Samsung and other manufacturers will want their displays to top Apple's. They'll need color management to keep up.

FIG 3.6: A wide-gamut image displayed on an older mobile device (left) and a newer one (right). Photograph by Jeff Carlson.

Responsive color

From the survey of mobile browsers, you know only some of your visitors will have color management. As a conscientious developer, you stick with sRGB. But wide-gamut images on a P3 screen (like on the iPhone 7) are a real marvel—rich and vibrant—and you'd like to offer better color to those who *can* see it.

You're in luck. Picking the right display gamut is just a variation on choosing an image based on screen size and density (@2x). The CSS Working Group has started to tackle this problem with a draft proposal that features a new media query: color-gamut. The media queries you use to check a browser's width and resolution are getting an upgrade for color management.

With the proposed query, your CSS could tailor a hero image on your site to a device's gamut as well as its resolution:

```
h1#hero {
  background-image: url(hero.jpg);
}
@media (min-resolution: 2dppx) {
  h1#hero {
    background-image: url(hero@2x.jpg);
  }
}
@media (min-resolution: 2dppx) and (color-gamut: p3) {
  h1#hero {
    background-image: url(hero-p3@2x.jpg);
  }
}
```

Don't embed profiles in hero.jpg and hero@2x.jpg, and they'll display correctly as sRGB. With hero-p3@2x.jpg, you can embed a profile with a wider gamut to take advantage of the DCI-P3 display.

If you're dealing with a product catalog or photo gallery, you'll want to do something similar using inline media. Since the venerable `img` tag doesn't support media queries, use the new hotness, `picture`:

```
<picture>
  <source media="(min-resolution: 2dppx) and
    (color-gamut: p3)"
    srcset="photo-p3@2x.jpg">
  <source media="(min-resolution: 2dppx)"
    srcset="photo@2x.jpg">
  <img src="photo.jpg" srcset="photo@2x.jpg 2x"
    alt="A photo">
</picture>
```

Each of the source elements provides a set of images for the browser to use. The media attribute lets the browser load the image that best matches the current display environment. On a high-resolution screen, photo-p3@2x.jpg will load if the device has a wide gamut; otherwise it would display photo@2x.jpg. If the browser doesn't support the picture element or can't find a source match, the img element acts as a fallback. In our example, that's the low-resolution photo.jpg.

Finally, you can incorporate the color-gamut media query into your JavaScript:

```
if (window.matchMedia('(color-gamut: p3)').matches)
{
  // do something with the wider gamut
}
```

If you're loading image resources dynamically, you can use the results of this test to adjust your server requests.

To see these techniques in action, take a quick visit to furbo.org/color/ResponsiveColor/. Viewing the source on that page will help you understand what's going on. Note that Safari 10 supports the new color-gamut media query on both iOS and macOS.

Responsive color gives you a way to future-proof your website: as mobile devices gain the power of their desktop counterparts, consistent color across platforms is possible. While you don't know when other browsers will catch up with Safari, you do know they'll follow web standards.

CONSISTENCY

In the meantime, with these different behaviors among browsers, achieving color consistency may seem a painful enterprise. Happily, it isn't if you follow one rule: *don't embed color profiles if you want your images to match your CSS colors.* This rule applies to most image files when you're building a website: leave out profiles for controls, widgets, and logos.

It's that simple: take another look at the test page in the browser screenshots. When we don't have a color profile, the CSS color and the image color match perfectly in every case. All modern browsers behave the same way. In fact, we should have omitted the color profile from the banner in Dr. Eyeful's site.

The corollary rule is: *embed color profiles in photos selected by a media query.* The query gives you the ability to pick the right image for display and provide backward compatibility.

Remember, there's no point in embedding a profile in a photo that'll use the default sRGB color space. And as we saw in some browsers earlier, embedding a color profile in an image can lead to mismatches with the CSS colors.

It takes extra work to create images with multiple color spaces, as it does to work with graphics in multiple resolutions. So when is it appropriate to make the effort? My guideline is to ask, *Am I selling something?*

Things like hero images that introduce your service to a potential client will look a lot better in a wider gamut. The same goes for photography that makes products appealing. You don't need it for your vacation photos. (To get an idea of how photography improves on a deeper display, I've compiled samples that let you compare sRGB with the wider color spaces of ProPhoto and AdobeRGB.)

One last factor to consider: image optimization. If you use a tool like ImageOptim to make your images mobile-friendly, be aware that these tools often make files smaller by removing color profiles. For example, see the "No profile" row on the Colorful test page. For images meant for a user interface, that's fine. But if you have embedded profiles in your photos, they'll be damaged.

MOBILE APPS

BECAUSE MANY MOBILE APPS begin their lives as websites, chances are good your web colors will someday become app colors.

The same limitations with memory and processing speeds that exist on the mobile web extend to native apps. Support for color management is limited, and the frameworks to build apps often rely on the display set to sRGB.

Android's specification forgoes color spaces or profiles—colors are specified in the old-school way with three bytes of red, green, and blue. You have to hope each individual manufacturer will present those bytes in something close to sRGB.

Apple, on the other hand, is shaking things up. In iOS 9, Apple added ColorSync support to Core Image, the code that lets you efficiently process graphics. The 9.3 release extended color management to user interfaces in the UIKit framework: UIImageView supported embedded color profiles, and UIColor included CGColorSpace for its RGB properties. iOS 10 continues these advances, with system-wide support for what Apple calls "wide color": you're now able to use profiles with an extended color range and process images with sixteen bits per channel.

The best way to get up to speed on these changes is to watch the videos from WWDC. Color management in iOS is first discussed in WWDC 2015's "What's New In Core Image [Session 510]," starting at 8:50 in the video. Slides 26 and 27 show excellent examples of how color management can improve the display of photography. From 2016, "Working with Wide Color [Session 712]" gives a brief overview of iOS 10's new color capabilities, the ways your development tools and workflows will change, and guidelines for better color in apps. Last, if your app features photographs, be aware the camera we carry in our pockets can now capture more vibrant imagery: see "Advances in iOS Photography [Session 501]" at the 44-minute mark to learn more.

Phew. Things are in flux, but the engineers at Apple are clearly working toward better color-management support in their OS. It's important to remember that these features are only available on devices with enough processing power—you'll need to consider backward compatibility with older devices.

When you're building an app, you'll face color management at every step of development. To help you understand the considerations involved, let's go through the process with a sample app for iOS 10. Download a ZIP file of the ColorfulMobile project to follow along (you'll need Xcode 8 or later to run it); you'll also see screenshots of the project in this chapter. Comments in the project's code explain options for handling color and resolving problems.

XCODE

The first step for any iOS app is to open Xcode. Since we've learned that sRGB is common on mobile devices, you might assume sRGB makes sense for your development environment too.

One can only dream. You'll be confronted with different color spaces as you work on your app. Even though iOS defaults to sRGB, storyboards sometimes use a generic color space, while the simulator mirrors your display's color profile. To get consistent color, you'll need to understand these distinctions.

If you haven't already, open the sample project and use the left-hand, dropdown navigation to locate the Main.storyboard file. We'll start the development tour with a common task in customizing a user interface: picking colors.

Picking colors

In View Controller Scene (the middle panel), click on the brown color bar labeled "123, 45, 67." On the right, select the Attributes inspector panel and click on Background; Xcode's color picker will pop up—make sure you're set to RGB Sliders. If you click on the gear icon, you'll see the color space associated with the chosen color (FIG 4.1). In our screenshot, the brown bar uses the default, sRGB. Use this dropdown menu to set color profiles for the elements in your design, and they'll appear correctly on any device that supports color management. (You can confirm this by firing up the Digital Color Meter.)

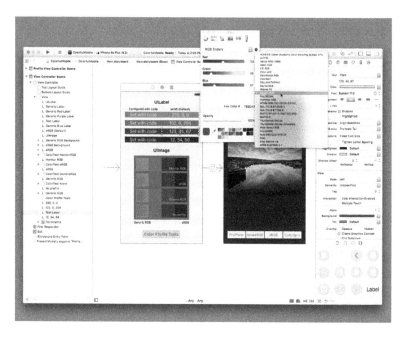

FIG 4.1: Xcode's color picker sets the color to the sRGB color space.

I built multiple apps in Xcode before I found this profile menu via the gear icon. In older versions, Xcode's default profile was Generic RGB—but most people didn't notice since iOS displayed all colors in sRGB. Here are some other Xcode tips and idiosyncrasies:

- What does this mean for projects from earlier versions of Xcode? When you open one of those storyboards with Xcode 8, it'll automatically convert colors from Generic RGB to sRGB. If you've set your colors to a different profile, Xcode will botch the conversion—because you've given it data it doesn't expect. If you see any color shifts, check both the values and selected profile.

- When you create a new control on your interface, the color space sometimes defaults to Generic RGB instead of sRGB. While this is likely a software bug, double-check via the gear icon before entering RGB values into the text fields.
- Along with the text fields for RGB values or hex codes, Xcode's picker lets you choose colors via eyedropper, crayons, or color wheel. Since these options are shared with other macOS apps, they work with the system's default color space, Generic RGB. Check, and convert to sRGB if needed.
- After you save your storyboard with Xcode 8, your version-control system will note several `colorspace="calibratedRGB"` modifications, as Xcode migrates your colors to `customColorSpace="sRGB"`. Once these changes go through, you won't be able to open the storyboard with an earlier version of Xcode. Make sure everyone on your team is ready to move to iOS 10.

Although you have a choice of color space, I recommend you still use sRGB with Xcode 8. Because the design tool doesn't let you specify more than one profile, working within the narrower gamut will provide the best compatibility across devices. Later in this chapter, you'll learn how to adapt your interface to wider color displays at runtime.

Compiling image assets

Like your code, an app's image assets are compiled—to optimize them for quick display on a mobile device. To support color management, Xcode brings a new twist to this build phase: wide color. Just as you adapted your design workflow for images with multiple resolutions, you'll now need to think about creating additional resources with new color specifications.

These new assets are wider in memory (with a depth of sixteen bits per channel instead of eight bits) and embed a wider color gamut (using the Display P3 profile). Good thing you got familiar with Photoshop's Color Settings in Chapter 2—you're about to put that knowledge to use!

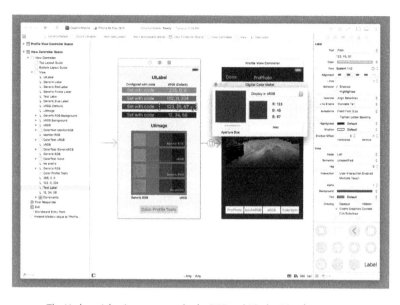

FIG 4.2: The Harbor_Adaptive asset uses both sRGB and Display P3 color spaces.

In the sample project, select the Images.xcassets folder, and the asset catalog will show all the graphics used in the app (for example, AppIcon, ColorTest-Adaptive, Harbor_Adaptive). The catalog has always let you specify images for different types of layouts and devices, and with iOS's new features, color gamut is now an option. Configure the gamut by opening the Attributes inspector (click the slider icon at top right), and choosing "sRGB and Display P3." Pick an image from the catalog, and you'll see outlines of extra assets that need to be filled (FIG 4.2).

So what goes in these image cells? Let's look!

Creating wider assets

The asset catalog supports two bitmap formats: PNG and JPEG. PNG offers lossless compression, which makes sense for smaller files, like controls and other interface elements. Photos and other larger images typically rely on compressed JPEGs that eat up less memory on a mobile device.

Our goal is an image that follows Apple's recommended settings for wide color, which will generate imagery with a higher dynamic range and smoother gradients. So let's loop back to Photoshop, and ready your levers for creating a new PSD document or converting an existing one.

When you're building assets from scratch, the only adjustment is in the New document dialog: set the Color Mode to "16 bit" and the Color Profile (under Advanced) to "Display P3," and you're done!

Sometimes, you'll need to convert assets from third parties, like a photographer or a stock service. These files are often in the JPEG format, which only supports eight bits per channel. To prep these for wide color, first open the file, go to Image > Mode, and set the depth to "16 Bit/Channel." (You can skip this step if you received a TIFF or RAW file saved with 16-bit color.)

(A note on terminology: the number of bits in an image has traditionally indicated its depth. Deeper images have more discrete values in memory, but Apple's documentation focuses on these extra bits working in conjunction with a profile to provide a wider range of color. In this context, deep and wide mean the same thing.)

Once you've adjusted the depth, consider the color space. As noted in Chapter 2, photographers often work in wider gamuts like Adobe RGB or ProPhoto. To retain as much of the original color as possible, use Convert to Profile... with a Destination Space of "Display P3."

Apple recommends saving an asset image as a 16-bit PNG, but, unfortunately, you won't be able to do so with Save for Web or Export As. (Yet. Adobe hasn't updated Photoshop's export features for wide color.) Instead, you'll need to return to Save As... to save the image as a PNG for your asset catalog. If you choose to save an 8-bit JPEG to get a smaller asset, just remember to embed a Display P3 color profile.

These techniques created the 16-bit PNG file for the Harbor_Adaptive asset in Xcode. (I made the 8-bit version with methods we all know by heart.) Since you'll deal with two files that look very similar, a handy way to verify an asset is to control-click on the cell (for example, "2x Display P3" for Harbor_Adaptive) and select Show in Finder. You'll see Harbor_DisplayP3_16bit.

png, and when you open the file in Preview and view the Inspector, you can check both the depth ("8" or "16") and the profile ("sRGB" or "Display P3").

Before you load your new 16-bit, Display P3 PNG file in Xcode, let's cover how the asset catalog handles an image, and weigh your options.

Converting colors automatically

Another difference between your UI graphics (PNG) and photos (JPEG) is color conversion. Xcode automatically converts PNG files to the color space a device needs; this conversion can be both a drawback (resulting in unpredictable colors) and a potential time-saver from doing manual work.

Let's start with how conversion can confuse: run the sample project on the iPhone 5s simulator. As this older device doesn't support color management, you'll see weird colors in the simulator's Asset Tests (**fig 4.3**). At the same time, the UIImage tests look fine—what gives?

As Xcode compiles the ColorTest images in the asset catalog, the software knows the iPhone 5s doesn't have color management and needs sRGB, so it converts the colors in the PNG files. The JPEG files remain unmodified and look wrong, because iOS ignores the profile. The PNG files appear correctly on screen, because they're no longer the files you put in the catalog.

You *can* use this automatic conversion to your advantage. If you specify a single, high-quality asset like 16-bit Display P3, Xcode will convert it to sRGB during your build. You're free from doing it by hand in Photoshop!

Unfortunately, this approach has a catch: the only way to see the results of Xcode's conversion is to run the app and view the results on screen, each time. You have no way to say, "Show me all the PNG files in the app I just built." If you target many devices, scales, and sizes, you'll launch a lot of simulators to do quality assurance.

And as you saw with Photoshop's Convert to Profile, the raw color values in your image will shift during the build. To ensure these assets match other elements in your interface, you must

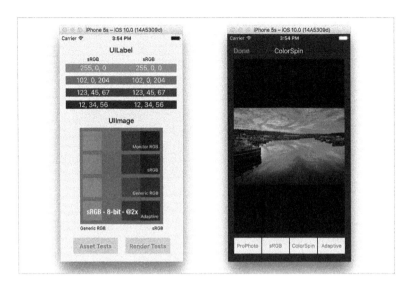

FIG 4.3: The UIImage samples (left) appear correct, but the simulator's profiles (right) are a different story.

specify Display P3 in code or the storyboard. UIColor is smart and will apply the same conversion Xcode did in the build.

If you're considering this technique, check out the sample project's **Harbor_Universal** asset as an example (see -setAdaptiveImage: in **AssetViewController.m**). You'll likely want to limit automatic conversion to new development, as existing code and storyboards make a lot of assumptions about sRGB.

Adapting images to displays

On the other hand, you might skip Xcode's automatic conversion, and opt for finer control: creating individual files for the sRGB and Display P3 slots, as you would with the 1x, 2x, and 3x slots for multiple resolutions. This scenario is similar to responsive color for the web—great news if you need to share assets between your website and mobile app.

When you run your app, Xcode will select images from the catalog based on a device's capabilities. Just as an @2x image will load for a Retina display, a 16-bit PNG file loads on a device that supports Display P3. Otherwise, you'll see the normal sRGB file. (This is also how Chapter 3's color-gamut media query works.)

See this for yourself by running the sample app on an actual iPhone 7 or iPad Pro (9.7-inch). You'll see how rich the colors appear—the red and purple colors depict the most change because they're at the extremes of the sRGB gamut. In the Asset Tests, both the ProPhoto and Adaptive samples show a sunset with a wider range of colors (especially with orange).

If you don't have one of these fancy new screens, track what's happening via the iPhone 7 simulator: "Display P3 - 16-bit" denotes when adaptive images appear in the bottom UIImage test and the Adaptive example in Asset Tests. If you run the sample on an older iPhone, you'll see "sRGB - 8-bit" instead.

At this point, you may think these extra resources will make your app download humongous. Luckily, the app-thinning feature introduced in iOS 9 removes unneeded resources before sending everything to the customer's device. The iPhone 7 receives the new wider images, while an iPhone 6s only loads the traditional images.

RUNNING YOUR APP

Now that your app is running, remember all devices won't handle your images the same way. You may see color shifts on devices that don't support color profiles (iPhone 5s), while other devices (iPhone SE) will display images perfectly (**FIG 4.4**).

Without support for ProPhoto, the iPhone 5s defaults to sRGB, and the colors become dull and muted. (The earlier ColorSpin example in **FIG 4.3** is admittedly a more extreme case of how colors can get mixed up without color management—but it does happen.) It's crucial to note that prior to iOS 9.3, all devices could not manage color.

What decides if a device is capable of enabling color management? The *Graphics Processing Unit* (GPU)! GPUs in mobile

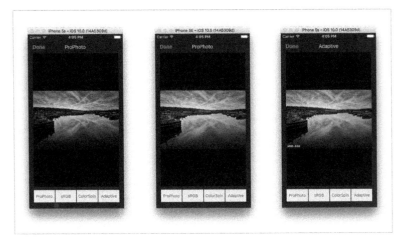

FIG 4.4: The iPhone 5s (left) doesn't support color management, the iPhone SE (center) does, and an adaptive image (right) fixes the problem on iPhone 5s.

devices have advanced rapidly. Starting with the A8 chips introduced in the iPhone 6, these processing units have had enough computing power to convert colors. (This line of chips is sometimes called "GPU Family 2." For a full list of devices that support A8 and up, check the iOS Device Compatibility Reference.)

Changing your view

Just as you did on the web, your mobile app can check if you're running on a P3 screen. For instance, you can define the red, green, and blue values in a UIColor as sRGB or Display P3, and you'll want to pick the ones that match your graphic. Or, maybe you're loading images over a network connection: the request to your server could include a parameter that tells the server to return a version with wider color.

Every UIViewController has a collection of traits, such as the interface idiom, display scale, and size class. These traits define the current environment for your user interface, and any view controller can use the displayGamut property to check if wide color is available:

```
UITraitCollection *traitCollection =
    self.traitCollection;
if (traitCollection.displayGamut ==
    UIDisplayGamutP3) {
    // current display is P3
}
else {
    // current display is sRGB or unspecified
}
```

To create colors in the new gamut, you'll use a variation on a trusty (older) method. Instead of colorWith Red:green:blue:alpha:, create a UIColor with colorWith DisplayP3Red:green:blue:alpha:. For instance, the sample app generates a fully saturated red for a background label with this code:

```
[UIColor colorWithDisplayP3Red:1.0 green:0.0
    blue:0.0 alpha:1.0];
```

On a display without a wider gamut, this code converts colors to sRGB. This automatic conversion process is identical to the one used on assets, so color matches between your images and UIColor are maintained.

To see how this plays out, check the sample project's ViewController.m—the same code adjusts the label's background colors when the view loads.

Rendering images

Data graphs, social network avatars, photo thumbnails: many of the images we use in our apps are *not* in the asset catalog. These graphics are created at runtime from a variety of user inputs, and you'll need to consider color management as you annotate, transform, and filter these pixels.

The sample ColorfulMobile app includes Render Tests you can access from the main screen. We'll do a quick overview of APIs old and new. (For more details, see the comments in the source code of **RenderViewController.m**, again in the sample project.)

Since iOS 4, the power combo of UIGraphicsBeginImage-Context, UIGraphicsGetImageFromCurrentImageContext, and UIGraphicsEndImageContext has generated dynamic images. Any code you've written in the past will continue to work as you adopt color management in iOS 10, but you'll soon stumble on a problem. These functions only support drawing in 8-bit sRGB: with no support for wide color, your app is going to look pretty dull on the newer screens.

Instead, check out UIGraphicsImageRenderer, a new block-based API, to create UIImage objects that match the screen's resolution and depth. For example, you can generate a 200-point red square in Display P3 like so:

```
const CGSize size = { 200.0, 200.0 };
UIGraphicsImageRenderer *renderer =
  [[UIGraphicsImageRenderer alloc]
  initWithSize:size];
UIImage *image =
  [renderer
  imageWithActions:^(UIGraphicsImageRendererContext
  *context) {
  [[UIColor colorWithDisplayP3Red:1.0 green:0.0
  blue:0.0 alpha:1.0] set];
  [context fillRect:context.format.bounds];
}];
self.imageView.image = image;
```

The first two buttons in the Render Tests show how your code will change. "Draw Old" is implemented the old-fashioned way in -setDrawOld:, while "Draw New" uses the newer techniques in -setDrawNew:. But as soon as you run the code on an sRGB screen, you'll wonder why you bothered: no visual difference exists between the old and new rendering code.

You'll understand why once you load the app on an iPhone 7. The colors achieved with the new image renderer are striking. Unfortunately, since you're reading this in a narrower gamut, I can only convey the relative differences via photo (**FIG 4.5**).

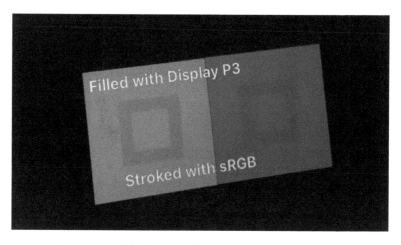

FIG 4.5: This photograph of the "Draw New" test on a 9.7-inch iPad Pro shows a dull sRGB box drawn on a bright Display P3 background.

Matching colors

When using UIGraphicsImageRenderer for wide color, your main challenge is getting the colors in code to match your assets as the screen depth changes. The "Colors Wrong" and "Colors Correct" rendering tests demonstrate the importance of choosing the right colors as you draw your assets.

Since images in the asset catalog can be either sRGB or Display P3, you need to watch for a few things:

- If you're drawing on an asset, the colors in the rendering context need to match the image's color space. You'll notice a color shift if you use sRGB to put a red rectangle on top of the same color in a Display P3 image—like with the swatches drawn on ColorTest.
- Update any colors that surround the asset. For example, the purple background that showcases the color strips in the ColorTest assets must change along with the display's gamut.
- The techniques to get an exact color match depend on whether you're using a universal image with automatic

conversion (ColorTest-Universal) or adaptive images (ColorTest-Adaptive). See both approaches in the sample code.

Again, these color shifts are difficult or impossible to see in the simulator. You won't realize you have a visual bug until you run the app on a device with a Display P3 screen.

As you're working with the extended color range in iOS 10, you may see a message like this in your debugging log: "UIColor created with component values far outside the expected range." This is your tip you're trying for a color that's out of gamut and likely to lead to an unwanted color shift. To find out where this is happening, set a symbolic breakpoint on UIColorBreakForOutOfRangeColorComponents and check the call stack when your app stops. (Learn more about setting up symbolic breakpoints with this guide from Big Nerd Ranch.)

Converting images

Let's loop back to a member of the old power combo, UIGraphicsBeginImageContextWithOptions, which offers parameters for controlling the opacity and scale of the resulting image. The image renderer upstart adds another parameter: prefersExtendedRange.

This extended-range parameter lets you control the color space of the converted image. By default, the image will use the same color space as the display, but sometimes you'll want to use a narrower gamut. The "Modify Image" rendering test shows one such case: generating thumbnail images.

Wider images take up twice as much memory than the ones we've used in the past. Each pixel in a traditional image uses four 8-bit integers for red, green, blue, and alpha. In a wide image, each deeper pixel uses a 16-bit floating-point value for the same data. If you're generating a lot of small images like thumbnails or avatars, that extra memory adds up. Your customer is unlikely to notice the benefits of wide color here, but they'll definitely notice a crash when your app runs out of memory. Save wide color for where it'll have the most visual effect: large areas with rich detail, like photographs.

Another neat feature of the image renderer is its ability to generate PNG and JPEG files with embedded color profiles. This gives you an easy way to create images that can be cached locally or uploaded to a network.

True Tone

Color management on iOS enables a key feature on some devices: True Tone.

The iPad Pro (9.7-inch) has an ambient light sensor built into the bezel of the screen that detects changes in your viewing environment. (Unfortunately, this feature is absent on the iPhone 7, presumably because the smaller form factor can't spare space for the sensor.)

iOS periodically checks the sensor and adjusts the profile of the display dynamically (based on the "white point" of the screen) so colors are more natural and reading stays comfortable.

For most apps, this constant adjustment is welcome and will make your app look better without extra effort on your part. Some apps, such as games or photo editors, may want to lessen the color-shifting effect by using `UIWhitePointAdaptivityStyle` in the `Info.plist` configuration.

To get an idea of how True Tone works, take an iPad Pro into a dark room and compare the white background in Photos with the same color in Safari. When you're viewing images, `UIWhitePointAdaptivityStylePhoto` makes the True Tone effect much less pronounced than the warmer colors in the web browser.

DO I REALLY NEED TO DO THIS?

No one likes to rewrite code that's working just fine. Even the engineers at Apple.

But the changes we're seeing in iOS are wide ranging: everything from the pixel formats in Core Graphics to the way Photos displays an image. This huge level of work is a clear indicator that Apple sees color management as a crucial part of their platform. It's more than likely other platforms, including Android, will follow Apple's lead—I suspect it won't be long before wide color is available on all new devices.

As these new devices proliferate, *a lot* of content *won't* be in sRGB. Remember that as of iOS 10, the camera takes photos in Display P3 for maximum quality. These images, in turn, will pass onto your app for editing, your server for storage, and your network for sharing.

To understand the scale of this change, note that in 2013 over 1.2 billion phones were taking pictures, a number that grew exponentially. In 2015, Apple sold over 26,000 phones per hour—and now those iPhones have wide color.

Adopting color management in your app won't be easy. You're going to find drawing code that's hard to update. Development tools are still evolving and may not be fully compatible with color management. Testing your code is also more difficult than it was with Retina displays: you can't just run your app at two or three times normal size. You need a display that can show a wider range of color, which is currently limited to the latest Retina iMac, an iPad Pro, and the latest iPhone.

But obstacles like these never get in the way of developers who want their apps to look the very best. My advice is to focus your efforts on the parts of your app where vibrant content has the biggest payoff—both you and your customers will be impressed with how much accurate color improves the experience.

5

DESKTOP APPS

YOUR IOS APP is a hit! Customers are craving a desktop version and you've created a new project in Xcode to build a Mac app. Let's examine color considerations on this platform. (Fortunately, after the in-depth changes for the web and mobile, this chapter will be quick!)

As you did in Chapter 4, download a sample app, Colorful, to follow along and do your own experiments—you'll also see it in the screenshots.

ANYTHING GOES

After seeing so many platforms that dictate a color space, we're now on an OS with no limits: your Mac displays any color space you choose (**FIG 5.1**).

The growing pains of iOS are bygones on macOS—Apple built ColorSync into the operating system's first release in 2001, making color management ubiquitous on the desktop.

You're also not limited to just one color space: multiple spaces can be mixed and matched as necessary. Any one of the choices from the color picker's gear menu is valid and will show up correctly at all points in the development process.

Like the rest of macOS, Xcode displays images using embedded color profiles, so make sure other controls in your interface have the same profile. For example, compare the test images created from ColorTest.psd with the Generic RGB and sRGB label-background colors in the sample project (**FIG 5.2**).

RESTRAINT IS IN ORDER

In spite of this newfound flexibility, you'll still want to be careful about how you use color in a Mac app.

Sometimes sticking with the system's default color space will make your development smoother. In other cases, your job will be easier if you use a common color space between your mobile and desktop apps. Let's look at your options.

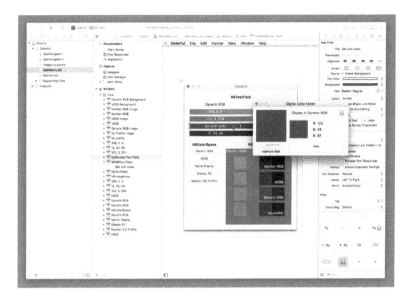

FIG 5.1: Interface Builder for macOS displays in whatever color space you select in the picker.

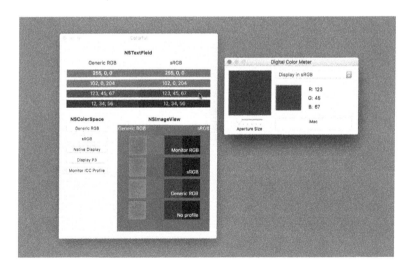

FIG 5.2: A Mac app using many color spaces simultaneously.

The default color

The AppKit framework to create Mac apps has traditionally used "calibrated" colors. This is just another term for Generic RGB, so if you want to create an NSColor in this color space, use colorWithCalibratedRed:green:blue:alpha:.

This de facto standard appears in a lot of our tools. Many developers, including your humble author, used the standard color picker numerous times before they noticed it had a gear icon to change profiles. Managed color is everywhere you look on your Mac, but that hasn't stopped any of us from creating apps without worrying about color spaces.

Common color

If you're developing an app for macOS as well as the web or iOS, working with sRGB color can make your life way easier. Cross-platform apps typically share a lot of assets: you'll spend less time making graphics and achieve a more consistent interface if you build everything in one color space.

To use sRGB in your controls, select it from the color picker's gear menu while entering your red, green, and blue component values. In the sample Colorful project, the NSTextField background colors on the right-hand side demonstrate this approach.

If you need to create sRGB colors in code, you have two choices:

```
[NSColor colorWithSRGBRed:(123.0/255.0)
    green:(45.0/255.0) blue:(67.0/255.0) alpha:1.0];
```

Or:

```
[NSColor colorWithRed:(123.0/255.0)
    green:(45.0/255.0) blue:(67.0/255.0) alpha:1.0];
```

These produce identical results, but the second form makes your life simpler because the name is very similar to its iOS counterpart.

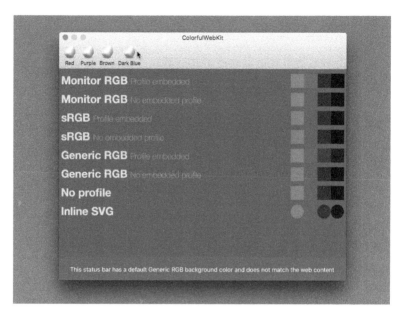

FIG 5.3: A color mismatch between and the native controls of a Mac app.

If you have more specific needs, you can create NSColor with any components and color space. For example, if you want to match the iMac's wide-gamut display, use a CGColorRef created with kCGColorSpaceDisplayP3. Check the sample project for details.

WebView

As we wind up our tour of development platforms, we're back on the web!

Since the introduction of Safari, the Mac has had excellent support for embedding web content in apps. Using the WebKit framework and a WebView object, apps can add HTML, CSS, and JavaScript to the user experience, while integrating with the desktop's unique capabilities.

When you use WebView in your app, you gain the same color management available in Safari. Everything you saw in Chapter 3 remains applicable. Your primary concern is to make sure that assets in the native part of your app match what's in your HTML and CSS (**FIG 5.3**). Sticking with sRGB is your best bet.

To learn more about ways to deploy WebView in a Mac app, download the ColorfulWebKit sample code. You'll also get a quick taste of the interaction between a native app and a web app.

Desktop apps often take a backseat to web and native apps running on our phones and tablets. Except in one major area: the development tools we use to create those mobile products. As the products we build become more color aware, you can avoid problems by knowing how your desktop tools handle color.

CONCLUSION

YOU'VE COME A LONG WAY since that first glimpse of Dr. Eyeful's website. Now that the pain has subsided, you're hopefully more comfortable with your tools and the colors they produce. You've also learned how to get predictable results while you work with color on any platform.

If I could offer one piece of advice at the end of this lengthy treatise: learn to love sRGB. It's the safest color space and avoids color shifts stemming from profile mismatches. Adopting this color space also makes saving assets less error prone, and lets you use the same files across a variety of environments.

But don't get *too* attached to sRGB. The displays on our existing devices will change in the coming years, and you'll want to move your workflows to these wider gamuts. The techniques in this book will ease that transition and make your products look even better on a desktop, tablet, or phone.

With the help of color management, your future looks bright!

ACKNOWLEDGMENTS

Any project that takes years to complete includes the contributions of many people. This book got its start in 2014, when my pals Jeffrey Zeldman and Ethan Marcotte showed enthusiasm for an early draft. That led to an introduction to Katel LeDû who, despite my repeated attempts otherwise, kept this project on track.

Tina Lee is a secret weapon. She finds vast swaths of words that aren't really needed, repairs my abuse of the passive voice, and generally makes me look like a better writer than I am. She'd probably like to get rid of this sentence and the prior one, but she told me I could do anything I want here, and aren't you glad the rest of the book isn't like this?

Work on this book was a constant reminder that I have awesome peers. Pieter Omvlee (Sketch), Tom Giannattasio (Macaw), Wade Cosgrove (Coda), and Simonas Bastys (Pixelmator) helped me understand how their excellent tools manage color. Marc Edwards, Troy Gaul, Gus Mueller, and Daniel Kennett provided excellent feedback on a complicated topic. Steve Troughton-Smith and his huge collection of devices helped with many screenshots. Thanks to you all!

Another group deserves special recognition: the folks at Apple who are leading the way with color management. Their knowledge and thoughtfulness show in videos, email correspondence, and blog posts. You know who you are, and you have my sincere thanks.

As this project neared completion, I sent an unfinished manuscript to Mike Krieger and the team at Instagram. It was a joy to hear that my book not only helped them get ready for iOS 10, but also played a part in their feature during the iPhone 7 keynote. Wow!

The last contribution to this book came from my friend John Gruber. I've been an admirer of his writing since that first fireball many years ago, and it's an honor to have him introduce my own work. :whiskey:

Finally, this whole thing couldn't have happened without Lauren Mayes, who's been by my side every day offering advice, motivation, and love. Thanks, sweetie.

RESOURCES

See my site for links to this book's sample color tests, Photoshop files, and Xcode projects, all in one spot.

More about color management

Photographers have been managing colors for years. Learn from folks who've explored how color management affects digital imagery:

- "Color Space and Color Profiles," Richard Anderson and Peter Krogh. From the American Society of Media Photographers. Discusses in depth the methods used to reproduce color in digital photography.
- "Digital-Image Color Spaces," Jeffrey Friedl. A multipart series exploring color spaces in digital images. Note that some of the information about how web browsers and operating systems handle color is outdated.
- "Overview of Color Management," Sean McHugh. An excellent three-part series showing how color management factors into digital photography.
- "Soft Proofing Photos & Prints," Sean McHugh. Explains the details of Photoshop's color-conversion support, including advanced options such as rendering intent and black point compensation.
- "SRGB vs. Adobe RGB 1998," Sean McHugh. Explores the differences between the two most common color spaces in digital photography.
- "The Role of Working Spaces in Adobe Applications" (PDF), Andrew Rodney. A great overview of how Adobe uses color spaces. Covers the origins and features of the options in the Color Settings dialog.

The web: past, present, and future

Get an idea of how color is evolving on the web:

- "Is Your System ICC Version 4 Ready?," International Color Consortium. Yet another color difference between browsers! A newer version of the ICC profile format is not supported in some browsers, including Chrome and Firefox.
- "Improving Color on the Web," Dean Jackson. This post on the WebKit blog shows all the ways Apple's browser is changing to match improved display technologies.
- "A Standard Default Color Space for the Internet - sRGB," Michael Stokes, Matthew Anderson, Srinivasan Chandrasekar, and Ricardo Motta. Although now obsolete, this original specification for sRGB was the first time many developers encountered color spaces and profiles.
- "CSS Color Module Level 3," W3C. The current CSS color specification.
- "CSS Color Module Level 4," W3C. This draft proposal includes support for color profiles and device-dependent colors. Note the new color() function and @color-profile rule. Although not directly related to color management, color-mod() will be helpful for adjusting colors in a web design.

Colors and code

Learn from the experiences of Mac developers:

- "Introduction to Color Management Overview," Apple. Oriented toward the Mac, but many of the concepts and techniques now apply to iOS developers as well.
- "Technical Note TN2035: ColorSync on Mac OS X," Apple. Covers all aspects of ColorSync support on Mac OS X. Much of the information also applies to iOS.

Tools, tools, tools

Color management will become a bigger part of your design and development workflow:

- "Color Management in Your Tools," Craig Hockenberry. A quick overview of how various design and development tools manage color.

Developers have special needs when it comes to picking colors. These free tools integrate with the standard color picker and let you output color as code for the web or native apps:

- Developer Color Picker, **Panic**
- Skala Color, **Bjango**
- xScope, **The Iconfactory.** This developer tool was the genesis for this book. It does a lot of things besides color too.

The gory details

Dive into the fascinating intricacies—terms and mathematics— of color science:

- "iPhone 6 Pixels," **Bryan Jones.** The way displays are manufactured affects how they display color. This retinal neuroscientist looks at various screens from Apple underneath a microscope.
- Planckian Locus. **That** weird curved shape you've seen throughout the book has a name, and it lies at the heart of the physics behind the electromagnetic radiation that reaches our eye.
- Trichromacy. **Red,** green, and blue. It comes down to light-sensitive proteins in our cone cells. This Wikipedia page is a great place to start learning more about the biology of our vision and how our retina responds to light.

Specifications

Explore the standards behind color management:

- "Introduction to the ICC Profile Format," **International Color Consortium**
- "Embedding ICC Profiles in Standard Image File Formats," **International Color Consortium**
- Adobe RGB specification **(PDF), Adobe**
- sRGB specification **(PDF), International Color Consortium**

REFERENCES: MAKING SENSE OF COLOR MANAGEMENT

Shortened URLs are numbered sequentially; the related long URLs are listed below for reference.

Introduction

00-01   http://xscopeapp.com/

Chapter 1

01-01   https://developer.apple.com/library/content/releasenotes/MacOSX/
WhatsNewInOSX/Articles/MacOSX10_11_2.html#//apple_ref/doc/uid/
TP40016630-SW1

01-02   http://www.macrumors.com/2015/10/16/new-4k-imac-teardown/

01-03   http://xscopeapp.com/

Chapter 2

02-01   http://furbo.org/color/Downloads/ColorTest.psd.zip

02-02   https://en.wikipedia.org/wiki/Loudness_war

02-03   http://furbo.org/color/Downloads/ColorTest-sRGB.psd.zip

02-04   http://furbo.org/color/Downloads/ColorTest-GenericRGB.psd.zip

02-05   https://developer.apple.com/library/mac/qa/qa1430/_index.html

02-06   http://furbo.org/color/Downloads/ColorTest-MonitorRGB.png.zip

02-07   http://furbo.org/color/Downloads/Image-ProPhoto.jpg

02-08   http://www.dpbestflow.org/color/color-space-and-color-profiles

02-09   http://https://fstoppers.com/pictures/adobergb-vs-srgb-3167

02-10   https://blogs.adobe.com/crawlspace/2015/06/save-for-web-in-photo-
shop-cc-2015.html

02-11   https://helpx.adobe.com/photoshop/using/export-artboards-layers.html

02-12   https://helpx.adobe.com/photoshop/how-to/design-with-artboards.html

02-13   http://furbo.org/color/Tools/

Chapter 3

03-01   http://www.w3.org/TR/css3-color/#rgb-color

03-02 https://www.w3.org/Graphics/Color/sRGB.html

03-03 http://www.w3.org/TR/SVG/color.html#ColorIntroduction

03-04 https://www.w3.org/TR/SVG/refs.html#ref-ICC42

03-05 https://www.w3.org/TR/SVG/painting.html#SpecifyingPaint

03-06 https://html.spec.whatwg.org/multipage/scripting.html
       #colour-spaces-and-colour-correction

03-07 http://furbo.org/color/CanvasTest/

03-08 https://github.com/whatwg/html/issues/299

03-09 http://furbo.org/color/Colorful/

03-10 https://webkit.org/blog/73/color-spaces/

03-11 http://furbo.org/color/Colorful/

03-12 https://bugs.chromium.org/p/chromium/issues/detail?id=44872

03-13 https://www.w3.org/TR/css3-color/#dropped

03-14 http://blogs.windows.com/bloggingwindows/2015/03/30/introducing-
       project-spartan-the-new-browser-built-for-windows-10/

03-15 http://www.apple.com/ipad-pro/

03-16 https://jeffcarlson.com/2016/04/21/the-9-7-inch-ipad-pro-color-gamut/

03-17 http://furbo.org/color/Downloads/Image-ProPhoto.jpg

03-18 https://drafts.csswg.org/mediaqueries-4/#color-gamut

03-19 http://caniuse.com/#feat=picture

03-20 http://furbo.org/color/ResponsiveColor/

03-21 http://furbo.org/color/WideGamut

03-22 https://imageoptim.com/

03-23 http://furbo.org/color/Colorful/

Chapter 4

04-01 https://developer.android.com/reference/android/graphics/Color.html

04-02 https://developer.apple.com/videos/play/wwdc2015/510/

04-03 https://developer.apple.com/videos/play/wwdc2016/712/

04-04 https://developer.apple.com/videos/play/wwdc2016/501/

04-05 http://furbo.org/color/downloads/ColorfulMobile.zip

04-06 https://developer.apple.com/xcode/

04-07 https://developer.apple.com/library/content/documentation/IDEs/
       Conceptual/AppDistributionGuide/AppThinning/AppThinning.html

04-08 https://developer.apple.com/library/content/documentation/
       DeviceInformation/Reference/iOSDeviceCompatibility/
       HardwareGPUInformation/HardwareGPUInformation.html#//apple_ref/
       doc/uid/TP40013599-CH106-SW1

04-09   https://www.bignerdranch.com/blog/xcode-breakpoint-wizardry/

04-10   http://petapixel.com/2015/04/09/this-is-what-the-history-of-camera-sales-looks-like-with-smartphones-included/

04-11   http://om.co/2016/01/27/what-in-2015-apple-sold-how-many-million-iphones/

Chapter 5

05-01   http://furbo.org/color/Downloads/Colorful.zip
05-02   http://furbo.org/color/Downloads/ColorfulWebKit.zip

Resources

06-01   http://www.dpbestflow.org/color/color-space-and-color-profiles
06-02   http://regex.info/blog/photo-tech/color-spaces-page1
06-03   http://www.cambridgeincolour.com/tutorials/color-management1.htm
06-04   http://www.cambridgeincolour.com/tutorials/color-spaces.htm
06-05   http://www.cambridgeincolour.com/tutorials/color-space-conversion.htm
06-06   http://www.cambridgeincolour.com/tutorials/soft-proofing.htm
06-07   http://www.cambridgeincolour.com/tutorials/sRGB-AdobeRGB1998.htm
06-08   http://https://www.adobe.com/digitalimag/pdfs/phscs2ip_colspace.pdf
06-09   http://www.color.org/version4html.xalter
06-10   https://webkit.org/blog/6682/improving-color-on-the-web/
06-11   https://www.w3.org/Graphics/Color/sRGB
06-12   https://www.w3.org/TR/css3-color/
06-13   https://drafts.csswg.org/css-color/#changes
06-14   https://developer.apple.com/library/mac/documentation/GraphicsImaging/Conceptual/csintro/csintro_intro/csintro_intro.html
06-15   https://developer.apple.com/library/mac/technotes/tn2035/_index.html
06-16   http://furbo.org/color/Tools/
06-17   http://download.panic.com/picker/
06-18   https://bjango.com/mac/skalacolor/
06-19   http://xscopeapp.com
06-20   http://prometheus.med.utah.edu/~bwjones/2014/10/iphone-6-pixels/
06-21   https://en.wikipedia.org/wiki/Planckian_locus
06-22   https://en.wikipedia.org/wiki/Trichromacy
06-23   http://www.color.org/iccprofile.xalter
06-24   http://www.color.org/profile_embedding.xalter
06-25   https://www.adobe.com/digitalimag/pdfs/AdobeRGB1998.pdf
06-26   http://www.color.org/specification/ICC1v43_2010-12.pdf

ABOUT THE AUTHOR

Craig Hockenberry has been making software since 1976 and built his first website at 14.4 kilobits per second. He's a principal at the Iconfactory, a company that's been changing the face of our computers for over twenty years. His writing has helped many fellow developers in their work, and that makes him happy. So does a Manhattan.

INDEX: MAKING SENSE OF COLOR MANAGEMENT

5

A BOOK APART

COLOR
ACCESSIBILITY
WORKFLOWS

GERI COADY

FOREWORD BY
DEREK FEATHERSTONE

Publisher: Jeffrey Zeldman
Designer: Jason Santa Maria
Executive Director: Katel LeDû
Managing Editor: Tina Lee
Editor: Caren Litherland
Technical Editor: Jon Hicks
Copyeditor: Kate Towsey
Proofreader: Katel LeDû
Compositor: Ron Bilodeau
Ebook Producer: Ron Bilodeau

ISBN: 978-1-937557-57-7

A Book Apart
New York, New York
http://abookapart.com

TABLE OF CONTENTS:
COLOR ACCESSIBILITY WORKFLOWS

FOREWORD

RESOURCES ABOUND FOR PEOPLE who seek guidance on how to make the web more accessible. Many of those resources specifically cater to a developer audience: they offer techniques for creating semantically structured templates, keyboard accessible date pickers, or accordion widgets that work well with screen readers. We web professionals tend to love these resources for a couple of reasons. First, they make our products easier for people with disabilities to use; second, they allow us to work a little more quickly, without reinventing the wheel every time.

What we need more of, though, are books like Geri's. If you write the perfect code for a flawed design, you may end up with parts that still aren't accessible. In *Color Accessibility Workflows*, Geri effortlessly puts accessibility into the hands and mind of the designer.

Geri's approach to color on the web is inspiring, methodical, and pragmatic. She shares the science of color and vision, and offers details about the tools she uses to create accessible color schemes. Although she concentrates on design, she gets nerdy enough for the developers out there, too. And, perhaps most crucially, she shares her reasoning, decision-making, and tried-and-true process for working with color and accessibility. This book is so much more than just a reference on color. Web design and development techniques will forever come and go. Geri's focus on thinking and workflow ensures that this book will last.

—**Derek Featherstone**

INTRODUCTION

In visual perception a color is almost never seen as it really is—as it physically is. This fact makes color the most relative medium in art."
—JOSEF ALBERS, Interaction of Color

The most talked-about dress in 2015 didn't appear on the red carpet; it surfaced as a viral photo that polarized the internet over whether it was white and gold, or blue and black. Although hypotheses abound about why the actual blue-and-black dress appeared to be white and gold for so many people, this seems beyond dispute: it all comes down to the perception of color.

German abstract painter Josef Albers, perhaps best remembered for his *Homage to the Square* paintings, was also a dedicated teacher who, in 1963, published an influential course on color theory that still has relevance today. He was right: color is relative—not just because it appears to differ across different surfaces, but also because it's seen differently by different people.

What comes to mind when you think of disabilities that affect how people interact with websites, apps, and video games? Maybe you think of physical disabilities that make traditional input devices, such as a mouse or game controller, impossible to use. Or maybe you think of a more extreme scenario, such as complete blindness, where a customer must rely on screen-reader technology to navigate the web. Or perhaps you think of the aging population, which finds small font sizes challenging to read.

Another disability, though, one that isn't talked about so often, affects a surprisingly large percentage of the population: color blindness. The so-called "Dressgate" phenomenon may have been a fun meme for plenty of people, but poor color perception is a frustrating part of many people's daily lives.

Compared to just a few decades ago, when most mass media was produced in black and white, color is increasingly used to impart information. Today, advances in technology allow us to view color everywhere—not just on television screens, comput-

FIG 0: Millions of colors surround us every day.

ers, and phones, but also in our cars, on our banking machines, appliances, and even watches—and the list goes on (**FIG 0**).

Color is a powerful tool that affords seemingly endless design possibilities, but far too many of us design with only one type of color vision in mind—our own. In this guide, we'll learn not only how to make accessible color choices, but also how to become better, more empathetic designers by discovering how other people see the world.

1

COLOR BLINDNESS

THE MISNOMER *color blindness* has led to false impressions about what someone affected by the condition experiences. Only in extremely rare instances does color blindness mean that a person can't see any color at all; *monochromacy* (also known as *achromatopsia*) affects an estimated one in forty thousand births worldwide. *Monochromats* experience not only a complete lack of color perception, but may have light sensitivity and reduced vision as well. By contrast, what most of us think of as "color blindness" is a very common condition referring to a decreased ability to see color, or a decreased ability to tell colors apart from one another (FIG 1.1). Because of this misconception, many people prefer to use the more accurate phrase *color vision deficiency* (CVD). Keeping this more nuanced understanding in mind, we'll use both terms throughout this book.

The majority of people who have color blindness inherit the condition as a genetic trait. This trait is more likely to occur in someone born chromosomally male (with XY chromosomes) than someone born chromosomally female (with XX chromosomes); the most common form of color blindness occurs in 8% of males, but in only 0.5% of females. Taken together, these statistics represent a significant portion of the population. We need to keep this demographic in mind as we work.

HOW COLOR BLINDNESS OCCURS

But first, let's grapple with the mechanics of color vision deficiency. Ready for some science?

Inside the human eye is a lining called the *retina*. The retina can be likened to a type of screen onto which an image is projected through other parts of the eye, including the pupil and lens (FIG 1.2).

Two types of photoreceptor cells, *rods* and *cones*, live inside the retina. Rods allow us to see dark and light, and shape and movement; cones allow us to perceive color. There are three types of cones, each containing a photopigment that is stimulated by red, green, or blue wavelengths in the spectrum. L-cones are sensitive to long wavelengths of light; M-cones are sensitive to medium wavelengths of light; and S-cones are

FIG 1.1: Top left: a person with normal color vision might see a website this way. Bottom right: how the same website might appear to a person with color blindness.

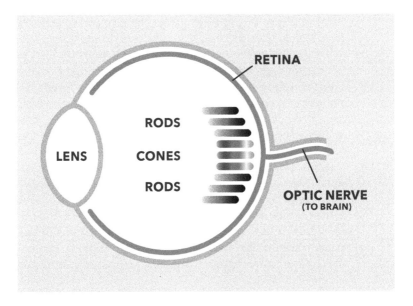

FIG 1.2: A diagram of the human eye.

sensitive to short wavelengths of light. When stimulated, the signals are combined in the brain and recognized as a color image—similar to how a computer mixes red, green, and blue light and emits it as an image on a screen.

Problems with color vision occur when one or more of these types of cones are defective or absent entirely. These problems can be inherited, or can be acquired through factors like trauma, exposure to ultraviolet light, degeneration with age, or as a side effect of diabetes.

People who have what is referred to as "normal" color vision are called *trichromats* because their color vision is based on all three types of healthy cones. In other words, they're capable of perceiving color detected from all three wavelengths of light. *Dichromats*, people who are missing an entire type of cone, can only perceive color detected from two wavelengths of light, a condition known as *dichromacy*.

Monochromacy is broken down into further distinctions. *Rod monochromacy*, the most severe condition, occurs when all three types of cones are faulty or missing and vision is dependent upon rods only, reducing color perception to shades of grey. People with rod monochromacy, who also experience reduced visual acuity and severe light sensitivity, may need to wear strong sunglasses both indoors and outdoors. *Blue-cone monochromacy*, a similarly severe condition, occurs when only blue cone receptors are functional. Blue-cone monochromats also experience reduced visual acuity and light sensitivity. *Cone monochromacy* is a less severe, extremely rare condition that does not affect visual acuity or light sensitivity. It occurs when only the red cone receptors or green cone receptors are present and functional.

To further complicate matters, a portion of one type of cone is faulty instead of completely absent in some people. Such people, called *anomalous trichromats*, have reduced sensitivities to color that may be less severe than what a dichromat experiences. They can be described as having a color *weakness* instead of color blindness.

Dr. Jay Neitz, a color vision researcher at the Medical College of Washington, states that trichromats with fully functional color vision can distinguish up to one million different colors, while a dichromat's palette is limited to just ten thousand colors. That's why dichromats are much more likely to be aware of their vision problem than anomalous trichromats, who might never know that they have mild color-defective vision unless they are tested.

WHAT COLOR BLINDNESS LOOKS LIKE

Have you ever noticed that it's much harder to discern color if you're in a dark space with no lighting? That's because our cones don't work as well in the dark; the rods are doing most of the work. Now imagine viewing the world this way under normal lighting conditions!

To convey what people with more severe types of color blindness experience, I'll focus on the different types of dichromacy. Remember that many people with deficiencies will see more colors than those shown in these simulated images, but not the full spectrum of color that most people with "normal" color vision see (FIG 1.3). Also note that because color blindness doesn't affect rod cells, people with color blindness can distinguish tones from light to dark (assuming they have no other vision problems).

Protanopia

Protanopia, or red-dichromacy, occurs when there's a total absence of L-cones. It's also one of the two types of color blindness commonly referred to as "red-green" color blindness. Affected people, called *protanopes*, have trouble distinguishing colors in the green-yellow-red area of the spectrum. In addition, the brightness of red, orange, and yellow colors is reduced. Reds often appear to be gray or black, and purples may be indistinguishable from shades of blue. A pink shirt, because it reflects both red and blue light, may simply appear blue. As the simulated images illustrate, the term "red-green" color blindness can be quite misleading, since protanopes often have trouble distinguishing many more colors beyond just red and green.

FIG 1.3: People with fully functional color vision are able to discern the full spectrum without significant confusion.

Protanopia-type deficiencies include *protanomaly*, a red-weakness, and together affect about 2% of chromosomal males (**FIG 1.4**).

Deuteranopia

Deuteranopia, or green-dichromacy, is the other "red-green" form of color blindness; it occurs when there's a total absence of M-cones. Affected people, called *deuteranopes*, have the same trouble distinguishing colors in the green-yellow-red area of the spectrum as protanopes do. Medium tones of red are more likely to be confused with oranges and yellows.

Deuteranomaly, a green-weakness, is by far the most common form of any color-vision deficiency, with roughly 5% of chromosomal males affected (**FIG 1.5**).

Tritanopia

Tritanopia is a much rarer form of color blindness. It is not inherited and is more likely to be acquired through old age, head injuries, or even alcoholism; it can potentially be reversed if the underlying cause is treated. Tritanopes, who lack S-cones, often confuse blue with green and yellow with violet.

FIG 1.4: People with severe protanopia have trouble distinguishing between reds, greens, and yellows. The brightness of colors may also be diminished.

FIG 1.5: People with severe deuteranopia also have trouble with reds, greens, and yellows, but brightness is generally unaffected.

Tritanopia and the related blue-weakness *tritanomaly* are not sex-linked traits, meaning they affect both chromosomal males and females equally. The number of people affected by tritanopia-type color blindnesses varies among different studies, but most say it occurs in less than 0.01% of the population (**FIG 1.6**).

FIG 1.6: People with severe tritanopia may confuse blue with green and yellow with violet.

TESTING FOR COLOR BLINDNESS

In the wake of 2015's viral "Dressgate" photo came an online test encouraging people to see if they belonged to "the 25% of the population" who are *tetrachromats*—that is, people born with an extra fourth cone who can potentially see up to one hundred million colors. As popular as the test was on social media, it was (perhaps not surprisingly) completely fake. While tetrachromacy is real, the condition in humans is so rare that the first scientifically confirmed case was only discovered in 2007. What's more, standard RGB computer monitors are incapable of displaying the range of colors required to accurately test for tetrachromacy—which raises questions about the accuracies of online vision testing in general.

Inaccurate, inconsistent color reproduction on home computer displays underscores the importance of getting properly tested for color blindness by a qualified vision specialist. Still, if you're curious, there are a few reputable online tests you might try on yourself. If they suggest you may be color-blind, it's best to follow up with a specialist for a confirmed medical diagnosis.

The most famous test is the Ishihara plate test, developed in 1916 and named after its creator, Dr. Shinobu Ishihara (**FIG 1.7**). The test consists of thirty-eight plates of numerals and lines hidden seamlessly within a field of dots. People who have

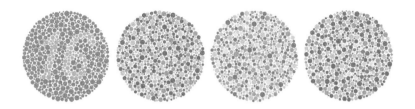

FIG 1.7: A selection of plates from the Ishihara color-blindness test.

trouble distinguishing the camouflaged numerals are known to have a color deficiency. Unfortunately, the test only evaluates forms of red-green color blindness, and even then with limited precision.

Alternatively, the Waggoner Computerized Color Vision Test (CCVT) is a paid test that provides more detailed information about which type of color blindness someone might have. The CCVT tests for protan, deutan, and tritan color vision deficiencies, and contains extra feedback about severity, if applicable.

HOW COLOR BLINDNESS AFFECTS PEOPLE

Although color blindness is surprisingly common, I had never met anybody who openly spoke about having the condition until I attended design school. Like many people with good color vision, I always took mine for granted; color blindness wasn't on my radar at all until my photography instructor, Ray Fennelly, opened up about it. As Ray recalled in an email conversation: "My design teacher, John Solowski, pointed it out to me in my first year at Ryerson University. I really was quite useless as a color printer. I guess that was why black-and-white photography appealed to me so much."

For my instructor, this meant he had to adapt to black-and-white photography—something he loved anyway—but for other people, being color-blind can have devastating effects on their career choices.

This may sound familiar if you've seen the 2006 film *Little Miss Sunshine*. Dwayne, the teenager who has taken a vow of silence until he fulfils his dream of becoming a test pilot, is horrified to discover he's color-blind; he realizes he'll never pass the screening test. Although the movie is fiction, this situation is a reality that many people have to face.

Screening tests are standard in many industries where color vision is a nonnegotiable requirement. Pilot, electrician, engineer, lab technician, and other career choices may simply be unattainable for those with color blindness. The topic is intensely debated by those who believe the concern is unwarranted. Many people feel discriminated against after failing vision tests when, in reality, they have no problem performing the job's day-to-day tasks.

In the United States, the Occupational Safety and Health Administration (OSHA) has no standards requiring normal color vision for any particular occupation; the standards are voluntary guidelines that are not regulated by federal or state government. Instead, each industry, employer, or vocational training program has final say about whether good color vision is a condition of employment, regardless of whether the person can perform the job functions safely or not.

This sort of prejudice abounds. In Japan, for example, color blindness has long been considered a disability for which affected people face widespread discrimination. The stigma derives from the publicity around a famous case within the Imperial Family. In 1920, the engagement of Hirohito, the eldest son of the Emperor of Japan, to Princess Nagako was vehemently opposed by Field Marshal Yamagata Aritomo, who alleged that Princess Nagako and her family were color-blind. He insisted that such a trait would damage the family's bloodlines, when in reality he wanted Hirohito to choose a bride from Yamagata's own clan instead. The effort to block the marriage failed (and it was proven that Princess Nagako was not color-blind at all), but the effect of perceiving color blindness as a negative trait persists in Japan today.

Yasuyo Takayanagi, an ophthalmologist and color-deficiency rights activist, conducted a survey in 1986 that revealed that nearly half of Japanese national universities discriminated against students and claimed that color-blind applicants were ineligible for admission "regardless of academic record." She states that although the number of universities observing this rule has decreased over the years, two national universities and one private university still retained the requirement as recently as 2014.

R-E-S-P-E-C-T

At this point you may be asking, "But we're just designing websites, right? Why does all this even matter?"

It's true that we may not have control over controversial rules and regulations in other industries. A designers and developers, though, we *do* have the ability to learn more about color blindness and make some simple changes to our workflows to mitigate the number of everyday frustrations faced by this significant demographic.

How often have you witnessed people who, attempting to use an app or website, blame themselves for being unable to comprehend or perform basic tasks? (Maybe *you've* even felt this way.) Too frequently, that feeling originates in design decisions that aren't the user's fault at all.

We have the capacity to make a website not just bare-minimum usable, but inclusive too—giving all readers the same confident, enjoyable experience, regardless of ability. This industry is ours, and we have the means—the obligation, even—to give all readers the respect they deserve.

Easier said than done, right? With so many businesses trying to take the easiest route from kickoff to launch day, it's clear that even essential accessibility is often not considered at all. Many well-meaning folks simply cannot understand the challenges faced by others unless they experience it themselves, and may not see the importance of baking in accessibility from the beginning. For those folks, making accessibility a business case will be a necessary tactic.

If someone finds it frustrating to navigate your website, use your app, or play your game because of a color problem, they'll simply find an alternative. With nearly 5% of the overall population affected, it's easy to see how this can translate into lost readership and sales.

If that still isn't enough to convince a more adamant skeptic, it's important to understand that poor accessibility can quickly become an unexpected and very serious legal problem. Perhaps the most infamous case occurred in 2006, when the Maryland-based National Federation for the Blind (NFB) sued retailer Target Corporation for not addressing that Target.com was inaccessible to visually impaired users. In 2008, Target settled the class-action lawsuit, agreeing to pay class damages of $6 million and make the website fully accessible by February 2009, under the monitor of NFB themselves. Would you be prepared to face the consequences if your business was sued for creating a product or service that was unusable by a color-blind person?

So far, we've gone deep into the particulars of color blindness. We've learned what it is, how it affects people, and why it's absolutely essential to consider it in every project we build. With a solid understanding of this relative perception of color, it's time to learn how we can keep color accessibility in mind while assembling thoughtful color palettes.

CHOOSING
APPROPRIATE COLOR

WITH SEEMINGLY ENDLESS CHOICES, deciding on a color scheme for a project can feel like an overwhelming task for many designers. Although color psychology, message and meaning, and color harmony are beyond the scope of this book, this chapter will help define a starting point for choosing *appropriate* and *accessible* palettes.

COLOR FUNDAMENTALS

The ability to discriminate between colors relies on three attributes: hue, saturation, and lightness. Let's look at these elements more closely.

Hue

Hue is a color property. It's what we refer to when we say that something looks red, yellow, green, or blue—like the colors we perceive in a rainbow (**FIG 2.1**). This natural gradient from one hue to another can look quite different to a person with impaired vision, which is why simply choosing two hues, like red and blue, often won't provide enough contrast to be discernible.

Saturation

Saturation refers to the strength of a hue. The most saturated hue is the purest hue; the least saturated appears gray (**FIG 2.2**).

Lightness

Lightness (also called *brightness*) refers to the lightness or darkness of a color. It's produced by adding white or black. A *shade* is achieved by adding black to increase darkness; a *tint* is achieved by adding white to increase brightness. Many colors are in fact darker or lighter shades of others: browns are darker shades of orange; pinks are lighter tints of red (**FIG 2.3**).

FIG 2.1: A range of hues from red to violet.

FIG 2.2: Saturation progresses from a pure color to gray.

Shades   Tints

FIG 2.3: A range of dark green shades to bright green tints.

CONTRAST

As an illustrator, I know that one of the most important keys to a good painting is effective use of *contrast*. Contrast can take many forms: contrast of shape, contrast of color, contrast of texture, or contrast of scale, for example. These techniques can create emphasis and attract attention to the most important part of an artwork; when used with rhythm and composition, they can draw the eye to the next interesting area. In web design, the same techniques apply to create an easy-to-follow arrangement of information, keeping readers engaged and guiding them throughout the site. Aside from being a powerful means of achieving visual hierarchy, contrast is also one of the best ways to increase the readability of individual page elements, particularly text.

Unfortunately, a low-contrast design aesthetic suffuses the web (FIG 2.4). This minimalist trend has real consequences for our audiences. It can create unnecessary eye strain, make readers with even minor visual impairments feel "old" and incapable, and be completely illegible for more affected people. A conscious decision to choose low-contrast colors for the sake of aesthetics is simply unacceptable when usability plummets as a result.

The good news is that contrast can be easily achieved in numerous ways, some more effective than others. I'll outline a few of these methods.

Light-and-dark contrast

The most effective contrast occurs between light and dark colors. If you can, try not to use colors of a similar degree of lightness next to each other in a design (FIG 2.5).

Furthermore, since red-green color pairs (particularly when placed next to each other) cause problems for the majority of color-blind people, avoid such pairs if possible.

Complementary contrast

You can also achieve contrast by choosing complementary colors (except, of course, red and green), which appear opposite each other on a color wheel. Complementary color pairs generally work better than hues that are adjacent on the wheel. Again, remember to adjust lightness and darkness as required (FIG 2.6).

Warm-and-cool contrast

Contrast also exists between warm and cool colors on the color wheel (FIG 2.7). Effective use of warm-and-cool contrast appears in the works of skilled painters who understand the phenomenon of *atmospheric perspective*—objects in the distance appear

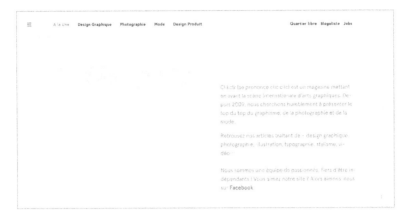

FIG 2.4: Some site designs prioritize style over legibility and readability, creating a challenge for readers with visual impairments.

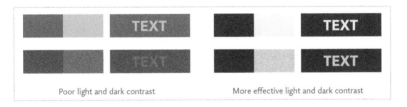

Poor light and dark contrast   More effective light and dark contrast

FIG 2.5: The sampled red and green colors share a similar degree of lightness and don't provide enough contrast on their own without some adjustments.

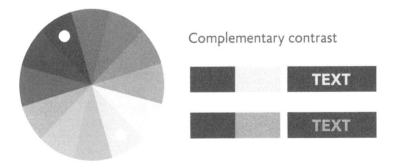

Complementary contrast

FIG 2.6: A complementary color pair can create more effective contrast than adjacent hues.

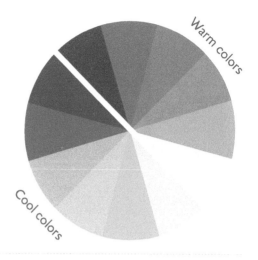

FIG 2.7: A color wheel divided into warm and cool colors.

to be cooler, while objects in the foreground appear to be warmer. A quick study of Leonardo da Vinci's *Mona Lisa*, for example, reveals that her hands—the closest point to the viewer—are the reddest and warmest, followed closely by the golden hues of her face, contrasted against the cool blue mountains of the background.

When designing with text, a dark shade of a cool color paired with a light tint of a warm color (**FIG 2.8**) provides better contrast than two warm colors or two cool colors (**FIG 2.9**).

Contrast of saturation

Contrast of saturation occurs when a dull color is placed next to a more intensely saturated color. Note that this technique is not as effective as light-and-dark contrast and should be avoided for important information (**FIG 2.10**).

We'll come back to contrast in Chapter 3, when we discuss how to achieve compliant contrast and implement color choices in our workflow.

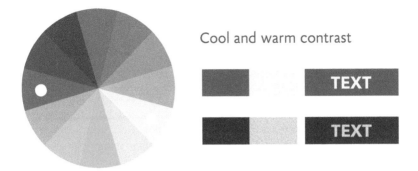

Cool and warm contrast

FIG 2.8: A dark shade of a cool color paired with a light tint of a warm color creates more effective contrast.

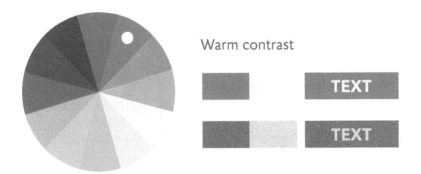

Warm contrast

FIG 2.9: A dark shade of a warm color paired with a light tint of a similar warm color creates less effective contrast.

Contrast of saturation

FIG 2.10: Placing a dull color next to a more saturated color is not recommended for creating effective contrast.

People often ask me if there are any "safe" color choices that can be seen by folks with all forms of color blindness. Unfortunately, there isn't a one-size-fits-all answer. Designing with only the most common deuteranopia-affected readers in mind could potentially exclude others with rarer conditions. Combined with the concerns of designing for low vision in general, the confusion could lead some designers to want to give up and design in grayscale instead! Of course, there are plenty of other ways to make color accessible without resorting to extremes, and there has been ample research and experimentation around which colors are most likely to be discernable by the greatest number of people.

The Japan-based *Color Universal Design Organization* (CUDO) developed a palette (PDF) containing colors that may be easier to discern individually by a more diverse color-blind audience. CUDO arrived at this palette by avoiding pure hues of red and green wherever possible; as a result, every color is easier to distinguish for people with deuteranopia, protanopia, and even tritanopia. These color choices are ideal for use in charts, wayfinding systems, and infographics, where color is key for interpreting information (**FIG 2.11**).

Designer Brian Suda has also experimented with color-blind-safe palettes. Not only does his palette translate well for a color-blind audience, but it also succeeds in grayscale, which can be helpful in some printing situations or on the monochromatic displays of various ereader devices (**FIG 2.12**).

Another useful tool I discovered has roots in a more traditional design industry—cartography. Professor Cynthia Brewer is a cartographer who developed an online tool called Color-Brewer, which provides color-palette advice originally intended for map design. One of the best things about this tool is that it also contains color-blind-friendly schemes that can be adapted for other applications (**FIG 2.13**).

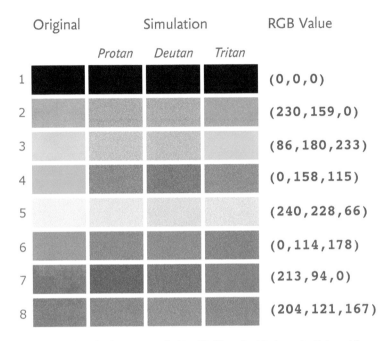

Original	Simulation			RGB Value
	Protan	*Deutan*	*Tritan*	
1				(0,0,0)
2				(230,159,0)
3				(86,180,233)
4				(0,158,115)
5				(240,228,66)
6				(0,114,178)
7				(213,94,0)
8				(204,121,167)

FIG 2.11: Examples of colors more easily identified by color-blind people. (Adapted from CUDO's research.)

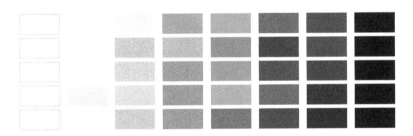

FIG 2.12: Brian Suda's set of color-blind-safe swatches.

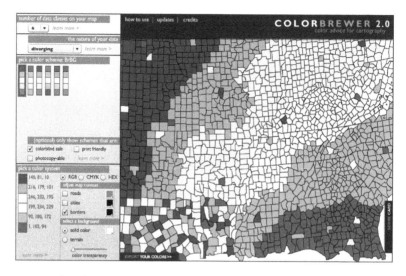

FIG 2.13: The ColorBrewer tool offers color advice for cartography.

Brewer explains that colors, including very similar colors, are much easier to differentiate when placed next to one another, much as they might appear in a map legend. It seems intuitive enough that comparing subtle color differences in close proximity is easier—think about how you'd overlap paint chips when picking out that perfect shade for your studio. A problem occurs, though, when the same colors are scattered in complex, random patterns: it becomes more difficult to locate which ones are unique. ColorBrewer demonstrates how a particular scheme will look when the color regions are close together, a little more spread out, or entirely random. If your scheme doesn't get a passing score, ColorBrewer will suggest reducing the number of data classes until you arrive at a clear and legible palette.

ColorBrewer lets you to choose color-blind-safe palettes in RGB, CMYK, and hex formats, and provides an ASE export function so you can load your generated palette straight into Photoshop or Illustrator.

We'll discuss additional tools to help you choose your palette in Chapter 3, after we learn about contrast compliance.

A word to the wise: choosing so-called "safe" and accessible colors may be met with opposition from higher-ups. In larger companies, such resistance may come from someone referred to in the industry as a "brand guardian". If forced to use on-brand color choices at the expense of legibility, try this counterargument: it's better to have a graph that looks slightly out of place but is easily deciphered than one that is on-brand but difficult to read. If customers can't make sense of something, they'll walk away.

CHECKING YOUR WORK

One of the first things I recommend to designers is integrating a color-blindness simulator into their workflow. Color-blindness simulators are indispensable tools for helping you assess whether you're on the right track from the start. Keep in mind, though, that not all color-blind people will see colors exactly as they appear in a simulator; simulators only mimic the vision of the most strongly affected people. Note that some differences in the simulated output may exist between different simulation applications—so be sure to remember the tips for choosing colors throughout your entire workflow and try not to rely on simulators as the only accessibility check in a project.

Mac OS X, Windows, and Linux users may want to try an application called Color Oracle. This indispensable tool displays common color-visual impairments as you use applications on your own screen. It's a full-screen filter that works throughout the operating system, independently of other software (**FIG 2.14**).

You can also proof for the two most common types of color blindness right in Photoshop or Illustrator (CS4 and later) as you're designing. This option is located under the View > Proof Setup menu in both applications (**FIG 2.15**).

Color simulators are excellent tools to have at your disposal—ideally, from the very beginning of a project—to help you make more informed color choices. Simulators alone, though, cannot guarantee your choices will be completely accessible. Next, we'll learn about color contrast ratios and compliance, which afford a more accurate way to evaluate your work.

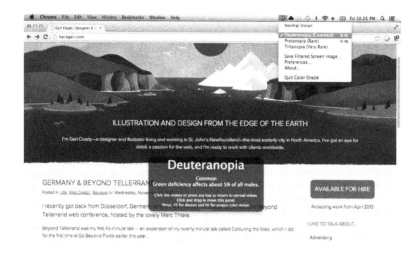

FIG 2.14: Color Oracle works throughout the operating system and can simulate color blindness in any application.

FIG 2.15: Photoshop and Illustrator (CS4 and later) offer native color-blindness proofing.

COMPLIANCE AND TESTING

THE WEB CONTENT ACCESSIBILITY GUIDELINES (WCAG) 2.0 contain recommendations from the World Wide Web Consortium (W3C) for making the web more accessible to users with disabilities, including color blindness and other vision deficiencies.

There are three levels of conformance defined in WCAG 2.0, from lowest to highest: A, AA, and AAA. For text and images of text, AA is the minimum level that must be met.

AA compliance requires text and images of text to have a minimum color contrast ratio of 4.5:1. In other words, the lighter color in a pair must have four-and-a-half times as much luminance (an indicator of how bright a color will appear) as the darker color. This contrast ratio is calculated to include people with moderately low vision who don't need to rely on contrast-enhancing assistive technology, as well as people with color deficiencies. It's meant to compensate for the loss in contrast sensitivity often experienced by users with 20/40 vision, which is half of normal 20/20 vision.

Level AAA compliance requires a contrast ratio of 7:1, which provides compensation for users with 20/80 vision, or a quarter of normal 20/20 vision. People who have a degree of vision loss more than 20/80 generally require assistive technologies with contrast enhancement and magnification capabilities.

Text that acts as pure decoration, nonessential text that appears in part of a photograph, and images of company logos do not strictly need to adhere to these rules. Nonessential or decorative text is, by definition, not essential to understanding a page's content. Logos and wordmarks may contain textual elements that are essential to broadcasting the company's visual identity, but not to conveying important information. If necessary, the logo may be described by using an alt attribute for the benefit of a person using screen-reader software. To learn more, check out accessibility specialist Julie Grundy's blog post on Simply Accessible, where she goes into the best practices around describing alt attributes.

Text size plays a big role in determining how much contrast is required. Gray text with an RGB value of (150,150,150) on a pure white background passes the AA level of compliance, as long as it's used in headlines above 18 points. Gray text with an

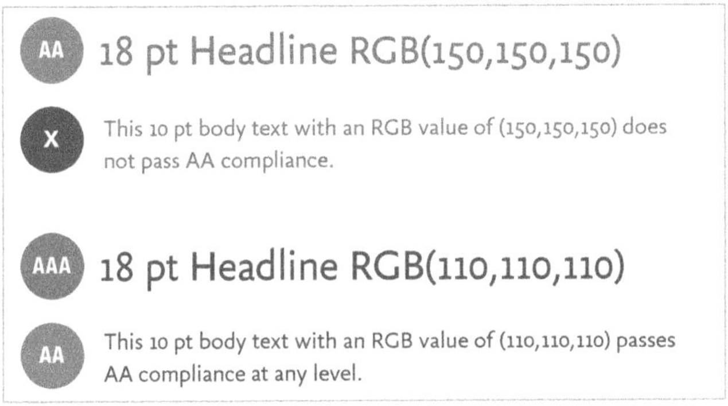

AA 18 pt Headline RGB(150,150,150)

X This 10 pt body text with an RGB value of (150,150,150) does not pass AA compliance.

AAA 18 pt Headline RGB(110,110,110)

AA This 10 pt body text with an RGB value of (110,110,110) passes AA compliance at any level.

FIG 3.1: Text size also plays a role when calculating compliance ratios.

RGB value of (110,110,110) passes the AA level at any text size, and will be AAA compliant if used as a headline above 18 points (**FIG 3.1**). A font displayed at 14 points may have a different level of legibility compared to another font at 14 points due to the wide diversity of type styles, so keep this in mind, especially when using very thin weights.

Personally, I recommend that all body text be AAA compliant, with larger headlines and less important copy meeting AA compliance as a bare minimum. Keep in mind that these ratios refer to solid-colored text over solid-colored backgrounds, where a single color value can be measured. Overlaying text on a gradient, pattern, or photograph may require a higher contrast value or alternative placement, such as over a solid-colored strip, to provide sufficient legibility.

These compliance ratios are often what folks mean when they claim that achieving accessible design by "ticking off boxes" can only come at the cost of stifled creativity or restricted color choices. But that simply isn't true. Experimentation with a color-contrast checker proves that many compliance ratios are quite reasonable and easy to achieve—especially if you are aware of the rules from the beginning. It would be much more frustrating to try to shift poor color choices into something compliant later in the design process, after branding colors have already been chosen. If you fight your battles up front, you'll find you won't feel restricted at all.

If all this talk of numbers seems confusing, I promise there'll be no real math involved on your side. You can easily find out if your color pairs pass the test by using a color-contrast checker.

CONTRAST CHECKERS

One of my favorite tools is Lea Verou's Contrast Ratio (**FIG 3.2**). It gives you the option of entering a color code for a background and a color code for text, and it calculates the ratio for you.

Contrast Ratio supports color names, hex color codes, RGBA values, HSLA values, and even combinations of each. Supporting RGBA and HSLA values means that Verou's tool supports transparent colors, a handy feature. You can easily share the results of a check by copying and pasting the URL. Additionally, you can modify colors by changing the values in the URL string instead of using the page's input fields.

Another great tool that has the benefit of simultaneously showing whether a color combination passes both AA and AAA compliance levels is Jonathan Snook's Colour Contrast Check (**FIG 3.3**).

At the time of writing, Colour Contrast Check doesn't support HSL alpha values, but it does display the calculated brightness difference and color difference values, which might interest you if you want a little more information.

COLOR PICKERS

If you need help choosing accessible colors from the start, try Color Safe. This web-based tool helps designers experiment with and choose color combinations that are immediately contrast-compliant. Enter a background color as a starting point; then choose a standard font family, font size, font weight, and target WCAG compliance level. Color Safe will return a comprehensive list of suggestions that can be used as accessible text colors (**FIG 3.4**).

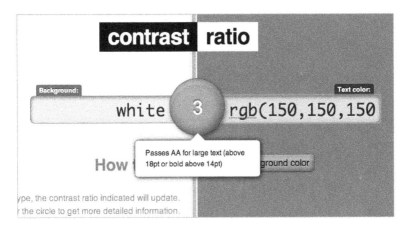

FIG 3.2: Lea Verou's Contrast Ratio checker.

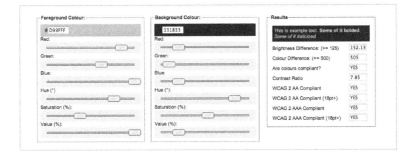

FIG 3.3: Jonathan Snook's Colour Contrast Check.

ADJUSTMENT TOOLS

When faced with color choices that fail the minimum contrast ratios, consider using something like Tanaguru Contrast Finder to help find appropriate alternatives (**FIG 3.5**). This incredibly useful tool takes a foreground and background color pair and then presents a range of compliant options comparable to the original colors. It's important to note that this tool works best when the colors are already close to being compliant but just need a little push—color pairs with drastically low contrast ratios may not return any suggestions at all (**FIG 3.6**).

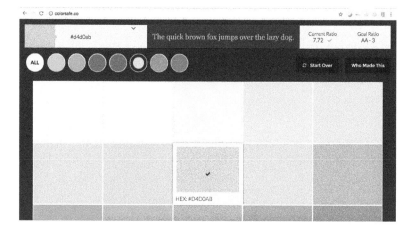

FIG 3.4: Color Safe searches for compliant text colors based on an existing background color.

Old contrast

Foreground	Background	Sample	Ratio	Distance
hsl(186, 38%, 55%) rgb(96, 175, 185) #60AFB9	hsl(178, 60%, 23%) rgb(24, 96, 94) #18605E	Title big size with words in bold Here is some text sample with some words in bold to illustrate the contrast.	2.89875	

FIG 3.5: This color pair is not AA compliant.

New contrast : 35 results (964 colors tested)

⇅ Foreground	⇅ Background	⇅ Sample	⇅ Ratio	⇅ Distance
hsl(187, 76%, 70%) rgb(122, 223, 237) #7ADFED	hsl(178, 60%, 23%) rgb(24, 96, 94) #18605E	Title big size with words in bold Here is some text sample with some words in bold to illustrate the contrast.	4.73462	64.54
hsl(188, 71%, 75%) rgb(147, 225, 237) #93E1ED	hsl(178, 60%, 23%) rgb(24, 96, 94) #18605E	Title big size with words in bold Here is some text sample with some words in bold to illustrate the contrast.	4.95319	73.57
hsl(187, 65%, 79%) rgb(170, 229, 237) #AAE5ED	hsl(178, 60%, 23%) rgb(24, 96, 94) #18605E	Title big size with words in bold Here is some text sample with some words in bold to illustrate the contrast.	5.26856	88.93
hsl(188, 53%, 84%) rgb(195, 231, 237) #C3E7ED	hsl(178, 60%, 23%) rgb(24, 96, 94) #18605E	Title big size with words in bold Here is some text sample with some words in bold to illustrate the contrast.	5.55873	108.76

FIG 3.6: A selection of Tanaguru's suggested AA-compliant alternatives.

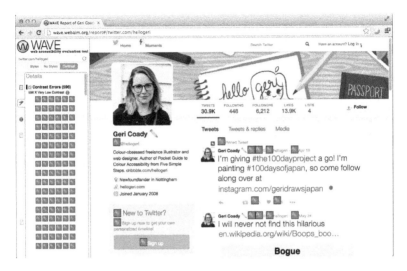

FIG 3.7: WAVE shows contrast errors by highlighting the relevant page elements.

TESTING TOOLS

If you'd like to test an existing website to see if it's up to par, check out a web-based service called WAVE. Although it evaluates for many different types of accessibility issues, it also features a contrast checker that pinpoints the exact location of any contrast hiccups on a given page. WAVE is also available as a Chrome Extension (**FIG 3.7**).

If Chrome is your preferred browser, try using Google's own Accessibility Developer Tools extension (**FIG 3.8**).

This tool allows you to inspect text elements and shows you the contrast ratio in a separate "Accessibility Properties" tab in the sidebar—very handy! You can run a full-page audit, too, for an extensive list of warnings (**FIG 3.9**).

Bear in mind, though, that it's important to take some of these warnings (or lack thereof) with a grain of salt. While audit tools like WAVE certainly can identify potential contrast errors in text, they only evaluate the issues they were programmed to evaluate; they can't predict exceptional circumstances. A site that passes such a test does not automatically mean it's accessible to a human being (**FIG 3.10**).

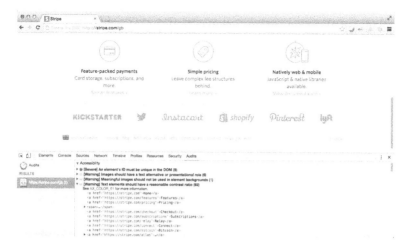

FIG 3.8: Accessibility audit screen in Chrome's Accessibility Developer Tools extension.

FIG 3.9: The accessibility properties inspector shows the insufficient contrast ratio warning for the gray text in the website's footer.

For example, because WAVE only checks for text contrast in relation to background colors, it doesn't notice that our red link in the introduction isn't underlined. For a person with protanopia or deuteranopia, this link will most likely blend into

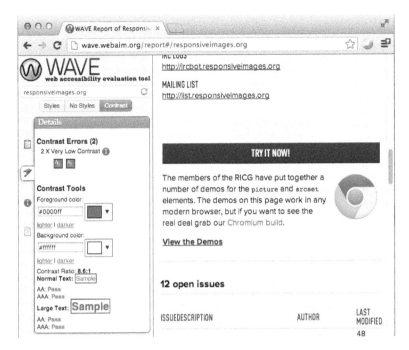

FIG 3.10: WAVE can't pick up on all color contrast issues, such as the non-underlined red link in this introductory paragraph.

the surrounding paragraph text; yet it will not return a contrast error in the test results.

A similar issue occurs when using text over a photograph. Consider a screenshot of a website with legible white text placed over a darkened photograph (**FIG 3.11**). Now imagine what that would look like with images turned off in the browser settings (**FIG 3.12**). In this example, because the parent container is white, the text completely disappears unless it's highlighted with a cursor, as demonstrated for the screenshot. Turning off browser images is not just for folks with visual impairments. Expensive roaming costs may force travelers to save data wherever possible. Slow internet connections and older devices may struggle to load images at all. For these reasons, too, setting a contrast-compliant background color is crucial.

FIG 3.11: A section of the Apple iPad website with legible white text over a photograph.

FIG 3.12: The same text (highlighted) appears to be invisible if background images are turned off or are unable to load.

In 2012, Twitter rolled out site-wide profile header images that were overlaid on a dark-gray (#444) background color, which provided plenty of contrast to pass a contrast checker. However, because image colors weren't taken into account, if a Twitter user uploaded a photograph with poor contrast against the white text, it would not raise any alarms in a contrast check.

To take another example, running this Weather Network profile through WAVE returned warnings for various design elements on the page, but no contrast issue was flagged for the header, even though the photograph does not provide enough legibility for a person with a vision problem (FIG 3.13).

After I sampled an average color of the photograph and ran it through Lea Verou's checker, it showed that the contrast was

FIG 3.13: WAVE returns contrast errors for some page text, but not all.

a very low 2.3—well under the minimum 4.5 required for AA compliance.

In addition, absolutely positioned text elements that appear outside of their parent containers can return false positives. I discovered an example of this on an older iteration of the Flickr homepage. Running a test on the page showed me that the Forbes quote at the top didn't pass the test, even though it looked acceptable over the dark blue sky graphic (**FIG 3.14**).

When I inspected the page, I noticed that the whole banner was absolutely positioned. Because the parent container was white, the white-on-white text returned a false alarm (**FIG 3.15**).

Although these little quirks can certainly impact the results of a test, it's still worth running your work through a checker to catch any potential oversights.

We've covered a fair amount of ground so far. Now that we're equipped with knowledge of the fundamentals of color-accessible design, let's turn to how we might combine what we've learned to finesse the user experience.

FIG 3.14: The contrast ratio of the Forbes quote is a low 1.01. Why?

FIG 3.15: The parent container is absolutely positioned and the background is white.

TIPS AND TRICKS

ALTHOUGH CERTAIN COLOR COMBINATIONS should be avoided where possible, try not to spend too much time worrying about achieving a so-called "perfect" palette. You can use plenty of other tips and tricks in combination with your color choices to improve the user experience.

NAMING

What's in a name? A lot, if you're color-blind.

For people with good color vision, simple words like "red" or "green" can seem unnecessary or unimportant when labeling items, but they can relay essential information to a color-blind person who cannot otherwise tell the two apart.

Color names

If you design websites that sell products, especially clothing, you'll need to pay close attention to how those products are labeled. One of the most common complaints I hear from people affected by color blindness is that they find it difficult to purchase clothing and accessories; they frequently need to ask another person for a second opinion on what the color of the item might actually be. While it's often easier for someone with color blindness to shop online than in a physical store (where it may be embarrassing to have to ask a staff member or other customer to confirm a color), many accessibility issues can still crop up on ecommerce websites.

Imagine you're designing a website that sells T-shirts. If you only show a photo of the shirt, it may be impossible for someone with color blindness to tell what color the shirt really is. For clarification, be sure to reference the name of the color in the description of the product.

T-shirt designers United Pixelworkers (inactive at the time of writing) did a great job at following this rule on their original website (FIG 4.1). Their Indianapolis shirt, for example, was clearly described as having a "navy Indy car on a red American Apparel 100% cotton tee" with a "navy UP logo on the back."

FIG 4.1: United Pixelworkers provided helpful descriptions of their T-shirts' colors and patterns.

Another common problem occurs when a color filter has been added to a product search. Here's an example from L.L.Bean's website containing unlabeled color swatches, and how they might look to someone with deuteranopia (FIG 4.2).

The color-search filter from an earlier version of the H&M website, which uses names instead, is slightly better, but this method can create unnecessary problems too (FIG 4.3).

The concept of completely stripping color from a design as a means of making things "easier" to comprehend for all audiences has been explored in other ways. Nathalie Dubé, a Canadian designer, experimented with this topic in a student project where she redesigned colored pencils to be all white, with a label printed on each stating the color name in French (FIG 4.4). Although this might make sense in theory, removing the color coating from each pencil also effaced a visual cue that could have made it easier to find the pencils at a glance.

It's important to remember that most so-called color-blind people can still see some color, and are capable of narrowing down such choices based on their own abilities. A color-blind person may not know which exact pencil is red, but they may know which pencils are *not* red, and therefore can eliminate many choices up front if a colored label exists. They can then

Good color vision   Deuteranopia

FIG 4.2: The color-search filter on L.L.Bean's website is no help at all to color-blind visitors.

FIG 4.3: On an earlier version of its site, H&M provided color names for its search filter, but matching swatches would have improved matters even further.

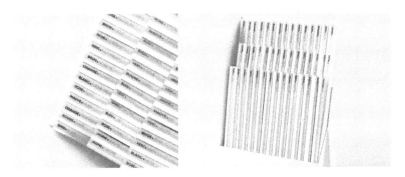

FIG 4.4: Nathalie Dubé's project erases color entirely, making pencil selection more difficult for everyone.

continue reading the labels to find the red in question. Removing color completely not only forces color-blind people to read every single label before making a choice, but forces everyone else to do the same.

The best solution is to use a combination of colors *and* names. Not only will that benefit people with good color vision, allowing them to scan swatches quickly, but it will also give color-blind users a reference and a name to work with. The American eyewear company Warby Parker has a robust search filter on its website, with a very effective combination of color swatches and names (**FIG 4.5**). The ability to increase the size of the swatch sample also helps reduce confusion.

"Creative" names

The color spectrum is continuous, and it is language that cuts it up. It is neither in nature nor in our eye that orange ceases to be orange and becomes red, nor in the speaking subjects who, faced with such a sample of color, decide its name. It is in the language that gave them the choice of words. If the English language had not placed orange between yellow and red, how are we to know that the perception of it would not have been different?
—THIERRY DE DUVE, Pictorial Nominalism: On Marcel Duchamp's Passage from Painting to the Readymade

As helpful as naming can be for describing the color of clothing or products, try not to get too fancy with your word choices. "Creative" color names, like the ones you might find on swatches of paint samples, can be just as confusing as not using any color name at all (**FIG 4.6**). Using a word like "grape" instead of "purple" doesn't really give the viewer any useful information about what the actual hue is. Is grape supposed to be purple, or could it refer to red or even green grapes? What about the name "smoke"? While you might intend for it to mean gray, smoke can also appear to be white, black, or brown, and colored smoke exists too. Stick with hue names as much as possible—there's

FIG 4.5: Warby Parker provides both color names and swatches—the most effective solution.

FIG 4.6: The color combinations of these men's sweaters are described on the Superdry website as Woodland/Sky, Iced Coffee/Apple, and Ashes/Coral, respectively.

a greater chance that the viewer will understand that a red shirt is red rather than brick, and it won't force them to ask another person for clarification.

This makes a huge case for why we always need to keep color-blind users in mind (**FIG 4.7**). How many potential customers might you lose because of a single design decision? Chances are, quite a few—especially if you're selling menswear!

FIG 4.7: How a person with tritanopia might view these sweaters. The color names carry little meaning.

IMAGES AND TEXT

Overlaying text on an image is an extremely common design technique that needs more consideration. Pay attention to the areas of an image where the text contrast and image contrast could become illegible to a person with vision problems (**FIG 4.8**). When in doubt, consider adding a solid background with the sufficient contrast necessary to keep the text visible no matter what kind of image is placed underneath (**FIG 4.9**). Alternatively, try making the image subtler by masking it with a darker color for lighter text, or a lighter color for darker text (**FIG 4.10**).

DATA AND INFOGRAPHICS

Designing accessible maps and infographics can be quite a challenge, especially since color is often chosen as the sole indicator of different data regions (**FIG 4.11**).

Don't rely on color-coding alone. Use a combination of color and texture or pattern, along with precise labels, and reflect this in the key or legend. That way, readers will always have two pieces of information to work with (**FIG 4.12**).

The patterns you choose can matter too. As a rule of thumb, a lighter shade of a background color should contain a subtler pattern design, such as a sparse dot or thin vertical line. A darker

FIG 4.8: In some areas of this photo, the text is illegible against the background.

FIG 4.9: Experimenting with placing text on a solid block or bar yields better results.

FIG 4.10: Stylizing images can help make text stand out.

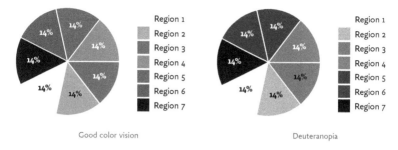

Good color vision   Deuteranopia

FIG 4.11: This chart contains colors that may cause confusion.

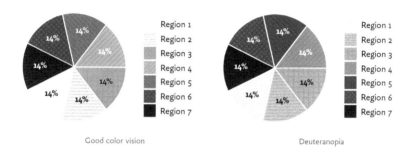

Good color vision   Deuteranopia

FIG 4.12: This chart contains improved color choices overall and adds a pattern to each type of data. The patterns are reflected in the key for improved legibility.

background color can contain a more complex pattern design, such as a square or diamond grid (**FIG 4.13**). When a complex pattern is placed over a lighter color, it can trick the eye into appearing darker than it really is. In general, consider making the pattern design darker in color than the background color it sits on, since a darker pattern may be easier to distinguish than a lighter one (**FIG 4.14**).

Line graphs can be difficult to read if they contain intersecting paths (**FIG 4.15**).

Try varying the thickness of each line, giving each a different style, and adding direct labels (**FIG 4.16**).

Introducing color to the backgrounds of infographics can also create confusion; avoid doing so if it negatively impacts legibility. Placing each chart on a solid white background can help keep the data as clear as possible.

FIG 4.13: Complex patterns can be difficult for people with low vision to distinguish.

FIG 4.14: Dark, subtle patterns placed over a lighter background color can be more effective.

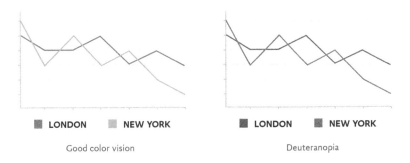

FIG 4.15: This graph's intersecting lines are difficult for people with deuteranopia to distinguish.

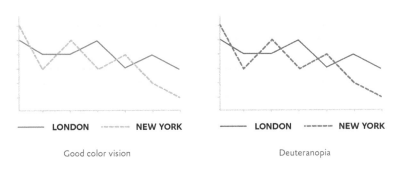

FIG 4.16: This line graph is improved by adding a second line style for redundancy.

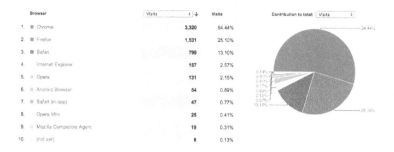

FIG 4.17: This simulated view of Google Analytics shows how labels pointing to each data region make the information easier to parse.

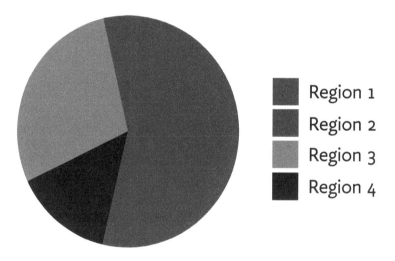

FIG 4.18: This simulated view shows unlabeled data regions, which can be confusing.

A pie-chart view for browser statistics on Google Analytics is color-coded with each slice directly labeled; it works well, even if many of the colors appear to be similar (**FIG 4.17**).

However, an example of an unlabeled chart demonstrates that even a simple chart with just three data regions can become confusing when colors look nearly identical (**FIG 4.18**).

The map of the London Underground is an iconic image not just in London, but around the world (**FIG 4.19**). Unfortunately, for a person with a vision problem, it contains some colors that appear indistinguishable from one another (**FIG 4.20**).

This is true not only for the London Underground, but also for any other wayfinding system that relies on color-coding as the only key in a legend.

Printable versions of the map exist online in black and white, using distinguishable patterns and shades of black and gray, but it's interesting to note that the actual wayfinding signage in place in the subway system is colored; the grayscale patterns can't be found in use. Still, this map is a helpful option for deciphering routes on paper (**FIG 4.21**).

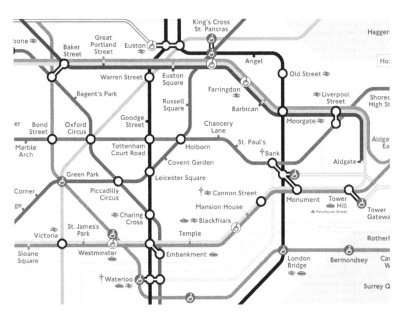

FIG 4.19: The map of the London Underground contains colors that can pose problems for a person with a color-vision deficiency.

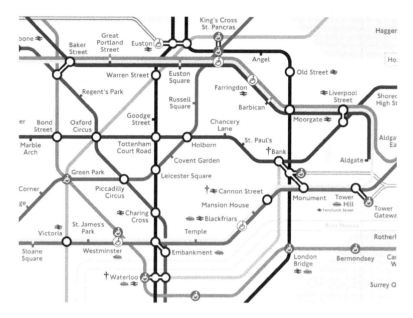

FIG 4.20: How a person with protanopia might view the London subway map.

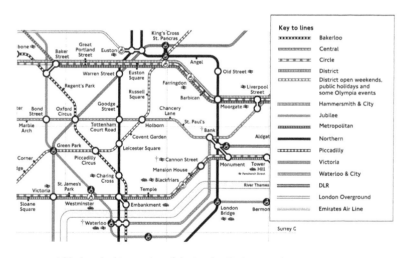

FIG 4.21: A black-and-white version of the London Underground map.

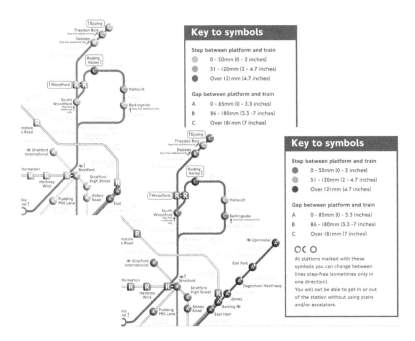

FIG 4.22: The step-free map as it might look to a person with deuteranopia.

If you're someone who has a physical disability as well as a vision problem, the step-free guide map has some very poor color-coding for step height between platforms and trains, and doesn't clearly indicate which stations have step-free line changes (**FIG 4.22**).

Paul Wynne designed a map to be used by both color-blind and non-color-blind people. He added a simple pattern to each line and reflected that in the key, and he attached color names to each line in case he received verbal directions from another person. He explains that now, if someone tells him to take the brown line and change to the red line, he can follow along with his version of the map (**FIG 4.23**).

By contrast, the Tokyo Metro map is designed to be accessible from the start. Although it too has different colors for different subway lines, each line is also given a letter of the English alphabet, and every station on that line is labeled with a

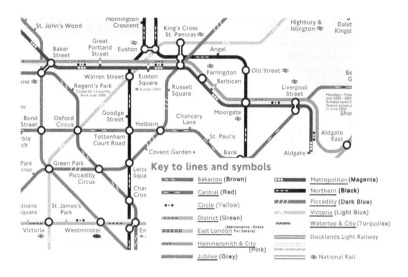

Key to lines and symbols

Bakerloo **(Brown)**	Metropolitan **(Magenta)**
Central **(Red)**	Northern **(Black)**
Circle **(Yellow)**	Piccadilly **(Dark Blue)**
District **(Green)**	Victoria **(Light Blue)**
East London (Maintenance - Check For Details)	Waterloo & City **(Turquoise)**
Hammersmith & City **(Pink)**	Docklands Light Railway
	Under construction
Jubilee **(Grey)**	National Rail

FIG 4.23: Paul Wynne's custom color-accessible London Underground map.

---

numeral. Takebashi station, also known as T-08, can therefore be intuitively understood as the eighth stop on the Tozai line. Not only does this make it easier for people with color blindness to understand, but it also helps non-Japanese speakers find stations based on letters and numerals rather than on unfamiliar words. Numerals also help riders understand the direction of the train when riding, as well as the number of stops left until their destination—an added benefit to travelers with low vision who must rely on announcements. The system's physical signage is consistent throughout the network, making wayfinding easier for everyone (**FIG 4.24**).

Some color-blind people have no difficulty navigating environments that depend on color-coding; others can decipher them after careful study. In a subway system, taking a little extra time to work out a map may not pose much of a problem, but remember to consider environments like hospitals and healthcare centers, where time can literally be a matter of life and death.

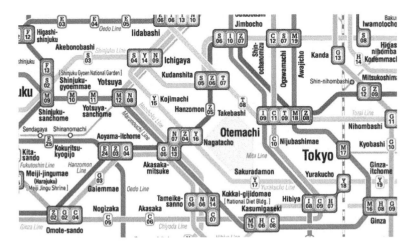

FIG 4.24: Every station on the Tokyo Metro subway is labeled with a color, letter, and numeral.

LINKS

One of the most common issues on the web occurs when, for aesthetic reasons, designers and developers remove the default `text-decoration: underline` CSS property on hyperlinks. Although many links are obvious based on context and location on the page (think navigation menus), links that appear within a paragraph of text can blend in if they lack another cue to make them stand out.

We ran into this problem when designing the website for the W3C's Responsive Image Community Group.

The red link contained in the black paragraph text was completely invisible. Although we had an underline on hover, it wasn't enough—we can't expect users to hover over sections of text with the hope that a link will come into view. Besides, hover states aren't perceptible on mobile devices (**FIG 4.25**).

If you don't want to underline the link, consider increasing its font weight or adding other visual cues, like framing or blocked background colors. Remember to be consistent—when using underlines as a link style, try to refrain from using underlines elsewhere in the design for other functions such as empha-

FIG 4.25: The link contained in this paragraph practically disappears in this protanopia-type color blindness simulation.

sis, since that could cause issues for folks with cognitive disabilities too. If all else fails, and you are for whatever reason required to keep links undecorated and differentiated purely by color, be sure to make the contrast between the link and surrounding text at least 3:1. An example of this would be standard #000000 black paragraph text, with a teal link color of #007777 that has a contrast ratio of 3.9:1; the #007777 remains legible on a white page background with a contrast ratio of 5.4:1.

In addition, for readers who rely on keyboard navigation to find their way around a website, remember to supply a different visual enhancement not only on mouseover, but also on focus states. Consider adding an outline or different background color to links to differentiate them when highlighted (FIG 4.26).

FIG 4.26: The website for An Event Apart adds yellow backgrounds to indicate focused links for visitors using keyboard navigation.

FORMS

Visual cues are important in form design too. Avoid labeling required fields with colored text only (**FIG 4.27**). It's safer to indicate required fields with supporting text in the label, or with a symbol cue like an asterisk, which is color-independent (**FIG 4.28**).

WCAG notes that asterisks may not be successfully parsed by all screen readers, and that they may be difficult for users with low vision to see, since they're often rendered in a smaller size than the default text. Furthermore, by introducing an extra layer of abstraction, asterisks may also pose difficulties for people with cognitive disabilities. A safer solution would be simply to label the field with direct instructions. If most fields are required but just a few are optional, mark the optional fields as "optional". If most fields are optional but just a few are required, mark the required fields as "required". This cuts down on the visual noise of a large number of labels and presents clearer instructions on how to complete the form.

Pay special attention to validation, too. If a form field is not filled out correctly, avoid highlighting the error with color alone; a red border may not be visible at all to some color-blind people and is meaningless. If you use a colored border, be sure to reinforce it with a clear error message.

Okay, enough theory. It's time to put everything we've learned into practice as we tackle color accessibility in our projects.

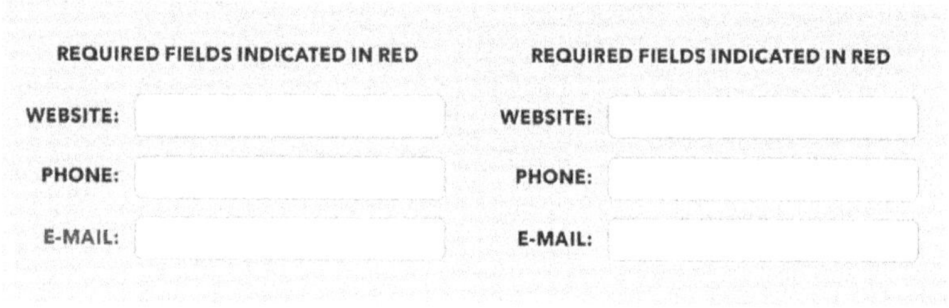

REQUIRED FIELDS INDICATED IN RED   REQUIRED FIELDS INDICATED IN RED

WEBSITE: WEBSITE:

PHONE: PHONE:

E-MAIL: E-MAIL:

FIG 4.27: Avoid designing forms with color as the only indicator of a required field.

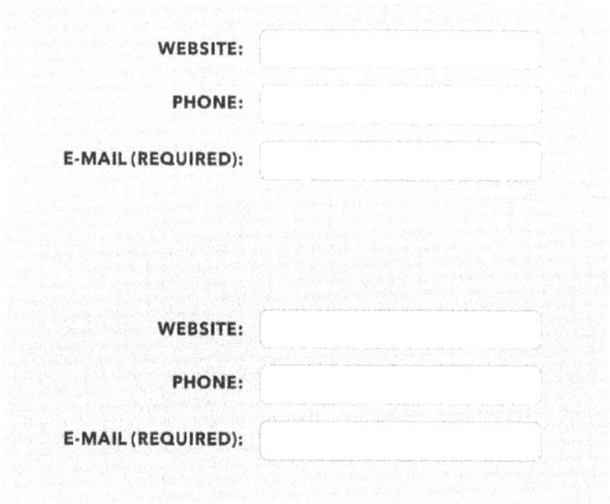

WEBSITE:

PHONE:

E-MAIL (REQUIRED):

WEBSITE:

PHONE:

E-MAIL (REQUIRED):

FIG 4.28: This form offers a better solution; its labels can be parsed by a screen reader.

5

IMPLEMENTATION

LEARNING THE VARIOUS TIPS AND TRICKS for making a website color-accessible may seem straightforward until the time comes to weave them into your existing workflow. Although project management approaches vary for every designer, developer, and team, it may be helpful to read a case study on how we tackled the website redesign for Simply Accessible.

Founded by Derek Featherstone, Simply Accessible is a group of accessibility specialists whose goal is to change the perception of accessibility on the web. A tired, outdated website lying fallow due to busy client projects provided the perfect opportunity for a total overhaul to show the world what the company really stood for: accessible design that is always inclusive but never boring.

CREATE A COLOR GAME PLAN

During the early stages of redesign research, I like to do a deep audit of the existing color usage across the entire brand. Gathering every instance of color and organizing it into a document can, at a glance, help you understand what should be dropped, added, or revamped. Almost certainly, it will show you just how many versions of a single color can creep its way into the code, especially in projects worked on by multiple people.

Some branding evolutions will keep an existing logo and introduce fresh colors (think Coca-Cola and its updated blacks, greens, and silvers for new bottles); others will preserve their iconic colors but usher in new logo styles (think Pepsi and its traditional red, white, and blue).

For Simply Accessible, both of these options proved difficult. There was no established logo to carry into the new design, and to call the name a "wordmark" was a stretch. The brand's typeface, Helvetica, lacked character by definition. The only feature left to work with was color. And even that was a challenge—the oranges looked murky and brown, and the blues looked far too corporate and "safe" for a company like Simply Accessible (FIG 5.1).

With our evaluation complete, we dug in deep and played around with some ideas to inject new life into our palette.

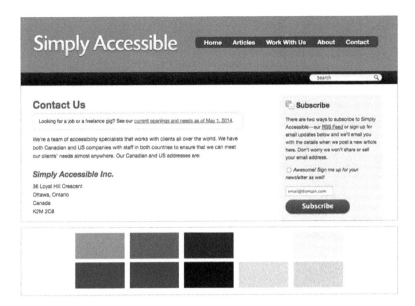

FIG 5.1: The original Simply Accessible website.

Develop color concepts

After much experimentation, we settled on a simple, two-color palette of blue and orange—a warm-cool contrast color scheme. We added swatches for call-to-action messaging in green, error messaging in red, and body copy and form fields in black and gray. Shades and tints of blue and orange were added to illustrations and other design elements for extra detail and interest (FIG 5.2).

If circumstances allow it, consider introducing new color choices to an internal, private project before jumping in and going public. Even applying fresh colors to something as simple as a report or presentation can allow plenty of time to get a feel for the design and work out any uncertainties. At Simply Accessible, we tested our initial palette on an internal report (FIG 5.3).

It's important to be open to changes in your palette; it may need to evolve throughout the design process. One of the biggest mistakes you can make at this stage is telling your client

FIG 5.2: Our first stab at a new palette.

FIG 5.3: Putting the test palette through its paces with an internal report.

that any given palette design is final—it's better to explain that it's actually a flexible concept that can adapt and grow. If you need to tweak the color of a button later because of legibility issues, the last thing you want is your client pushing back because it's different from what you promised.

As it happened, we did tweak the colors after the test run, and we even adjusted the new logo—what looked great printed on paper looked a little too light on device screens.

Consider how colors might be used

If you haven't had the opportunity to test your palette in advance, don't worry. As long as you have some well-considered options, you'll be prepared to think about the various ways that color might be used on your site or app.

Unless you're designing a small, static, one-off project that will never grow or evolve, it's unlikely you'll know every design element required for launch date, or what could potentially

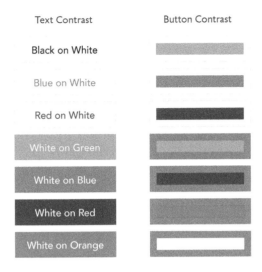

Text Contrast	Button Contrast
Black on White	
Blue on White	
Red on White	
White on Green	
White on Blue	
White on Red	
White on Orange	

FIG 5.4: A variety of potential combinations of text color and background color, and button color and background color.

be introduced to the site down the road. There are, of course, plenty of good places to start.

For Simply Accessible, I mocked up some examples in Illustrator to get a handle on the elements where contrast and legibility matter the most: text and background colors (**FIG 5.4**). While it's less crucial to consider the contrast of decorative elements that don't convey essential information, it's still important for a reader to be able to discern elements like button shapes, empty form fields, and focus states.

Run initial tests

Once these elements were laid out, I manually plugged the HTML color code of each foreground and background color into Lea Verou's Contrast Checker. I added the results from each color pair test to my document so we could see at a glance which colors needed adjustment and which colors wouldn't work at all (**FIG 5.5**).

As you can see, this test exposed a few problems. To meet the minimum AA compliance, we needed to slightly darken the green, blue, and orange background colors for text—an easy

Text Contrast

Black on White	Ratio: 21.00 AA Large: Pass AA Small: Pass	AAA Large: Pass AAA Small: Pass
Blue on White	Ratio: 4.7 AA Large: Pass AA Small: Pass	AAA Large: Pass AAA Small: Pass
Red on White	Ratio: 8.23 AA Large: Pass AA Small: Pass	AAA Large: Pass AAA Small: Pass
White on Green	Ratio: 3.26 AA Large: Pass AA Small: *Fail*	AAA Large: *Fail* AAA Small: *Fail*
White on Blue	Ratio: 4.66 AA Large: Pass AA Small: Pass	AAA Large: Pass AAA Small: *Fail*
White on Red	Ratio: 8.23 AA Large: Pass AA Small: Pass	AAA Large: Pass AAA Small: Pass
White on Orange	Ratio: 3.36 AA Large: *Fail* AA Small: *Fail*	AAA Large: *Fail* AAA Small: *Fail*

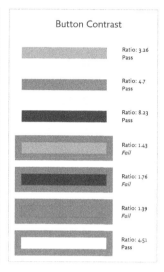

Button Contrast

Ratio: 3.26 Pass

Ratio: 4.7 Pass

Ratio: 8.23 Pass

Ratio: 1.43 Fail

Ratio: 1.76 Fail

Ratio: 1.39 Fail

Ratio: 4.51 Pass

FIG 5.5: This diagram revealed that three text- and background-color combinations had contrast-ratio issues.

FIG 5.6: This diagram showed that three button and background-color combinations had contrast-ratio issues.

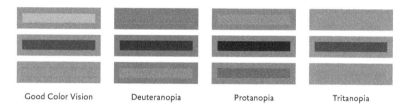

Good Color Vision   Deuteranopia   Protanopia   Tritanopia

FIG 5.7: How our proposed color pairs might look to people with three types of color blindness.

fix. A more complicated glitch emerged with the button colors. Although I had envisioned some buttons appearing over a blue background, the contrast ratios ended up being well under 3:1 (**FIG 5.6**). Although there isn't a guide in WCAG for contrast requirements of two non-text elements, the *International Organization for Standardization* (ISO) and *American National Standards Institute* (ANSI) standard for visible contrast is 3:1, which is what we decided to aim for.

We also checked our color combinations in Color Oracle, which confirmed that colored buttons over blue backgrounds simply wouldn't work. The contrast was much too low, especially for the more common deuteranopia- and protanopia-type deficiencies (**FIG 5.7**).

Make adjustments if necessary

We adjusted our colors using the Tanaguru Contrast Finder to achieve accessible versions of our green, blue, and orange background-text colors. We also opted to change all buttons to white when they were used over dark backgrounds; this increased contrast and made the button design across the site more consistent. It also helped us avoid introducing a lot of unnecessary color variants, which could cause potential confusion when navigating the site.

You'll probably find that putting more effort into achieving compliant contrast ratios at this stage will make the rest of implementation and testing much easier. When you've got your ratios looking good, you can move on to implementation.

IMPLEMENT THE PALETTE IN A STYLE GUIDE AND PROTOTYPE

Once I was happy with my contrast checks, I created a basic style guide and added all the color values from my color exploration files (**FIG 5.8**), introduced more tints and shades for use in detail work and illustrations, and added patterned backgrounds. I created examples of every panel style we intended to use on the site, with sample text, links, and buttons—all with working hover states and focus states (**FIG 5.9**). Adding color to a working style guide not only makes things easier for the developers, but it also facilitates further contrast checks and testing in an actual browser.

White #FFFFFF   Light Blue #EEF8F9   Blue #008AB4   Dark Blue #0C4C6F

Light Orange #FCEDE3   Orange #C9472D   Red #AF2D2D   Dark Red #991F1F

Light Grey #DDD   Grey #BBB   Dark Grey #333   Black #000

FIG 5.8: Adding basic color swatches to a style guide.

FIG 5.9: A variety of panels with text, button, and background-color combinations in a working style guide.

FIG 5.10: Designing in grayscale may help you focus on contrast between important elements before introducing color.

WORKING IN GRAYSCALE

Gray has no agenda... Gray has the ability, that no other color has, to make the invisible visible.
—ROMA TEARNE, Mosquito

In the early stages of designing actual page wireframes or layouts, it can be helpful to ignore your newly chosen color palette and work in grayscale instead. If you can strike the right balance and create a legible, attractive design here, chances are it will work when you introduce your color choices, and will have a better chance of retaining the contrast necessary for the needs of a wider audience (**FIG 5.10**).

Many of the initial concepts for the Simply Accessible website were designed this way, in grayscale, even though we already had a palette in mind. It allowed us to focus on the content that mattered most and let us push out faster page layouts, rather than worrying too much about where each particular color should go.

PREFLIGHT CHECK

Before launch day, it's a good idea to do a final check for color accessibility issues to ensure that nothing has been lost in translation from the intended design to the actual code, especially when working with a large team. Fortunately, at this stage, unless you've introduced massive changes to the design in the prototype, it should be fairly easy to fix any issues that arise, especially if you've stayed on top of updating any revisions in the style guide. If it isn't feasible at this point in time to check every single page, particularly on a large website, select a representative sample of various types of pages to evaluate instead.

WAVE is great to use here because it works in any browser. However, if your site doesn't have a public link, it's better to use the built-in Chrome Accessibility Tools (**FIG 5.11**).

THE HUMAN TOUCH

Ultimately, no amount of careful planning or evaluation reports can compare to the feedback received from real humans with abilities and disabilities of all kinds. If you're unsure of how something may be viewed by people with a color-vision deficiency, reach out and ask for their opinions and experiences. Involve them in the early stages of design and development— not just as an afterthought. At the same time, remember not to jump to conclusions based on a single person's advice, since disabilities cannot be generalized. Combining user feedback with evaluation tools and best practices is your safest bet.

Although Simply Accessible's final palette diverged from our initial ideas, we were pleased that it wasn't merely compliant, but also showed the company's true personality, with plenty of room to expand and evolve (**FIG 5.12**).

Keeping these pointers in mind should help you gain a better understanding of how to weave color accessibility into a project from the start. Next, we'll discuss how to tackle less-than-ideal implementations of color accessibility—when it arrives as an afterthought, fix, or add-on feature. And trust me, it will. Life is messy that way.

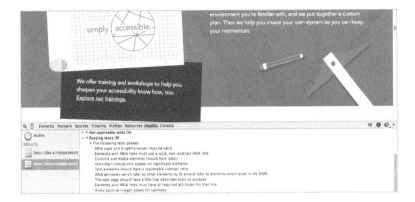

FIG 5.11: Chrome's Accessibility Tools audit feature shows no immediate issues with color contrast in our prototype.

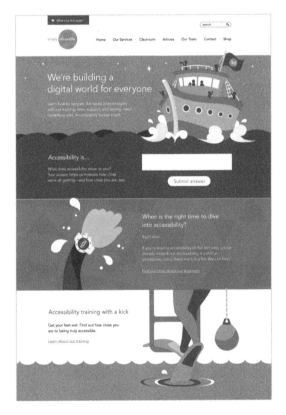

FIG 5.12: The redesigned Simply Accessible website.

6

PROVIDING ALTERNATIVES

"EASIER SAID THAN DONE!" That's what some of you may be thinking about the actual implementation of color-accessible design. In the real world, circumstances sometimes hinder designers or developers from influencing the opinions of higher-ups, like skeptical bosses or clients who refuse to back down from poor design decisions. On top of that, you may already have a product with major accessibility issues in need of fixing. If that's the case, consider providing alternative styles or allowing users to edit their own colors.

WEBSITES AND APPS

The iChat application for macOS is no longer available, but it remains a good example of such features (**FIG 6.1**). Although, by default, it used colored bubbles to indicate a user's status (available for chat, away or idle, or busy), the preferences included a Use Shapes to Indicate Status option, which changed the standard circles to green circles, yellow triangles, and red squares, respectively (**FIG 6.2**).

If the style of your app, website, or game is low-contrast by default, consider adding a style switcher either as a setting or as a button in a visible location. Check out the example on Belgian designer Veerle Pieter's blog. She drops the colored backgrounds, inverts the text color, and changes link colors—simply by loading a new style sheet (**FIG 6.3**).

Some operating systems, like Windows, have built-in high-contrast modes that are popular among readers with low vision. Unfortunately, because of limitations in the way such modes handle images, some website icons and images don't translate well and may disappear completely when a high-contrast mode is enabled.

If SVG icons or images are essential to your website's design, consider using Boston-based developer Eric Bailey's method for modifying them through CSS media queries, using a lesser-known feature that allows you to directly target Windows' High Contrast Mode:

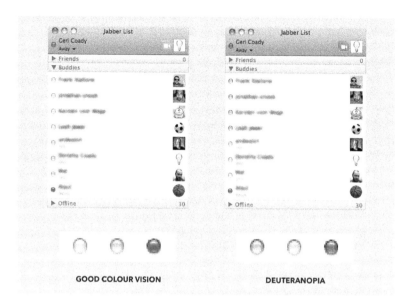

FIG 6.1: The default status bubbles of the iChat application were not color-blind-friendly.

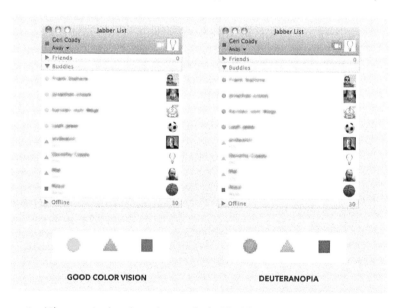

FIG 6.2: iChat contained an alternative set of color-blind-friendly icons consisting of shapes in addition to colors.

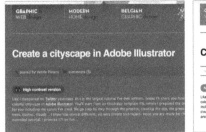

Normal view

High contrast

FIG 6.3: Adding a high-contrast style sheet to your website can help many readers.

Default High Contrast view

Corrected using media queries

FIG 6.4: Example of two side-by-side icons with High Contrast Mode enabled. One is poor; the other has been tweaked using media queries.

```
/* Targets displays using any of Windows' High
   Contrast Mode themes: */
@media screen and (-ms-high-contrast: active) { }
/* Targets displays using Windows' High Contrast
   Black theme: */
@media screen and (-ms-high-contrast: white-on-
   black) { }
/* Targets displays using Windows' High Contrast
   White theme: */
@media screen and (-ms-high-contrast: black-on-
   white) { }
```

Using this code, a problematic icon can be targeted and given higher-contrast colors that will retain their contrast when High Contrast Mode is active (**FIG 6.4**).

Let's talk more specifically about game design. At the time of writing, Niantic's Pokémon GO, an augmented-reality game that was awarded five Guinness World Records in August 2016 and became an overnight social media phenomenon, contained problematic gameplay elements for people with color-vision deficiency. PokéStops, a feature where players must physically visit locations to restock on game items, relied only on color to show players if the stop had already been visited (**FIG 6.5**). This poses obvious problems for someone with red-green color blindness (**FIG 6.6**).

Niantic isn't the only developer guilty of poor color accessibility; it's a major issue in video game design. I asked a group of color-blind people which medium or form of entertainment was the most difficult to read or use, and multiple people noted that video games needed the most improvement. One man argued that game developers don't seem to pay much attention to color at all, even when it's an essential part of gameplay. It's easy to understand why he might feel this way: game developers often focus on flashy graphics designed to impress, but leave humbler interface design elements as an afterthought. This results in a poor user experience, even for a person with good vision. Combine that with the fact that many games rely on the use of color as an essential game mechanism, and you end up with some games being completely unplayable for a significant part of the population.

Color-blind gamers have been increasingly vocal online, urging developers to release updates to enhance games that weren't designed with color-vision deficiencies in mind. A 2011 BBC article interviewed Kathryn Albany-Ward, founder of the UK group Color Blind Awareness, who suggested that game developers place warnings on the game packaging or download page if good color vision is a requirement for enjoyable gameplay. "It's like a 'contains traces of nuts' label," she explained, "so at least you know you're not wasting your money."

Fortunately, some companies are starting to listen to this feedback. Every release in Activision's popular *Call of Duty* series since *Modern Warfare 3* allows players to change team

FIG 6.5: How unvisited and visited PokéStops look to a person with normal color vision.

FIG 6.6: Unvisited and visited PokéStops can appear the same for a person with red-green color blindness.

indicators from a confusing red-and-green pair to a more legible light-blue-and-orange pair. Blizzard's huge title *World of Warcraft* now includes three sets of filters to assist people with all three forms of color blindness, and can be personalized with a "strength" slider depending on how severe one's condition is (**FIG 6.7**).

The developers of the game *Faster Than Light* created an alternate mode for color blindness and asked for public feedback to make sure it passed the test. And for the most part it

FIG 6.7: World of Warcraft games include customizable color-blind filters to improve the gaming experience.

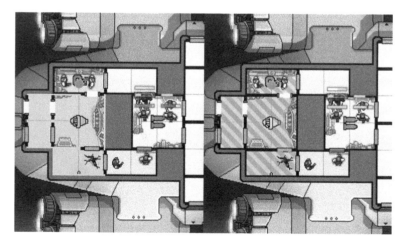

FIG 6.8: Normal game mode and color-blind game mode in *Faster Than Light*.

FIG 6.9: AudioSurf allows gamers to choose their own colors.

did—though adding stripes to the red zones and changing outlines to blue instead of green made all the difference (**FIG 6.8**).

The game AudioSurf from indie developer Dylan Fitterer uses players' own music to create the puzzles in each level. Players gain points by clustering blocks of the same color on the highway, and the settings include an option for people to choose their own colors, whether out of personal preference or out of necessity due to visual impairment (**FIG 6.9**).

Many game developers are heading in the right direction and understand the importance of color accessibility; others, alas, still have a long way to go. In the 2011 BBC article I mentioned earlier about color blindness in gaming, industry giants Nintendo told the BBC that while its developers do try to make their games as accessible as possible, it was "not possible to cater to the needs of all the players 100% of the time." Although there may be some truth in that statement—designing interfaces to support those with color deficiencies will still leave out many people who are completely blind—it sounds quite defensive and dismissive. In my opinion, that's the wrong attitude to take.

CONCLUSION

IN DISCUSSIONS AROUND ACCESSIBILITY, you may hear people ask "how much work" is required or "how many features" are necessary to make a website accessible, as if that can be quantified. Let's think more positively. Let's ask: "How can I make this as inclusive as possible?" And: "How can I make this more accessible than before?"

Accessibility expert Derek Featherstone explains that many people believe doing "something" is better than doing nothing at all, even if that "something" means subpar accessibility with less than optimal access. He states that we all need to aim for the stars, set a high standard, and keep pushing ourselves to do more to include as many people as we can. I couldn't agree with him more.

Maybe we should all take a cue from developer Mat Marquis, who, in a 2012 talk on responsible design, declared:

> When I build a website, my goal is to build a website for anyone who cares to use it. Maybe I don't always get everything 100% right, but I'm going to keep trying. And when someone asks me why I couldn't make something work? "I'm trying" is a damn sight better answer than "because I didn't have to."

Like elegant typography, engaging content, and efficient code, color is yet another powerful tool at our disposal for crafting enjoyable user experiences on the web. I hope these color accessibility tips will become an important part of every responsible designer's workflow as we strive to make the web accessible to all. Let's not leave anyone behind.

ACKNOWLEDGMENTS

SPECIAL THANKS GO TO Emma and Mark Boulton and the original Five Simple Steps team for publishing my first book on color accessibility before they closed their doors. I'm so grateful to be able to continue writing about this important topic for A Book Apart.

To my team—Katel LeDû, Caren Litherland, Tina Lee, and Jason Santa Maria, you have been an absolute pleasure to work with. Thank you, Jeffrey Zeldman, for giving me this wonderful opportunity.

Thank you, Jon Hicks, for being my technical editor. Your input as a colorblind designer has been invaluable. Thank you, Dr. Meghann Mears, for helping me explain the more scientific side of things and for your support as a friend.

Thank you to Derek Featherstone and the whole Simply Accessible team for all the incredible work that you do to make the digital world a better, more inclusive place for everyone.

And, of course, thank you Simon (and Bearface) for your love and support.

Articles

- "Are colour blind gamers left out?" by Dave Lee for *BBC News*
- "New Outlook on Colorblindness" by Melinda Beck for the *Wall Street Journal*
- "Say What You See: How does colour-blindness affect the property sector?" (PDF) by Noella Pio Kivlehan for *Estates Gazette*

Research

- "Cognitive Disabilities" by WebAIM
- We Are Colorblind
- Colblindor
- Colour Blind Awareness
- "Colour Vision: Almost Reason Enough for Having Eyes" (PDF) by Jay Neitz, Joseph Carroll, and Maureen Neitz

Tools

- Web Content Accessibility Guidelines 2.0
- Contrast ratio by Lea Verou
- Colour contrast check by Jonathan Snook
- Color Oracle by Bernhard Jenny
- Tanaguru Contrast Finder
- WAVE Web Accessibility Evaluation Tool
- "Color Design for the Color Vision Impaired—Mapping: Methods & Tips"(PDF) by Bernhard Jenny and Nathaniel Vaughn Kelso
- "Accessible Color Swatches" by Brian Suda
- Colblindor compilation of tests
- Waggoner Computerized Color Vision Test
- EnChroma online test
- DanKam—an augmented-reality application for color-blind users

REFERENCES:
COLOR ACCESSIBILITY WORKFLOWS

Shortened URLs are numbered sequentially; the related long URLs are listed below for reference.

Introduction

00-01 https://en.wikipedia.org/wiki/The_dress

Chapter 1

01-01 http://www.neitzvision.com/

01-02 http://www.color-blindness.com/protanopia-red-green-color-blindness/

01-03 http://www.color-blindness.com/deuteranopia-red-green-color-blindness/

01-04 http://www.color-blindness.com/tritanopia-blue-yellow-color-blindness/

01-05 http://discovermagazine.com/2012/jul-aug/06-humans-with-super-human-vision

01-06 http://www.eyemagazine.com/feature/article/ishihara

01-07 http://www.testingcolorvision.com/

01-08 https://www.osha.gov/pls/oshaweb/owadisp.show_document?p_table=INTERPRETATIONS&p_id=24865

01-09 https://www.theguardian.com/news/2000/jun/17/guardianobituaries

01-10 http://www.shikikaku.com/en/shikikaku/

Chapter 2

02-01 http://jfly.iam.u-tokyo.ac.jp/html/manuals/pdf/color_blind.pdf

02-02 http://optional.is/required/2011/06/20/accessible-color-swatches/

02-03 http://colorbrewer2.org/#type=sequential&scheme=BuGn&n=3

02-04 http://colororacle.org/

Chapter 3

03-01 https://www.w3.org/WAI/intro/wcag.php

03-02 https://www.w3.org/WAI/WCAG20/quickref/#qr-visual-audio-con-trast-contrast

03-03 https://en.wikipedia.org/wiki/Luminance

03-04 https://en.wikipedia.org/wiki/Visual_acuity

03-05 simplyaccessible.com/article/descriptive-alt-attributes/

03-06 http://leaverou.github.io/contrast-ratio/

03-07 https://snook.ca/technical/colour_contrast/colour.html#f-g=33FF33,bg=333333

03-08 http://colorsafe.co/

03-09 http://contrast-finder.tanaguru.com/

03-10 http://wave.webaim.org/

03-11 http://wave.webaim.org/extension/

03-12 https://blog.twitter.com/2012/because-you-have-more-to-show

Chapter 4

04-01 http://content.tfl.gov.uk/standard-tube-map.pdf

04-02 http://content.tfl.gov.uk/bw-large-print-map.pdf

04-03 http://paul-wynne.blogspot.ca/2010/07/london-underground-colour-blind-map-mark.html

04-04 https://abookapart.com/products/design-for-real-life

04-05 http://responsiveimages.org/

Chapter 5

05-01 http://jasonsantamaria.com/articles/the-sweatpants-of-typefaces

Chapter 6

06-01 http://veerle.duoh.com/design/article/all_about_masks_in_photoshop
06-02 https://css-tricks.com/accessible-svgs-high-contrast-mode/
06-03 http://www.bbc.com/news/technology-13054691
06-04 http://www.colourblindawareness.org/
06-05 http://store.steampowered.com/app/12900
06-06 http://www.bbc.com/news/technology-13054691

Conclusion

07-01 http://simplyaccessible.com/article/pragmatism-transcripts/
07-02 https://beyondtellerrand.com/events/duesseldorf-2012/speakers/
       mat-marquis

Resources

08-01 https://www.wsj.com/articles/SB10001424052970204349404578100
       942150867894
08-02 http://www.colourblindawareness.org/wp-content/uploads/2010/07/
       EGA_160711_083.pdf
08-03 http://webaim.org/articles/cognitive/
08-04 http://wearecolorblind.com/
08-05 http://www.color-blindness.com/
08-06 http://www.neitzvision.com/img/research/CV-ReasonForEyes.pdf
08-07 https://www.w3.org/TR/WCAG/
08-08 http://colororacle.org/resources/2007_JennyKelso_ColorDesign_hires.pdf
08-09 http://www.color-blindness.com/color-blindness-tests/
08-10 http://enchroma.com/test/instructions/
08-11 https://dankaminsky.com/dankam/

H

Helvetica 60
Hirohito 12
H&M 42
HSLA 30
hue 16

I

iChat 71
Illustrator 24-25
images and text 46
infographics 46, 48
International Organization for
    Standardization (ISO) 64
Ishihara, Dr. Shinobu 10
Ishihara plate test 10

L

lightness 16
shade 16
tint 16
links 55
Linux 25
Little Miss Sunshine 12
L.L.Bean 42
London Underground 51
luminance 28

M

macOS 71
Mac OS X 25
maps 46
Marquis, Mat 78
minimum color contrast ratio 28
Modern Warfare 3 74
Mona Lisa 20
monochromacy 4
blue-cone 6
cone 6
rod 6

N

National Federation for the Blind
    (NFB) 14
Neitz, Dr. Jay 6
Niantic 74

O

Occupational Safety and Health
    Administration (OSHA) 12

P

patterns 48
Pepsi 60
photoreceptor cells 4
cones 4
L-cones 4
M-cones 4
rods 4
S-cones 4-5, 8
Photoshop 24-25
Pieter, Veerle 71
Pokémon GO 74
Princess Nagako 12
protanopia (red-dichromacy) 7

R

Responsive Image Community Group
    55
retina 4
RGB 24
RGBA 30

S

saturation 16
screening tests 12
Simply Accessible 28, 60, 63, 67
Snook, Jonathan 30
Suda, Brian 22
SVG 71

Geri Coady is a color-obsessed illustrator and designer from Newfoundland, Canada who now lives in Nottingham, UK. A former ad agency art director, she currently works with companies like Simply Accessible, Withings, and Scholastic. She is the author of *Pocket Guide to Colour Accessibility* published by Five Simple Steps, an occasional illustrator for *A List Apart*, and was voted *net Magazine's* Designer of the Year in 2014. Geri has spoken at design and tech events around the world, including Smashing Conference and Future of Web Design.

6

 A BOOK APART

ANIMATION
AT WORK

———

RACHEL NABORS

FOREWORD BY
DAN MALL

BRIEFS

Publisher: Jeffrey Zeldman
Designer: Jason Santa Maria
Executive Director: Katel LeDû
Editor: Lisa Maria Martin
Technical Editor: Kirupa Chinnathambi
Copyeditor: Kate Towsey
Proofreader: Katel LeDû
Book Producer: Ron Bilodeau

ISBN: 978-1-937557-59-1

A Book Apart
New York, New York
http://abookapart.com

TABLE OF CONTENTS: ANIMATION AT WORK

FOREWORD

WHEN I FIRST SAW *Toy Story* in 1995, I immediately knew I wanted to be an animator. Years later, I went to college for it, where I learned a lot—including the fact that, although I liked animation, it didn't like me back. I took, and enjoyed, classes that talked to me about squash and stretch, anticipation, secondary actions, and all the principles that drew me to cartoons and movies in the first place. But I just didn't like *being* an animator.

Luckily, I stumbled into a blossoming field then called "interactive design." I finished school with knowledge of typography and HTML and Flash and white space, and spent the next decade designing websites instead of animations. During that same time, Flash animation was gratuitously used and abused, often getting in the way of what people actually wanted to do on the web—and giving digital animation as a whole a bad name.

Then the iPhone came out.

Suddenly, we realized that animation isn't just a nice-to-have; it can actually help us. It can show us where things come from and where things go. It can calm us down and excite us. We've now seen the value of animation in interface design, and we're primed to integrate it into our own work.

If words and phrases like "animatics" or "frame rates" aren't familiar to you, have no fear: this book will get you up to speed in no time. Rachel's thorough approach doesn't just tell you what animation is but, more importantly, why it works. She'll show you how brains and eyes work, the historical context of web animation, tips for collaborating with colleagues to get the work done, and much more.

Without further ado, welcome to animation at work.

—Dan Mall

To Joe, the best cheerleader and support crew I could ask for.

INTRODUCTION

BEFORE I WORKED IN WEB DEVELOPMENT, I was an award-winning cartoonist. I always wanted to see my comics moving on a screen—but I ended up moving interfaces on a screen instead!

It was a long journey to get from telling stories with words and pictures to sharing other people's stories with code and pixels. And, at first, I struggled to explain the importance of purposeful animation, to justify expending effort on it to stakeholders burned by Flash. This is the book I wish I'd had when I started.

This is not a book about what JavaScript library to use, how to write CSS transitions, or how to create performant animations with browser developer tools. There are a great many wonderful books about those topics already.

What this book *does* contain is distilled, timeless advice on why animation matters and when to put it to use on the web: where to incorporate it into designs, how to communicate it across teams with different skillsets, and how to implement it responsibly. My intention is for this book to empower you and your teammates to make informed, long-term decisions about what to animate—or not animate.

It answers all the questions bosses, clients, and workshop attendees have asked me about UI animation over the years. It shines a light on the things we do know, and—perhaps most crucially—it points out what we don't know. (And there's a *lot* we don't know.)

Before we go too far, let me clear up some terminology. We are bandying about the terms "motion design" and "UI animation" and "web animation" a lot these days. Sometimes we even use them synonymously! But there are some big differences worth clarifying.

- *Animation* is the act of changing something—animating it. Animation is not limited to motion: you can change something's color or opacity or even morph it into a new shape without moving it.
- *Motion design* is a branch of animation and/or graphic design, depending on your perspective. You could say that motion

design is to animation what graphic design is to illustration: the latter serves as a form of expression and communication, storytelling, and art, whereas the former exists to convey and serve the information it's delivering to its audience. Motion designers create a wide range of animations, from movie credit sequences to interstitials for television news to explainer videos.

- *UI animation* refers to animating user interfaces on any device, from DVD menus to iPhone apps to dropdown menus on the web. Even a light swirling on your smartwatch or a screen wipe on your eInk reader is a kind of UI animation.
- *Web animation* encompasses animation, motion design, and UI animation used on the web. Web animations are implemented with technologies like CSS, HTML, WebGL, SVG, and JavaScript.

To fully understand animation and its implications for the future of web design, we must first examine the roots of animation itself.

The illusion of life

When most folks think of "animation," the first thing to spring to mind is often a cartoon character like Mickey Mouse or Sailor Moon. But those are just examples of animation applied to illustration. Animation itself is a visual representation of change over time. And it has some powerful applications. Applied with precision, it can enrich digital environments and help users make smarter, faster decisions. But, like so many of humankind's greatest tools, before we put animation to work, we used it for entertainment.

In the early 1920s, the popularity of theatres propelled booms in both movie-making and animation. New York advertising firms scrambled to create entertaining ads and bumpers for cinemas around the country, causing animation studios to sprout like weeds. One young man chose to head west and start his own animation studio closer to Hollywood, where housing and labor were cheaper. His name was Walt Disney.

Disney did have rivals and equals—animation giants in their own right, like Chuck Jones of Warner Bros. fame. But Disney outpaced them all. He was a shrewd businessman who fiercely guarded his studio's intellectual property and invested heavily in technology like Technicolor and the multiplane camera that allowed for shooting parallax effects. He made deals to secure international distribution, thus reaching animators and artists across the globe like Osamu Tezuka, who would become the father of Japanese animation.

Some of Disney's "Nine Old Men"—Disney's core animators turned directors—wrote a book about the techniques used under their watch. *The Illusion of Life* contained the "Twelve Principles of Animation" espoused by these animators to help breathe vitality into their illustrations. In the early 1990s, computer scientists began applying these principles to interface design (PDF).

Animation at work

Windows and Macintosh operating systems had been jostling for pole position for years when researchers began studying how animation impacts human computer interaction. Soon, subtle motion design started showing up in both systems, from the "genie effect" in Macs to the "minimize window" animation on Windows machines. Quietly, without fanfare, animation became a core offering for both platforms.

Meanwhile, animation on the web was overt, in your face, experiential, entertaining. Flash plugins enabled games, cartoons, even overblown "flashy intros" users had to sit through before they could access the content. While it did become common courtesy for such sites to provide a "skip intro" button—and many people, myself included, enjoyed the entertainment Flash provided—animation on the web got a reputation for style over substance.

It has been said *so* many times before that I'm loath to say it again, but the iPhone changed everything. Earlier touchscreen interfaces had been attempted, but none had coupled the input of a user's fingertips with immediate, visual feedback—animation. The iPhone's expert use of animation created natural-feeling app interfaces that maximized use of space and responded to users' gestures.

Since then, apps have been influencing many web design trends, down to hamburger menus and horizontal scrolling on websites. And with touchscreens replacing point-and-click interfaces on many devices, users expect the web to look and feel more like apps. The line between "the web" and "app" has blurred so much that we use "web app" to refer to sites that are more than just HTML documents.

For anyone building sites that look, feel, perform, and serve as well as an app, animation is an essential tool. Operating systems, apps, and video games have shown us that animation cannot just differentiate products but must also serve our users. Animation provides critical context and guidance for users flooded with information. It can mask slow performance and even be used to increase perceived performance. Good motion design provides a sheen of polish and branding that can engender users' trust with as much strength as a professional logo. And smart companies are paying attention.

The following chapters are the culmination of my experiences: from consulting with Silicon Valley tech companies to giving workshops around the world to studying studio animation, motion design, and UI animation. I've reached out to animation evangelists, front-end developers, product designers, and UX researchers at companies like Intuit and Etsy to provide that in-house perspective so often missing from books written by consultants.

For some folks, animation is still a dirty word—something decorative to be slapped on at the end of the project if there's enough budget left over, or avoided altogether. But there is power in animation. The power to create experiences that go beyond mere linked documents. The power to immerse users in an illusion of life. And that power is about to be yours.

HUMAN PERCEPTION
AND ANIMATION

WE HAVE A TENDENCY in the web industry to relegate animation to the very last moment in a project's production, tacking it on at the end as a nice-to-have. But animation is so much more than window dressing! UI animation can reduce cognitive load and increase perceived speed for users, giving our projects that competitive edge.

In order to make powerful animations that help users, first we have to learn a little more about the human visual system. Buckle up, because we're about to get science-y!

THE HUMAN VISUAL SYSTEM

We humans have a very special visual processing system. Whereas most mammals' vision is largely motion-based, primates have an additional color component to their vision. This extra component of vision changed our brains as we evolved.

Now consider that we can animate three things:

- **Position or location:** We can move an element in relationship to its surroundings (like sending it across a page); or we can move it in relationship to itself (like making it spin in a circle).
- **Form or shape:** We can change an element's form by scaling its size up or down; or we can fundamentally change its shape into something new, from a triangle to a square.
- **Color:** At its simplest, we can animate an element's transition from one color to the next. We can also change the opacity of a color, which the human eye perceives as a change in density or material.

Conveniently, these three properties translate into two visual processes in our brains (**FIG 1.1**):

- An older system present even in our most ancient ancestors for tracking location, motion, and physical relationships.
- A newer process for distinguishing things by their properties—like color and shape—that evolved when our primate ancestors acquired color vision.

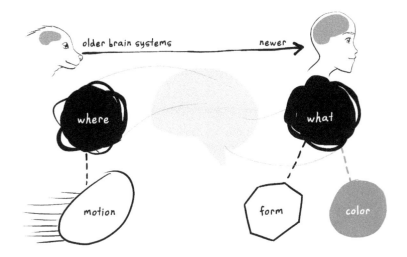

FIG 1.1: The human visual system differs from that of most other mammals: color vision means we're not completely bound to motion like our primitive ancestors, but motion remains a strong and ancient component of how our brains construct our perception of reality.

Margaret Livingstone called these the "Where System" and the "What System" in her book *Vision and Art: The Biology of Seeing,* which I highly recommend to anyone nerdy enough to be reading *this* book.

Interfaces and designs tickle the more recently evolved What System, helping users identify elements on a screen by their shape and color. But when we design with motion, too, we tap into the older Where System. We can use motion to orient users in an information space and shore up spatial hierarchy.

Designing with motion can be very powerful for guiding users. For instance, when a user is navigating through a site, using a sliding motion between pages can help them keep track of where they are in a linear list of items. Motion jacks directly into the Where System, which interfaces with all kinds of orienting mechanisms. Meanwhile, having a list item change colors to indicate its availability will tap into the What System, helping users recognize that an overall state of being has changed.

CUTS AND CONTEXT SWITCHING

Animation can add critical context to seemingly disconnected elements and events. Offloading this context to the visual cortex reduces cognitive load and increases perceived speed. But most websites are built around instantaneous transitions with little to no context.

Consider the simple act of navigating a website: after a user clicks a link, information is painted onto the screen as quickly as possible. If the render time is particularly slow, users might see a flash of white between clicks.

Each time the new page is rendered, users must re-evaluate where they are and their context. Each time, their brains must determine, "Does this page look like the last page I looked at? Yes? Okay, now where is the part that changed…"

A "cut" is a term from cinematography that dates back to when directors would literally cut and splice pieces of film together to connect shots from different angles and shoots to create a narrative. This works well on screen because audiences instinctively watch actors' hands and gaze, which directors can use to connect two disparate shots (**FIG 1.2**). And audiences are trained! It works like a charm.

The web remains largely cut-driven, much to our users' detriment. User interfaces lack faces, hands, and other cues. Sweeping screen changes can be disorienting, while smaller changes might go unnoticed entirely. During testing, we might hear a user sheepishly ask, "What just happened?"

Establishing shot of a man and woman talking.

Cut to the man looking up at the woman.

Cut to what the man sees: the woman looking back.

FIG 1.2: Cuts in film allow the camera to quickly ping-pong between faces in a conversation without motion.

FIG 1.3: This dropdown goes from one state to the other, no animations—just a cut from one to the other.

Early operating systems were entirely cut-based. This was partly because early processors couldn't handle animation, and partly because software was often designed with a "read the manual" mentality. Since then, users have learned to adapt: after clicking on a long box, the box that appears underneath must be a dropdown (**FIG 1.3**). But it still takes quite a bit of mental work and training to get there.

But there are some interactions, whether new to us or ambiguous, that no amount of training or previous experience can prepare us for and no amount of inference can reveal. In these instances, animation adds context that still images and cuts can't give us.

Imagine an image of three spheres in a row—the "before" state—and a second image in which one of the spheres has moved—the "after" state. The after state can be achieved through multiple relationships between the spheres, and each possible relationship changes the meaning of that state (**FIG 1.4**).

Which ball is on the upper right? This important relationship cannot be inferred without animation (or judicious amounts of color coding, labeling, and explanatory text—which generally makes for a cumbersome design!). Even if we did use a diagram or a second color to clarify, our users would still waste time having to decode the information on the screen.

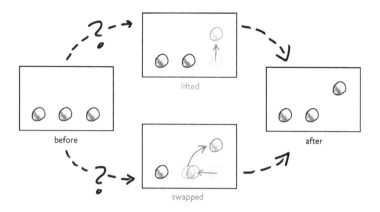

FIG 1.4: There are many ways to achieve the same after state, but only by animating the process will the true nature of the spheres' relationship become crystal clear.

Alternatively, if we make the relationship explicit through animation, that's time users can spend thinking about what to do next, not *What just happened?* And it's all thanks to the magic of the brain's visual cortex.

THE HIGH ROAD THROUGH THE BRAIN'S GPU

A cut-based interaction forces the user's brain to imagine all the in-between states that could have been. "In-betweening" comes from animation: it's when an animator takes two key poses (or frames) and draws all the states in between them (**FIG 1.5**).

In-betweening is very time consuming and not very glamorous, so it's often dumped on interns or sent overseas. No one wants to grow up to be an in-betweener: it's a dead-end job. And the human brain doesn't do so great at in-betweening either (**FIG 1.6**). It takes a lot of bandwidth for the brain to connect the dots between cuts. People like you and I—who work on computers day in and day out—have adapted, but new users, casual users,

FIG 1.5: In this sequence of drawings, the extreme left and right cats (in blue) are in "key poses." The grey cats in transitional states between them are "in-between" frames. You may have heard Flash developers refer to these intermediate states as "tweens."

FIG 1.6: When we see a cut in our UI, our brains do the in-betweening for us.

incapacitated users, and folks just not in the mental prime of their life can get snagged on these cognitive bottlenecks.

Fortunately, animation can help. Researchers Scott E. Hudson and John T. Stasko found in the early '90s that sudden changes could distract users (PDF) from what they were doing, and that animation "allows the user to continue thinking about the task domain, with no need to shift contexts to the interface domain. By eliminating sudden visual changes, animation lessens the chance that the user is surprised."

There is research in film narrative that seems to support this as well, indicating that cuts between actions cause a sort of internal reset for the viewer's mental model of what is going on. This aligns with observational evidence that cuts between human interaction and computer reactions are especially dis-orienting, and helps explain why animation was so crucial to touch interface development.

Let me elaborate. Computers have two processors: one for complex system tasks, the Central Processing Unit (CPU), and the other for tackling the major number-crunching involved in processing and displaying graphics, the Graphics Processing Unit (GPU). In this analogy, because cuts require in-betweening, they get processed on the main thread—what we might call our brain's CPU—where *everything* is processed: from what you are currently doing to what you need to do next to what things you need to pick up at the grocery store tonight. This bogs your cognitive system down and slows reaction times.

Using animation to explicitly show users the in-betweening keeps those processes on the brain's visual cortex instead (**FIG 1.7**). This lets users stay focused and on task. In this way, you can think of animation as a shortcut through the brain's GPU, so to speak.

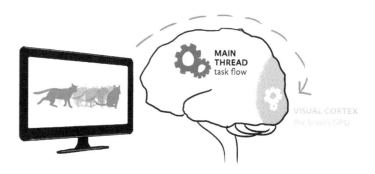

FIG 1.7: Animation lets the visual cortex handle spatial association and content change, freeing up the rest of the brain to stay on task.

THE CONE OF VISION

The human eye is most sensitive to color and details in a very small spot called the foveal region. Meanwhile, our peripheral vision, while blurry and lacking color, is highly sensitive to movement. In fact, on the very outer edges of our retina, it doesn't even transmit visual information to the brain. It only detects movement and sends a signal to jerk our eyes in that direction.

So how are we not living in a blurry monotone world? What we perceive as vision is not actually a one-to-one representation of what we perceive with our eyes. It's more like a simulated picture based on patches of information. You're not aware of it, but your eye moves constantly in *saccades*—tiny, jerky movements that send snapshots of information from different areas back to the brain, letting it repaint and update our picture of the world around us.

These physical realities have real-world ramifications for motion design and animation in web and interface design. For instance, a person cannot focus on two independently moving objects on opposite sides of a screen at the same time. They're also less likely to notice color changes happening in their peripheral vision.

I like to think of the interplay of peripheral and central vision in terms of a "Cone of Vision," with the center of vision reacting more to changes in color and the peripheral being more sensitive to motion (**FIG 1.8**). This is very helpful when deciding what kinds of animations to use where in a design. If a user is looking directly at an element, a color fade or small movements might be enough to attract their attention during one of those saccades. But if a user isn't looking directly at something, we might need additional measures to get their attention.

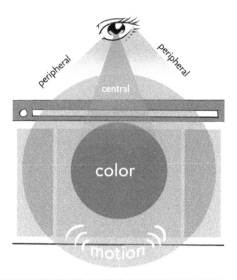

FIG 1.8: You can think of human sight as a Cone of Vision, with color sensitivity at the center and motion sensitivity toward the edges.

Change blindness and animacy

Change blindness is when a person's Cone of Vision doesn't pick up on a visual change. This happens offline all the time—you've probably returned to your desk or a familiar room before and didn't notice that an object was moved or taken away. But when change happens on a web page, we want users to be aware of it. One of the most effective ways to get change to register is to increase an item's *animacy.*

Animacy refers to a quality of "aliveness," usually tied to motion, shape, and other animatable properties. Studies show that the more alive something appears, the more likely it is to capture attention and thus break change blindness.

Change blindness is often a problem in cut interfaces with repeating patterns, like spreadsheets. It can take a few moments for users to reorient and see, *Oh yes, there's a new item right there.* But by animating an element, just a bit, we can harness the Cone of Vision to help users register the change.

FIG 1.9: Future generations will not remember these ads that wiggled and shook and sometimes even blared sounds at honest citizens of the Internet. (Watch the accompanying video.)

But animacy can be overdone. Cut interfaces are mentally taxing, as we've seen, because reorienting and puzzling out *What just happened?* are microdistractions. But high-motion animation can also be mentally taxing: users' brains work overtime to separate signal from noise. Remember back when banner ads blinked and shook and screamed at users to get them to click (**FIG 1.9**)?

Much like New Yorkers don't notice the huge flashing LCD signs that advertise shows on Broadway, users quickly become blind to unimportant change. To brains, high-animacy advertisements become nothing more than the wind rustling leaves.

In short, be considerate in your use of animacy. Respect the Cone of Vision.

DESIGNING WITH ANIMATION ISN'T ROCKET SCIENCE! (BUT IT IS NEUROSCIENCE.)

I've only introduced a small and vastly oversimplified sliver of the rich and deep bounty that neuroscience and cognitive psychology have to offer the field of web design. These are fascinating fields and a joy to study. Scientists are discovering new things about how the brain works *every day*. With better science we can build better things for a brighter tomorrow. If you want to learn more about how the human mind perceives the world around it, check out the Resources section.

That said, if you're feeling a little intimidated by all this "hijacking the human visual system for your own purposes" stuff, I've put together some starting points that are sure to apply to most any site or web app you find yourself working on. In the next chapter, we'll distill UI animation into five distinct categories and see when and how to apply them. Armed with the knowledge of how animation works with the human brain, you'll be even better able to decide when and where to use these types of animations for your users' benefit.

PATTERNS AND
PURPOSE

SO WE CAN USE ANIMATIONS to tap into users' visual systems and give them a cognitive speed boost, terrific! But before animating every element of our designs, we must learn when and how to use this new tool: with great power comes great responsibility, and so forth. And as animation must vie with many other concerns for development and design time, it makes sense to spend our resources where they'll go the farthest.

This chapter sets you up with some core animation patterns and shows you how animation applies to a greater system. Then you'll learn how to spot cognitive bottlenecks and low-hanging fruit, maximizing the impact of the animations you do invest in.

COMMON ANIMATION PATTERNS

If you've looked at as many examples of animation on the web and in app interfaces as I have, certain patterns start to emerge. These patterns are helpful for identifying and succinctly verbalizing the purpose of an animation to others. Here are the categories I've found myself using the most:

- *Transitions* take users from place to place in the information space, or transition them out of one task into another. These tend to have massive impacts on the content on the page, replacing large portions of information.
- *Supplements* bring information on or off the page, but don't change the user's "location" or task. They generally add or update bits of additional content on the page.
- *Feedback* indicates causation between two or more events, often used to connect a user's interaction with the interface's reaction.
- *Demonstrations* explain how something works or expose its details by showing instead of telling.
- *Decorations* do not convey new information and are purely aesthetic.

Let's have a look at each of them and see how they impact the user's experience.

Transitions

The web was originally designed as a series of linked documents. Clicking on a link caused the browser to wipe the screen, often causing a telltale flash of white, before painting the next page from scratch. While this made sense in the context of linked text-based documents, it makes less sense in an era where pages share many rich design elements and belong to the same domain. Not only is it wasteful of the browser's resources to be recreating the same page layout over and over, but it also increases users' cognitive load when they have to reorient and reevaluate the page's content.

Animation, specifically motion, can facilitate the user's orientation in an information space by offloading that effort to the brain's visual cortex. Using a transition between changes in task flow or locations in information architecture ideally reinforces where the user has been, where they are going, and where they are now in one fell swoop.

For example, on Nike's SB Dunk page, when a user clicks a navigation arrow, the current sneaker moves out of the way while the next sneaker moves in from the opposite direction (FIG 2.1). These transitions clearly show the user how they are navigating along a linear continuum of sneakers, helping them keep track of their place and reinforcing the spatial model of perusing a real-world row of sneakers.

On another shoes site, fluevog.com, transitions move the user from task to task (FIG 2.2). After a user starts typing in the search field, the results are animated on top of a darker backdrop. This transitions the user from the browsing context to refining their search results, streamlining their focus while also reassuring them that they can get back to browsing without much effort.

When a user clicks one of the side arrows...

...the next sneaker slides in from the corresponding direction to show progression through the sneakers and reinforce their spatial locations.

FIG 2.1: On this Nike page, transitions are used to navigate forwards and backwards along a linear continuum of sneakers. (Watch the accompanying video.)

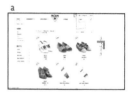
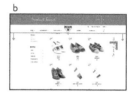

When a user clicks on the search icon...

...the search bar slides out of hiding, pushing the nav bar down from the top, its input field already in focus.

When the user starts typing, the search results overlay fades in to help them focus on live results.

FIG 2.2: On Fluevog's website, transitions move users from the browsing context to the searching context. (Watch the accompanying video.)

Supplements

While transitions move the user *from* state to state, supplemental animations bring ancillary information *to* the user. Think of times when information complementary to the main content of the page appears or disappears in view: alerts, dropdowns, and tooltips are all good candidates for a supplemental animation on entry and exit.

Remember that these animations need to respect the user's Cone of Vision: will they be looking directly at a tooltip appearing next to their cursor, or will their attention need to be directed to an alert on the side of their tablet?

a

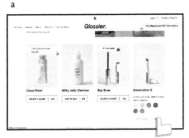

When a user clicks the Add to Bag button...

b

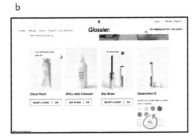

...the button gets a spinning loading icon to let the user know that the server is handling their request...

c

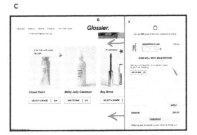

...when the request is done, the shopping cart sidebar slides out over the page...

d

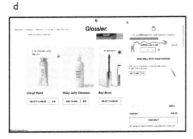

...then the free shipping meter animates to attract the user's attention to how much more they need to spend.

FIG 2.3: Glossier.com uses supplemental animation to show and hide the user's shopping cart, keeping them in the shopping context longer without forcing them into the purchasing context. (Watch the accompanying video.)

When a user adds a product to their shopping cart on glossier. com, rather than taking them to a whole new shopping cart page, the site merely updates the user as to their cart's contents by popping it out as a sidebar (**FIG 2.3C**). While a transition would snap the user out of browsing mode, this supplemental animation lets the user dismiss the shopping cart and continue shopping.

The shopping cart sidebar uses an additional supplemental animation to quickly and subtly attract the user's eye: a progress meter gradually fills to show how much the user needs to spend to get free shipping (**FIG 2.3D**).

This shopping cart process has a third animation pattern going on: the Add to Bag button gains a spinning icon when clicked, which gives the user feedback as to its loading state (**FIG 2.3B**). Speaking of feedback...

Feedback

Animation can give users direct feedback about their interactions. A depressed button, a swiping gesture—both link a human action to an interface's reaction. Or the flip side: a loading spinner on a page indicates that we're waiting on the computer. Without visual feedback, people are left wondering if they actually clicked that "pay now" button, or if the page is really loading after all.

On the Monterey Bay Aquarium's site, hovering over a button causes its color to fade from red to blue, indicating that the element is interactive and ready to react to user input (**FIG 2.4**). Button hovers are classic examples for this kind of animation,

a

b

When a user hovers over a button...

...the button's color changes to indicate the element is interactive.

FIG 2.4: On the Monterey Bay Aquarium's site, hovering on a button triggers an animation that gives the user feedback that the element is interactive. (Watch the accompanying video.)

a	b	c
When a user visits the site, a <u>loading bar progresses across</u> the top of the page to show how much longer till load.	When the page has fully loaded, <u>the logo writes itself</u> to indicate the wait is over and attract the user's attention to the middle of	...before the <u>background fades in</u>.

FIG 2.5: Design studio Animal uses a progress to let users know how much of the page has loaded, and an animated logo to indicate when it's fully loaded. (Watch the accompanying video.)

partly because the gain of giving users visual feedback on buttons is so measurable and important to business.

Design studio Animal's site uses a bar of color across the top of the page as well as an animated version of their logo to indicate the page's loading and loaded states *while* providing interest and reinforcing their "wild" branding (**FIG 2.5**).

Demonstrations

Demonstrations are my personal favorite use of animation. They can be both entertaining *and* insightful. These animations put information into perspective, show what's happening, or how something works. This makes demonstrative animations perfect partners for infographics. One thing all demonstrative animations do is tell a story, as you'll see.

"Processing..." pages are an opportunity to explain what's happening to users while they wait. TurboTax makes good use of these processing pages (**FIG 2.6**). After users submit their US tax forms, it banishes any remaining anxiety by showing them where their information is headed and what they can expect—all while reinforcing their brand's friendliness and accessibility. (It also helps that the animation distracts users from a rather lengthy page load with something visually engaging!)

a

When the user submits their taxes by clicking the "transmit" button...

b

...the form fades to white and then the office scene fades in and slides down...

c

...then an envelope representing the users taxes pops into view.

d

The envelope opens as, within the circle, files begin to fall into it...

e

...and when full, the envelope closes to show that their tax information has been gathered.

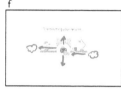

f

Then the envelop moves up and down as clouds whisk by within the circle, giving a feeling of transmission through the sky.

g

The envelope comes to rest and a checkmark pops up to show that its contents have been received

h

Then the envelope scoots out of the circle...

i

...and the whole scene simultaneously fades out while sliding up while the circle shrinks.

FIG 2.6: TurboTax both informs their users and masks long page loads by demonstrating what's going on after the user submits their US tax forms. (Watch the accompanying video.)

Coin famously uses demonstrative animations to explain their consolidation card's value proposition to curious visitors as they scroll through the site (**FIG 2.7**)—no need to press play

a

When a user visits the site, they're presented with an autoplaying video demonstrating the value proposition.

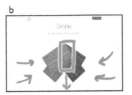

b

As the user scrolls, they see visual demonstrations of the same proposition, starting with many cards merging into one...

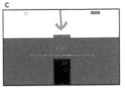

c

...then the one card slides underneath the next section.

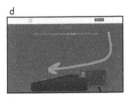

d

As the user continues to scroll, the card follows and swipes the card reader...

e

...then comes to rest next to the iPhone before flicking away casually to

f

At the very bottom of the page, the card slides up as if saying it was there for us all

FIG 2.7: As visitors scroll through Coin's site, the company's value proposition plays out in front of them. (Watch the accompanying video.)

and sit through a video ad or wade through paragraphs of expository content. This page is the very essence of "show, don't tell."

Decorations

It's not hard to mistake decorative animations for demonstrative animations. But there is a key difference: where demonstrations bring new information into the system, decorative animations do not. They are the fats and sugars of the animation food pyramid: they make great flavor enhancers, but moderation is key.

The best way to spot a purely decorative animation is to ask, "What can a user learn from this animation? Does this guide them or show them something they wouldn't know

a

On page load, the door is closed.

b

Then the spotlight shines down as the bright patch expands...

c

...then the door opens to reveal a symbol representing women.

HOLD for a beat.

d

She rises up slightly as suddenly a hole opens up beneath her!

e

She falls down the hole.

f

Then the door swings closed as the spotlight recedes.

g

The hole shrinks to nothing.

h

And we're back at the first frame like nothing happened. Like she was never there.

FIG 2.8: Revisionist History's site uses decorative animations to add visual interest to non-visual media. (Watch the accompanying video.)

otherwise?" If the answer is no, you might have a decorative animation on your hands.

Even though they get a bad rap, decorative animations can help turn the ordinary into the extraordinary. Revisionist History's site uses decorative animations judiciously to bring flat illustrations to life. The animations add just enough interest to

a

Users at first see a blank, green screen.

b

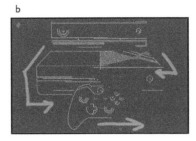

Promptly the console draws itself in.

c

When the illustration is complete,
its buttons press...

d

...then the illustration shrinks upward
while the article rises to meet it.

FIG 2.9: Polygon uses decorative animations as a showstopping feature to stand out from the competition. (Watch the accompanying video.)

allow for the visual content on the page to be more austere, letting users focus on the podcast (**FIG 2.8**).

Polygon.com epically used animated illustrations to create centerpieces for a series of console reviews. These decorative animations may not have added new information, but they crucially reinforced the Polygon brand. They also helped each console review stand out from the competition, which at the time sported indistinguishable photographs of the same devices.

PURPOSE

Once we've started noticing patterns, it's easier to talk about purpose. All of these patterns (with the exception of maybe the decorative ones) do something important: they supply context in a context-poor environment.

The world around us is alive with information in the form of noises, smells, and movements, and it responds when we interact with it. The web is rich with information, but it's not inherently rich with context and feedback. Animation can and should help with that, from providing feedback about the status of your tax return submission to attracting your attention to a crucial update. That is animation's true purpose: to add context.

An easy way to check if an animation provides context is to use your words to describe what benefit or new information it supplies. From the Nike example (**FIG 2.1**), we could say, "The sneakers move forward or backward to show the user where they are in a linear list of shoes, and what direction they are moving in along that list."

The more easily we can describe how an animation enriches the information on the page, the more context it likely provides. And the more context an animation provides, the more justified we are in supplying it. Context-rich animations have purpose and real meaning on the page, as opposed to existing solely to "delight."

Thinking about animation early

To make sure that our animations are purposeful, it pays to starting thinking about them as early as possible in a project. When web projects are in the planning stages, it's important to have conversations about animation with as many stakeholders as possible, from development to design and UX. Look for opportunities to bring animation into the discussion.

- **Information architecture and navigation structure** can be augmented with motion design. How can you reinforce a user's location in the site's data space? How can you convey their transition from location to location within that space, or their progression through tasks?

- **Interaction design** opens up when animation comes to the table. Static interfaces tend to require much more wording to explain relationships that animation can visually demonstrate. What interactions are you overexplaining?
- **Branding** can be reinforced by animations—both overtly with decorative animations, and discreetly with easing and animation language (more on those in the next chapter). What kind of emotions should your brand evoke, and how can animation reinforce them?

We'll talk more about generating buy-in and collaborating in a little bit, but for now, know that the more folks are listening at the start, the more your animations are likely to make it into the final product.

Spotting cognitive bottlenecks

Not all of us are so fortunate as to be at the start of a new project when it comes time to implement animations. When tasked with adding animations to an existing project, we run the risk of only implementing "delighters"—decorative animations that reinforce branding or live up to stakeholder expectations, but don't necessarily improve cognitive flow for users.

Don't give up hope: seize this opportunity! The cut interface of most websites gives off plenty of "cognitive bottleneck smells" that we can home in on and mitigate with animations:

- **Flashes of white** happen when a new page is loaded and painted into the browser window. Why replace the whole page when you can change and animate just the parts that matter? If the new content is different from the old in purpose or location, consider using a transition to take the user there. If the design of the pages is identical and its content the same, a supplemental animation might be just the trick to bring the changes into play.
- **Content insertion or removal** is a prime candidate for animation: tooltips, menus, dialogs, sequenced information.

- **Wordy descriptions** can indicate something being told instead of shown. Can a demonstration do it better?
- **Videos**, in the same vein, can be overkill for demonstrations in some cases and require user interaction to stop or start. Can an animated demonstration convey the same information passively and with fewer megabytes?

Prioritization

In his book *Creativity, Inc.*, Pixar's Ed Catmull mentions a phenomenon their producers have dubbed "the beautifully shaded penny." This refers to how creative folks tend to pour a lot of energy into a feature that is actually quite small in the greater scheme of the project. Katherine Sarafian, a Pixar producer, called it "the equivalent of a penny on a nightstand that you'll never see." For instance, a scene in *Monsters, Inc.* included a stand of alphabetized CDs—each one with a carefully designed cover—but in the actual film, we only see three of them.

It's easy for me, as an animation wonk, to walk in on a project and see all the opportunities to animate. But animation has to jostle with many other features for developer time—from performance to typography—and resources are not limitless. So we have to prioritize to make sure we get the most impactful animations into the project while leaving some of the nice-to-haves for another day.

Just because an animation makes something look nicer doesn't mean it's worth the effort to implement from a development standpoint. Consider whether or not it's adding information back into the system. Is it a working animation or an entertaining animation? We can weigh it and find out!

First, find out what patterns the animation falls into. If something is both a transition and a demonstration, that's a double-whammy: it's providing *even more* valuable context.

Then, to help quantify that context, ask the following questions:

- Does it show the user where information came from or went to?
- Does it indicate progress?
- Does it move the user through an information space?
- Does it reinforce physics or branding?
- Does it explain something faster than words or a video could?

The more boxes an animation ticks and patterns it fulfills, the more likely it is to provide a net gain for your users, and the more justifiable it becomes. This is how you know it's not just a nice-to-have.

But not all justifiable animations are feasible within the scope of a project. You may lack resources to implement a new framework to allow page transitions, for instance. To help visualize which animations to focus on, I create a graph with "ease of implementation" on the X-axis (ranging from easy to implement to difficult) and "justification" on the Y-axis (ranging from nice-to-have to necessary), and plot the animation features on it accordingly (**FIG 2.10**). Every animation you'd like to use will rank somewhere on this chart.

Does the animation tie into another priority, like performance or a highly anticipated new feature? When an animation ties in with another effort, it's more likely to involve more parties and resources may be more or less available because of that. I give these kinds of efforts a bigger size on the graph to visually indicate the weight of their undertaking.

Next, I draw a cross over the graph (I know, it's sad to mar such a beautiful graph, but this is the important part) (**FIG 2.11**). Usually we end up with the following categories of importance:

- **Low-hanging fruit** represents big wins at low cost. There are few good reasons to delay working on these, and they should be moved to the top of the priority heap across the board. Prioritizing them will net you big wins.
- **Long-term investments** represent animations that will help people a lot, but require more effort to execute. To make sure the result is what you expect, run some prototypes by users and gauge their reactions. The animation may not be

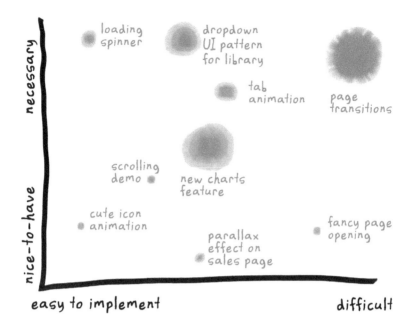

necessary

nice-to-have

loading spinner

dropdown UI pattern for library

tab animation

page transitions

scrolling demo

new charts feature

cute icon animation

fancy page opening

parallax effect on sales page

easy to implement　　　　　　　　　　　　**difficult**

FIG 2.10: Plot your potential animations on the chart according to how necessary and difficult to implement they are.

as important as thought, or if it is, use the results of the test to help justify prioritizing the time for it in the future. Try not to leave long-term investments in the icebox for too long, though! Ignore them, and your project won't be all it can be.

- **Pet projects** are great to keep around for slow days (they happen) and to hand out to new recruits as a special challenge. (Who wouldn't jump at the chance to animate a "favorite" icon on their first day?)
- **Hopeless causes** are both unnecessary *and* difficult to implement. Just accept that you will never have the time or the justification to work on them. If someone else magically gets them done, have a long talk with them. Maybe they

FIG 2.11: Divide your chart into quadrants to help identify your priorities.

know a technique worth learning—or they might need their priorities adjusted.

Larger dots that touch more teams will need to be brought up earlier in a project. When it comes to animation, the more planning and integration time people have, the more likely the animation is to make it into the feature. Think of these bigger dots as opportunities to collaborate across teams and build something everyone is proud of.

USEFUL AND NECESSARY, THEN BEAUTIFUL

The Shaker people have a design philosophy that suffuses their craftsmanship: "Don't make something unless it is both necessary and useful; but if it is both necessary and useful, don't hesitate to make it beautiful."

We have a tendency to talk about animations as "beautiful" or "delightful," but delight alone is not a reason to use an animation. When crafting for delight, we risk creating a purely decorative animation that will wear on users' nerves after the fiftieth viewing. Animation is not in and of itself delightful. But when used considerately with all the other pieces in the system—the typography, the interface, the voice and tone of the site, the speed of content delivery—the *whole* experience becomes delightful.

Now you should be able to distinguish useful, necessary, and even beautiful animations from one another, and be able to spot opportunities to use them. But great animation ideas must be conveyed across great teams. And to do that, we need a technical vocabulary developers understand. In the next chapter we're going to focus on the terminology of web animations and how their different components work together.

3
—

ANATOMY OF A WEB ANIMATION

I ONCE HAD A PROJECT where a designer gave me an animated GIF to recreate in CSS. (Please, please do *not* send developers animated GIFs and no guidelines to work from at 4:30pm. It's a form of cruelty, I'm certain.) I stayed up all night remaking it in CSS until it looked like a perfect replica—to *my* eyes. However, when the designer came back in the next morning, the first thing they noticed was that I hadn't translated an almost imperceptible bounce!

If only they had provided me with a little extra information, I would have been able to recreate that GIF perfectly and in much less time. To do that, I would have needed to know three things about the animation:

- *Easing*: The rate at which the visual changes occur—for instance, going from slow to fast.
- *Duration*: How long the animation should last, often in fractions of a second.
- *Properties*: What visual aspects you want to change, like width or color.

Let's have a closer look at these three comrades.

EASING

Easing describes the rate at which something changes over a period time. When applied to motion, easing can describe an element's acceleration or deceleration. The term has its roots in traditional studio animation, where it was called "cushioning" or even "slowing."

In CSS, easings are called *timing functions* and are described in a few ways. Every browser understands the default CSS timing function keywords:

- ease-in (acceleration)
- ease-out (deceleration)
- ease-in-out (speed up then slow down)
- linear (constant rate of change)

Each of these easings works best in different situations:

- Acceleration is good for system-initiated animations, like a pop-up asking users to sign up for a newsletter. If this unannounced animation starts slowly, it's less likely to startle users, even if it takes the same amount of time as an animation with an ease-in.
- Deceleration starts quickly and gives a UI a snappy, responsive feeling. It's great for user-initiated interactions, like button clicks and page transitions.
- Speeding up then slowing down is useful for interaction models when moving an element toward another.
- A constant rate of change works best for fades and color changes, which can look jarring with a steep curve.
- Bounces can add extra animacy to draw attention to elements or to add an air of "fun" to the brand.

These easing values look and feel the same from browser to browser, site to site. But if you want your animation to stand out, to feel unique to your site, you'll want custom easings. CSS has a special format for customizing easing: the *cubic Bézier curve*.

Cubic Béziers are a formula used to mathematically describe a rate of change. When plotted on a graph, a cubic Bézier will form a curve with steepness indicating a quicker rate of change. This formula can be shared in CSS by putting the curve's coordinates into the cubic-bezier(w, x, y, z) timing function. Because of its flexibility, this formula also lets us create single and double bounces. Even CSS's default timing functions can be described as cubic Bézier curves (**FIG 3.1**)!

Cubic-bezier.com is a great tool that lets you tug and pull the handles of the curve in real time, updating the formula while you watch. Both Chrome and Firefox have similar tools, which I highly recommend trying out. Playing with tools like these is a fun way to get a feel for the way easings work.

But you might prefer starting with the tried and true formulae at easings.net. These have been used in interaction design for years. Is your brand gentle and elegant like a Sine curve, or fast-paced and bursting with energy like the steeper Expo? Give

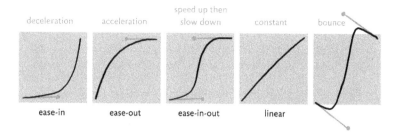

FIG 3.1: CSS's default easings described as   curves.

them all a spin, and copy and paste the formulae for the ones that feel the most like your brand.

Speaking of branding, it's best to keep animations looking uniform throughout your site's experience. The best way to do that is to create a collection of harmonious easings for reuse. It's helpful to keep them all in a chart detailing their purpose, their cubic Bézier formula or CSS keyword, and where said formula came from (**FIG 3.2**).

PURPOSE	ORIGIN	CSS TIMING FUNCTION
Acceleration	EaseInCubic from easings.net	
Deceleration	EaseOutCubic from easings.net	
Ease-in-out	EaseInOutCubic from easings.net	
Subtle curve	Browser default keyword	
Bounce	Custom-made at cubic-bezier.com	

FIG 3.2: An easings chart can tamp down on proliferating easing usage and provide a unified feel for your site's animations.

DURATION

Animation is change over time. To create any animation, it helps to know its duration. While easings tell us the rate of change, the duration tells us how long the animation lasts. But how long *should* an animation last? We can make some inferences. Perhaps you're familiar with Jakob Nielsen's "Three Important Time Limits" post from 1993? In it, Nielsen referenced a 1968 study that measured human reactions to computer response times. The results of the study showed that:

- Response times of 100 milliseconds or less felt instantaneous.
- Response times of up to 1 second still felt connected.
- After 10 seconds, users began to feel disconnected.

These durations are referenced by many UX community members to this day for gauging human-computer interactions. But remember that this research was done in 1968, and it was already almost three decades old when Nielsen wrote about it.

People use computers very differently from how they did in the late 1960s, and it appears their patience is running out. In 2009, Google ran experiments where they slowed down their search results pages by 100 to 400 milliseconds. The slower response times had a measurable impact on the number of searches per user. Even weeks later, users from the slowed pages were not searching as much. Another Google study from 2016 indicates that 53% of mobile site visits are abandoned if they take longer than three seconds to load. Previous research *really* should be revisited in this new era of touchscreens and beefy graphics cards.

Fortunately, we have some other resources to draw from, and the time units involved are all under one second long. While CSS can accept both seconds and milliseconds, JavaScript only takes millisecond values. Thus it makes sense to think of and document our animation durations in terms of milliseconds first.

The average time it takes people to react to visual change is about 215 ms. Thus, it makes sense that 200-300 ms is a recurring sweet spot among game and interaction developers. Durations in this range tend to be the workhorses in an interface.

The Model Human Processor (a system used to quantify human computer interactions) clocks the time it takes a user's eye to move at between 70 and 700 ms. It follows that animations in the center of the user's Cone of Vision do better with shorter durations (closer to the 70-200 ms spectrum) because the eye has less distance to travel. Animations on the edge of the Cone of Vision benefit from additional time for the user to move their eye, over in the 300-700 ms spectrum.

If something is moving across a screen, it will need more time than something providing immediate feedback, like a color change on hover. The eye is quite sensitive to color changes when it's looking directly at the animation. For that reason, I've found that color and opacity changes under the user's finger or cursor can feel slow if they take more than 100 ms. But if you're moving something across the page, 100 ms is too fast, and going over 300 ms may be necessary. It's important to try out various durations with real users to find the "Goldilocks duration" that feels "just right" for your use case.

Production speed

Studio animators working tirelessly on scenes week after week get pulled into a warped sense of time and space where their animation's playback seems faster than it really is. This is why animators have a saying: "Whatever your pre-production duration is, halve it. Then halve it again!"

This happens to us on the web, too. When preparing an animation, we also tend to perceive it as running faster than it really is. It's not uncommon to slash a production animation's duration to 25% of its development length. Just be sure that you're still giving the animation enough time to run if the user blinks or the animation doesn't render perfectly smoothly. The developer tools in both Chrome and Firefox can help you run animations faster or slower for debugging (FIG 3.3).

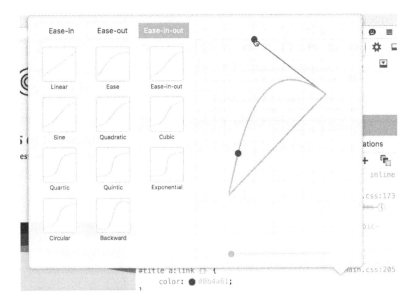

FIG 3.3: Firefox's developer tools offer presets as well as customization options for cubic Bézier curves. Dragging the handles on the curve changes the playback rate of the animation, with steeper segments running faster than more gradual slopes. (Watch the accompanying video.)

Timing scales

Just as with easings, durations can be arranged into reusable sets, with different durations for color changes, localized reactions like button presses, and large movements. But we don't have to select numbers out of thin air; we can use timing scales. The concept is similar to modular scales in typography: all values are related, and if you combine them with a vertical rhythm, a piece exhibits overall harmony.

Amy Lee, prototyper at Salesforce by day and musician by night, first introduced me to the concept of reusable and interlocking timing values on Salesforce's Lightning Design System.

KEYWORD	DURATION IN MILLISECONDS	USE
Immediate	100 ms	For fades and color-based animations
Fast	300 ms	For interacting with elements that need to feel responsive and peppy
Slower	400 ms	For moving elements on the page
Deliberate	700 ms	For large movements across the screen or self-contained demonstrations

FIG 3.4: This timing scale is inspired by the Fibonacci sequence: 100 + 300 = 400, 300 + 400 = 700. Referring to a chart like this will, once again, help standardize animations across a site.

[It] is about an agreed-upon synchronization of animation choreography. Imagine how an orchestra might play together. Without a common timing system, each player would drift through the score at their own rate. However, if we agree that a quarter note is 400ms long, then we all can play together at a peppy tempo of 150 beats per minute.

You can generate a timing scale the same way you generate a typographic scale. Salesforce's Lightning Design System uses timing scales to let developers tokenize their timing values. It's easy to line overlapping animations up to end at the same time with a system like this (FIG 3.4).

PROPERTIES

Properties describe *what* is changing over time. Color and opacity changes convey fades. Changes in location convey motion. Changes in scale or shape convey deformation and transformation.

Having a record of what CSS properties change is very helpful to developers—and for long-term documentation. When we record all this information in storyboards (we'll get to those in the next chapter), it leaves a clear blueprint for others to follow tomorrow.

Performance

Not all properties are as easy to animate for different browsers. Many of them trigger costly layout and painting operations in the browser, which on an overworked or underpowered device can cause an animation to drop a few frames—aka stuttering, or what studio animators refer to as "juttering" or becoming "janky." Jank breaks the illusion of life, so it's important to stick to performant properties. Properties like opacity and transform (which *transforms* scale, position, rotation) are currently pretty safe bets. Many browsers optimize their rendering pipeline to process opacity and transform animations on the computer's GPU.

But there will be times when we want to animate less performant things like width or borders. Browsers are working hard to improve their animation performance, so while it's great to try to stick to transform and opacity, don't be afraid to push boundaries where it has negligible impact on the animation's overall performance.

John Lasseter of Pixar said, "The art challenges the technology, and the technology inspires the art." It's true that what we do with animation today impacts what browser vendors build for tomorrow. It's a beautiful push and pull of needs.

PUTTING IT ALL TOGETHER

Now that we have all the building blocks required to describe and document an animation, we'll dive into how to turn animations into deliverables for your teams. We'll meet some old tools from studio animation and learn how to rally support for an animation agenda.

COMMUNICATING ANIMATION

ANIMATION SITS AT THE INTERSECTION of UX, development, and design. This means it can bring teams together—or drive them apart! Communication issues and inadequate deliverable documentation can make it hard for teams to design and build out animations quickly, leaving things like motion design and gestures at the bottom of the pile for implementation. Lack of respect and deference to one another can lead to deprioritization, and exclusionary gatekeeping can keep animation from being fully embraced across an organization.

Fortunately, animation can be nestled into our existing design and development processes and documentation. We have been using things like UI pattern libraries to document microinteractions and style guides to contain our typography and color palettes. With a systematic approach, we can bring animations to heel as well.

This chapter is all about communicating your animation patterns across teams, and getting everyone on board the "animation train."

CRAFTING AN ANIMATION LANGUAGE

The key to any interaction model is consistency. When I was new to web animation, I wanted to animate all the things. UI animation was new and exciting and looked so polished! But when I looked at all my animations working on the same site, they weren't working together. Was I going to get a modal fading in or sliding in? Were all the icons animated, or just the ones I had time to get to and thought were clever? Was every page going to transition in, or just this set over here?

UI animation works best when it conforms to predetermined sets of rules. And if you're working on a large project with a long-term growth plan, you'll want to use animations that can be adapted to multiple uses while maintaining cohesion and consistency. This is where animation language comes in.

We can combine the three components of animation that we discussed in Chapter 3—easing, duration, and properties—to create microanimations with descriptive names like "pop," "fade," and "slide." A microanimation can be used as part of a

FIG 4.1: Salesforce provides a rich vocabulary of predefined microanimations for developers to use and combine into new patterns. (Watch the accompanying video.)

greater design pattern, or combined with other microanimations to create macroanimations—for instance, a modal that fades onto the screen then pops to grab user attention. We might then label that combined animation as an "alert," and use it over and over again.

Many of these microanimation names start as friendly onomatopoeias around a meeting room table: swoosh, zoom, plonk, boom. Something I've noticed at many companies around the world is that participants will hold a sound longer to indicate extended duration: "Can you make it more like *voooooosh* and less like *voosh?*" It makes sense to "pave the cowpaths" and adopt the words your company is using already.

When codified, these microanimations can form animation vocabularies that yield huge benefits when it comes time to document visual deliverables with text. Salesforce's Lightning Design System provides developers with a host of these microanimations to compose whatever custom designs or interfaces its users create. In this way, Salesforce engenders brand compliance by providing easy-to-reach-for defaults (**FIG 4.1**).

Salesforce could have provided lengthier documentation explaining the choices their design team made, but the Lightning Design Team chose to lead by examples and easy, composable presets, providing a path of least resistance for developers who are probably more interested in getting a product out the door than learning the intricacies of UI animation that you are (and you are so awesome for it).

DOCUMENTING ANIMATION FOR DESIGN SYSTEMS

There are two reasons to document design decisions:

1. To create deliverables for developers to implement.
2. To create guidelines for designers and developers to follow in the future.

Nowhere is this more important than with animation. Animation cannot be conveyed in a single screenshot. And while it can be demonstrated in a GIF or a video, developers have to pick apart those formats with more or less fidelity. None of these alone are good formats for communicating animation deliverables in the present or future. They cannot be passed to an external agency as one would a branding bible or style guide. They cannot be referenced when creating choreographed systems that look and feel the same across a user's journey.

To build scalable, maintainable, integrated designs, we need to document not just the anatomy of their animations (as seen in Chapter 3), but also how those animations should be choreographed in the context of user interaction. Lucky for us, we have a couple of tools that can help.

Storyboards

In 1933, Disney Studios crafted the world's first storyboards in preparation for working on the world's first feature-length animated film, *Snow White and the Seven Dwarfs*. The storyboards reduced time spent on poorly planned shots, and helped directors and writers visualize the final story and edit it on the fly, taking studio animation from a waterfall workflow to an agile one. Storyboards made *Snow White* possible, and the Hollywood directors who had mocked Disney's dream of an animated movie soon found themselves adopting storyboards for their own projects.

These days, storyboards are used not only in cinema but also in game design, interaction development, and—you guessed it—even in web design. Storyboards are useful because they put words, even values, next to snapshots of an animation.

Storyboards can help explicitly state how an interaction is expected to be implemented. They can reduce the load on developers and are a great place to document *why* a decision was made (**FIG 4.2**).

I like to make my initial storyboards the old-fashioned way: with index cards and corkboards or Post-Its and sketchbooks. But even I use an officious, cleaned-up template (PDF) for client deliverables and archival purposes. For those with a completely digital workflow, boords.com provides a promising solution, with PDF exports and a simplified interface (compared to cinematic storyboarding software!).

Storyboards are great for archiving design decisions and setting standards, but they fall short in a few ways. You can't demonstrate or test an animation's look and feel with them, and they are clunky to integrate with existing online design guidelines. But, as far as quantifying what changes when, tried and true storyboards can't be beat.

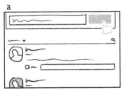 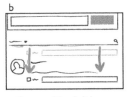 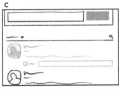

a

When a user adds a new friend by clicking the button...

b

...the new friend slides down from the top of the list over 200ms with an ease-in...

c

...displacing the friends below, drawing attention to where the new friend can be found while confirming that the friend was

FIG 4.2: The second frame describes the animation's duration and easing, and the third frame explains what benefit the animation provides. (Watch the accompanying video.)

Animatics

Where storyboards excel at providing deliverable values and inline reasoning, they fall short at conveying an animation's "mouthfeel." Stakeholders are unlikely to be satisfied with a presentation of a storyboard. If a picture is worth a thousand words, then an animatic must be worth a thousand meetings.

Once again, studio animation provides a solution in the form of *animatics*: videos of the storyboard panels set to an audio track with the actors reading their lines and the soundtrack playing. Animatics can be shown to a test audience to see how they respond to a plot twist, or presented to investors as proof of progress.

For creating animatics, Adobe After Effects is the current software of choice in the motion design industry. Web designers may be more accustomed to creating animatic-like demos in Keynote, which can be clicked through in meetings or recorded with screencasting software like Quicktime or Camtasia. And some visual prototyping tools, like Principle, export to video achieving two things at once. You can also make animatics as small videos or GIFs. If you're a paper prototyper, you can even use a stop-motion app on your phone to record an animatic (FIG 4.3)!

FIG 4.3: Animatics come in all shapes and forms, from super-polished designs made in After Effects to stop-motion films. I made this one with Post-Its and a stop-motion app on my phone. (Watch the accompanying video.)

Prototypes

Animatics can provide a visual "aha!" moment for stakeholders, but they are impossible to test in the field. Something that sounds good in theory and looks good on a big screen in a meeting room can still frustrate users in practice. Prototypes give us the chance to observe real people doing real things with our animations.

There are two approaches to prototypes: prototyping frameworks that require a knowledge of HTML and CSS, and prototyping software that offers a visual interface to work with. Developers tend to prefer the former, often leaning on frameworks like Framer, while many designers prefer the latter in the form of software like InVision.

Both approaches require team members to invest time in learning a new system, thus increasing the commitment factor. Essentially, prototyping involves making the site twice: once as a working mockup and then again as product-ready code. While large companies can afford entire prototyping teams and reap the benefits of "measure twice, cut once," this is prohibitive for many small businesses and agencies. But for those who can afford it, it's a solid approach to designing with animation.

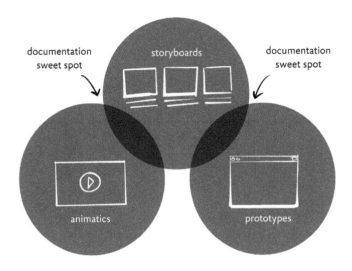

FIG 4.4: The best approach to documentation is to couple verbal and visual descriptions together.

Verbal and visual documentation

Prototypes, unlike storyboards, are terrible for documentation: only code-savvy team members can read them, and the files must be organized and sometimes compiled or served before inspection. On the other hand, animatics are terrible for developers to work from because they don't provide values for an animation's easing, duration, and properties. An external agency would struggle to deliver a fully branded experience riffing off a pile of non-production code or animated GIFs. And storyboards, while archival, convey nothing of motion in action.

So what do we do? The best approach to get both deliverables and archival information is to combine two of these approaches: coupling animatics with storyboards, or adding live microinteractions to design systems along with the values necessary to reproduce them (**FIG 4.4**). The former works great on smaller teams and projects on a shoestring budget, while the latter reinforces the authority of a larger enterprise.

GENERATING BUY-IN

Now we know how to share animations in formats that communicate their actions and the technical details required to recreate them. But as anyone who's tried to create a style guide alone has learned, "if you document it, they will come" is a fallacy. We need to get our teammates excited about animation!

Focus on the benefits

First you might be inclined to argue with numbers and facts. But this can be tricky. Understanding the inherent value of animation requires an understanding of how the human visual system works, something even renowned academics struggle with.

What's more, arguing for or defending animation can cause friction with some folks who don't like being challenged over seemingly unimportant "decoration." So why not skip combat mode altogether and talk benefits? If stakeholders collaborate, document, and codify their efforts together, their animations will pay off with:

- **Lighter code.** When animation is normalized, it's unlikely to be repeated in numerous permutations throughout a codebase.
- **Reliable interaction patterns.** Consistent interactions bolster user confidence and trust. Dropdowns that slide down alongside ones that fade in, for instance, make an interface feel shifty and unfinished.
- **Maintainability.** Reliable, repeatable, consolidated animations are easier to maintain than their fly-by-the-seat-of-their-pants counterparts.
- **On-brand interaction.** Animations can reflect the brand's voice and tone, reinforcing branding.
- **Shorter design and development time.** If animations don't need to be tooled from scratch for every bit of interaction, spinning up rich new experiences is that much faster.

Show, don't tell

There's one sure way to drive home how much difference animation makes: show it. As Robert Greene wrote in his Machiavellian book, *The 48 Laws of Power*, "It is much more powerful to get others to agree with you through your actions, without saying a word. Demonstrate, do not explicate." So often when animation is picked up for a project, it's because someone placed an animated version next to a static comp so stakeholders could see the difference for themselves.

From big companies like Google to small ad agencies, showing beats telling. Getting the animations out of your head and in front of the eyes of people who matter beats lobbying. Trust human intuition to convince a skeptical audience. The brain's GPU can't be denied.

Spread the love

An animation-friendly mindset must be cultivated and championed around the workplace. Someone has to keep it top of mind when it would be forgotten during prototyping. Someone has to keep an eye on the latest research and performance tricks. Why can't that person be you?

But be wary of falling into the trap of trying to own animation for your team or company. I've watched companies lose all momentum on bringing animation into their UI when the one person who internally evangelized motion design left. Setting yourself up as a lone gatekeeper is dangerous—not just for the company, but also for you. You could be seen as the obsessive animation wonk who thinks the world revolves around "silly decorative stuff." It's easy to ignore one person, but a group of allied experts is a force to be reckoned with. You'll have a better chance of getting animation on the table at the start of a project.

Look for collaborators outside your own department. If you're in design, a developer can help you prototype ideas or build out UI patterns. If you're in UX, a designer can help you make animatics that win over managers. And don't forget about accessibility, branding, and performance folks. Because animation touches so many disciplines, it has the magical power to bring people together who otherwise might never collaborate. Find these people and befriend them.

Animation as a team sport

Once again, think of yourself more as a gardener, not a gatekeeper. When working on animations, share your work with your teams. Let them get excited. Take their feedback. If they want to help document or prototype, no matter how briefly, let them touch the project and feel part ownership. When everyone feels like this is their baby, they're less likely to throw it out with the bath water.

WHEN A PLAN COMES TOGETHER

For animation to be a part of a balanced design, many different moving parts need to come together—literally! You must be attentive to details, consistent in your approach, and document every decision. But none of this matters if no one adopts these guidelines. Providing an animation vocabulary helps: it gives your partners useful, on-brand defaults to get started with. But more than anything, it's up to you to bring people together, which requires setting egos aside and solving problems greater than any of us can tackle alone.

BEST PRACTICES AND OTHER EDUCATED GUESSES

ANIMATION ON THE WEB is nothing new, but it's enjoying a comeback at a time when we care deeply about accessibility and usability. This is a good thing because it reminds us to put animation to work *for* our users, instead of just using it for our own entertainment and delight.

Unfortunately, past web animators from the Flash era didn't leave many best practices or guidelines for us to follow. We are new to using animation in this purposeful, respectful way. Not a month passes that I don't learn something new about how different people perceive motion and change, or how we can create even more useful animations.

As such, the following "best practices" are more like guidelines to follow and test while we uncover more and more about how animation works—and doesn't work—on the web.

NO ONE SHOULD NOTICE THE WAITSTAFF

There is nothing so satisfying as hearing a beta tester remark, "Oh, that's delightful!" upon seeing your first UI animations. However, this could be a red flag. It means that they have noticed an animation, and that means they are spending cognitive power on it—the exact opposite of what animations should do. There are some circumstances, such as demonstrative animations, where we want people to really notice the action. But for the majority of microinteractions, we don't want animations to distract users.

I like to think of animation as the waitstaff at a fancy restaurant. You come to eat and drink, and to have good conversation with your companions. A good server facilitates this. No sooner have you set your fork down than your dinner plate seemingly disappears and is replaced with a dessert dish. As Heather Daggett, senior experience design prototyper at Intuit who works regularly with animation, put it:

Users should only notice your animation if you need to attract their attention in that moment. Otherwise, micro-interactions and other transitions should be so seamless, users don't even notice that there is animation.

When testing with users, pay attention to when they notice animation and when they don't. We know we're reducing their cognitive load when they don't notice something.

CONSISTENCY IS KEY

I mentioned in the previous chapter that consistency is important to creating a unified experience for our users, and that extends to animations. Beyond just using the same easings across a site or adhering to an animation language, we want to make sure that animations behave consistently as well.

Every entrance needs an exit

When a piece of information animates onto the screen, it should also animate as it leaves the screen. Because of how HTML, CSS, and JavaScript are often used together, it is often easier to animate an element's entrance than its exit. As such, many alerts beautifully animate into view, only to cut back into the void as soon as the user dismisses them (**FIG 5.1**). This gives a UI an unfinished, unreliable feel.

To provide a user with a consistent experience, we must invest early and wisely in a system that waits for an exit animation to finish before removing an element or changing state.

When a user goes to point at a navigation menu item...

...the menu expands downward when hovered over...

...and stays expanded until the hover is moved...

...whereupon the menu disappears immediately from the page without animation.

FIG 5.1: Sights like this are unfortunately commonplace: on Duluth Trading Company's site, the dropdowns expand downward when users hover over their link. But when the mouse moves away, those submenus disappear. (Watch the accompanying video.)

Avoid FOULS

You may have heard of flashes of unstyled text, or FOUT, that happen when a page's fonts haven't loaded yet so it displays default system fonts. Perhaps you've also met its cousin, FOULS: Flashes of Unloaded/ing States. These are often glimpsed when first loading or leaving a page on sites rich with transitions and supplementary information: briefly there's a flash of a page with no content, possibly followed by a loading state, then a page with the loaded content. These can happen in any order,

FIG 5.2: The "Facebook Shimmer" uses lightly animated or "shimmering" bars and blocks for placeholder content until the real content loads. (Watch the accompanying video.)

and when they do, they leave users wondering (again!), "What just happened?"

Loading states can mask empty pages bereft of content from users by providing an indication that the content is on its way. Ideally it flows like this:

1. A user lands on a page with no loaded content. But rather than showing an **unloaded** page...
2. ...the page starts in a **loading** state, showing indicators that content is coming and/or where it will be soon. (Facebook's "shimmer" pattern is a good example of this (**FIG 5.2**). Spinners in place of loading images are another example.)
3. Finally, the newly arrived content transitions to a **loaded** state.

a

When a user clicks on a link to another part of the site...

b

...the content fades out and slides up...

c

...but then the same content fades in and slides down, flashing an inappropriate loading state...

d

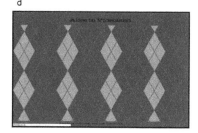

...before the new page with a very different design cuts into place.

FIG 5.3: This example of FOULS comes from a version of my own site, RachelNabors.com. So very embarrassing! (Watch the accompanying video.)

Loading states are very useful, but only if they actually hide the unloaded content from detection. We must ensure that users always see loaded states in the correct order—loading to loaded—and never see the unloaded state. This requires building with an "always be loading" mentality, where the default state of content in a JavaScript-enabled environment is a loading state. If you use automated testing in your development pipeline, test for these different states.

For an embarrassing example of a FOULS, look no further than my own site (**FIG 5.3**). As of this writing, I use JavaScript to dynamically load content and update the address bar without repainting the page, a technique sometimes called PJAX. This lets me use transitions between "pages" as a user navigates. But sometimes a user navigates to a part of my site that looks very different. They get the transition for unloading the page's content, but then the same content reappears right before they visit the other part of my site.

PAY ATTENTION TO FRAME RATES

Frames per second (FPS) measures how many different images can be rendered onto a surface in the space of a second. Early silent films were shown with as few as 16 FPS. Modern films are shown at 24 FPS, while in the web development community, we aim for 60 FPS. But why is this gap so wide? How can 24 FPS look fine in a movie theatre, but anything less than 60 FPS on our phones looks "janky" or choppy?

First we have to understand a little bit more about how the human eye perceives change. It can take as little as 13 milliseconds for our brains to "see" an image. That's close to 80 FPS. But we're already noticing the need for frame rates closer to 90 FPS in virtual reality development. These are much higher than the standard 60 FPS touted by performance experts as "good enough" to look smooth for the human eye. So what's happening here?

The human eye doesn't perceive "frames," it perceives motion as a continuum. One of the happy accidents of filming movies with cameras is that they also record "motion smears" that mimic this continuum. If you've ever paused an action sequence or taken hurried vacation photos, you can see these smears (**FIG 5.4**). You can show the eye a series of images with these motion blurs at a low frame rate, and it will look much more fluid than the same series without blur at a higher frame rate. Even Pixar adds motion blur to its films to help fast movements register better at low frame rates.

FIG 5.4: This young chicken was moving so fast that her leg disappeared into a smear of motion when I photographed her. When something moves quickly in our field of vision, it will stimulate a continuous smear of photoreceptors in our retina, not unlike what you see here.

On the web, we don't have motion blur. But we do have hardware constraints: 60 FPS happens to be the upper limit of what modern systems can interpret and display at a reasonable clip *today*. So we run all our animations as fast as the system will allow and hope the user won't notice. But there are cases when they will notice:

· **When moving a small graphic across a large area.** If we have a 60-foot-long screen and animate a ball moving across it at 60 FPS in the span of a second, the eyes of the audience will see 60 separate, sequential balls, appearing one after the other, one per foot. This is an extreme example of an effect called *strobing* (**FIGS 5.5A-B***)*. As web animation starts showing up on increasingly large screens, this will become an issue.

- **When the frame rate varies.** When an animation jumps from 60 FPS to 34 FPS then back again—even quickly—it can disrupt a user's flow. A 30 FPS animation that consistently runs will appear smoother than a 60 FPS animation that dips from time to time. The human visual system is always looking for inconsistencies. Inconsistencies bog down the brain.

In these instances, you may have to manually add motion blur using SVG filters or sprites and/or throttle the page's frame rate. Both techniques are beyond the scope of this book but may be worth considering for some special projects.

Alternatively, for moving graphics across large distances, you might also try fading the object out in the middle part of its trajectory, then back in at the destination. This gives the impression that the element moved so fast that it didn't register.

For the time being, try to keep your frame rate as steady as possible, either using throttling and motion blur techniques or by optimizing your performance, and be wary of moving things over large areas.

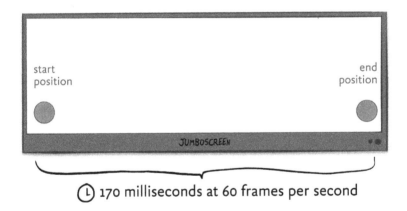

Ⓛ 170 milliseconds at 60 frames per second

FIG 5.5A: Imagine moving an image across a large screen like a TV or a billboard in a short amount of time. At 60 FPS, the ball only has 10 frames to move from its start position to its ends position.

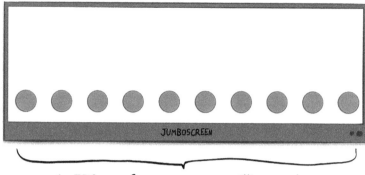

60 FPS = 10 frames per 170 milliseconds

FIG 5.5B: Ten frames mean ten individual orange balls are rendered onto the screen. The human eye is so sensitive, it will register each and every one of them. This makes the ball look like it's jumping across the space, making the animation feel janky, not smooth.

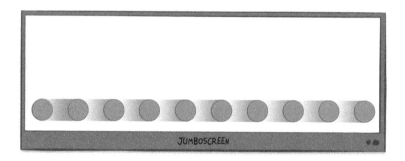

FIG 5.5C: But if we add motion blur to each of those frames, they create that "smear of motion" we saw in the image of the chicken. Although your retina can perceive change at much higher rates, this artificial smear fools your retina into seeing a more smooth and continuous motion.

RESPECT USER COGNITION DIFFERENCES

Not everyone experiences the world the same way. This has become more and more apparent in the web development and design community as we increasingly rely on user testing to try out ideas and prototypes. With animation, we must be aware of these differences—some of them are downright dangerous.

- **Time warps** occur for some people who physically experience time running faster or slower. A common example is older folks experiencing the world as racing by faster and faster while still remembering that summer seemed to last forever when they were kids. Different substances and mental states impact our perception of time, as well. Time seems to slow down for people in emergency situations, and speed up for people who are drunk. (This Wikipedia article on time perception is a fascinating place to dig in on the topic.)
- Everyone experiences time on a different scale, meaning that for some folks, the animation timings we use may seem too fast or too slow. Maybe one day, operating systems will offer time dilation controls. But until then, we can create alternate CSS with different duration values or use the Web Animations API to speed up or slow down animation playback rates across the board. Then we can let the user reduce or increase animation durations right alongside setting their motion preferences.
- **Seizures** are an increasingly concerning side effect as animation on the web becomes more common. Large, flashing red areas are the most triggering, but any on-screen change that flashes rapidly could lead to a headache, if not an outright attack. In 2008, the W3C created Web Content Accessibility Guidelines to help us build a better web for all. The current guidelines advise that elements flash no more than twice per second. Because this is a known quantity and seizures are so dangerous (and who wants to put a seizure warning on their site?), it makes sense to eliminate this kind of animation from our designs.

- **Vestibular disorders** describe a host of disorders of the human visual and balance systems. People suffering from these can have symptoms ranging from headaches to dizziness to nausea brought on by motion and animation. For some folks, a parallax effect might cause mild discomfort. For others, simply scrolling a web page can cause the room to spin. As many as 35% of Americans aged 40 years or older have experienced vestibular dysfunction in some form.

It's important to accommodate all these users, but it's impossible to design lowest common denominator animations that satisfy them all. You might be wondering if animation is worth the trouble. Those cuts are looking pretty accessible right now... But remember that the cognitive boost animation can give the majority of people is often well worth the trouble of accommodating stress cases.

Put the user in charge of their experience

Thanks to the world of operating system design, we know a bit about accommodating these folks. Remember, it's been in companies like Microsoft and Apple's best interests to make sure 100% of the population can use computers.

When iOS7 introduced zoom effects, many iPad and iPhone owners complained vociferously about dizziness. Apple developers accommodated them by releasing a patch that tucked a "reduce motion" option into the settings panel (**FIG 5.6**). This option replaced many other motion-based animations with fades, which do not trigger vestibular disorders. These options aren't limited to iOS7: earlier operating systems like Windows ME even had settings to turn off individual UI animations.

What it all comes down to is empowering our users to choose how they want to experience the web. And we can

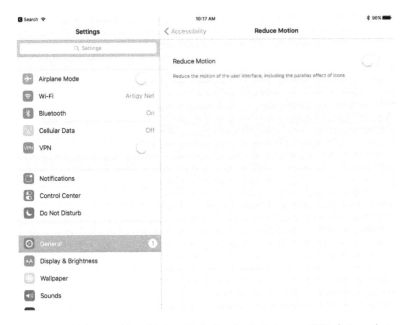

FIG 5.6: Apple's iOS provides a "Reduce Motion" option in their accessibility features that replaces the system's zooms with fades. (Watch the accompanying video.)

let those users choose for themselves whether they want full, partial, or no animation, and what speed it plays at.

We could do this with a preferences bar (a la the EU's "cookie bar"), or a settings panel shown on landing, or within the options of a web app, where we might keep other accessibility settings tucked away (FIG 5.7).

Someday browsers might offer some of these as global settings for users. There is even discussion of a "reduce motion" media query. But until then, we have options, and we *can* accommodate all users without leaving animation out of the equation.

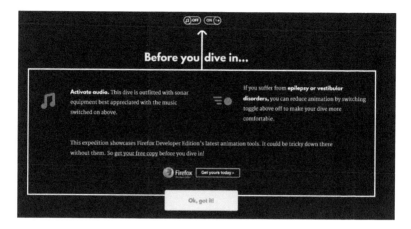

FIG 5.7: At DevToolsChallenger.com, visitors are greeted with the option to reduce animations as well as turn on music.

a

When a user hovers over a navigation element...

b

...the navigation bar rises slightly to indicate that clicking on the menu item...

c

...will hoist a new panel onto the screen.

d

When the menu panel is open, if the user hovers over a navigation element...

e

...the panel will sink lower slightly to indicate that clicking that navigation

f

...will cause the panel to slide back off the screen.

FIG 5.8: At DevToolsChallenger.com, hovering over the menu bar option causes the bar to "lift up," signaling, "if you click me, expect me to slide further up." Hovering over the same options when it's open causes the panel to "nudge downward," saying, "if you click me, I will slide further down." (Watch the accompanying video.)

Signal oncoming animations

One thing that can be helpful for all users is signaling what things are going to animate. For instance, hovering over an expandable sidebar might cause it to slightly shift in the direction it will expand if the user clicks it (**FIG 5.8**). This sort of anticipatory animation lets users mentally prepare themselves for what happens next.

ANIMATING RESPONSIBLY

I have given you the tools you need to decide when an animation provides a solid benefit to your users and when it's a nice-to-have. You know the cost of animation to development and device performance. You know the risk involved in shipping disruptive animations to an audience with differences in their visual perception systems. Hopefully you are equipped to spot and evade trendy, unnecessary effects that will no doubt come and go just as they have since the days of Flash, from "skip intro" buttons to parallax effects.

I also want you to be wary of outdated research. It's an exciting time to be working with animation on the web. We're actively reading all the research papers that have come before in our sister industries of game and software design. But most of this research is very old and needs to be revisited.

I caution you, dear reader, against holding anything as written in stone because there was a paper published on it years ago or because someone famous has talked about it, so it must be true. I have been that person on the stage, accidentally espousing something later proven false. I would rather be challenged than put on a pedestal.

I encourage you to do your own research and share what you find. One of the strengths of our community is how eagerly and quickly we share our findings with each other, helping us all learn and iterate faster. Unlike other industries who hoard their company secrets, the web thrives on openness. We are constantly iterating, shipping, speaking, writing, tweeting, coding, forking, pushing. We share our triumphs, our research, our knowledge. We test more, iterate faster, and spread knowledge farther than anyone else. And with UI animation, we have the opportunity to uncover new discoveries and great truths, going beyond mere hackneyed rules of thumb.

This openness means that the next big breakthrough will come from someone like you, someone picking up this book and looking at it with fresh eyes. You're going to uncover new truths, truths that other communities may learn from. I look forward to the day when we can see an entire book dedicated to the science and best practices of animation for the web. Until then, may these notes serve you well.

Go forth and animate... responsibly!

ACKNOWLEDGMENTS

This book might never have come to be if it weren't for the unending encouragement and support of many people, both folks near and dear to my heart as well as people I only know through the magic of the internet. I'm surely going to leave someone out, and I hope they'll forgive me. They are wonderful people.

I'd like to personally give a shout-out to Pablo Defendini for giving me a safe place to land and cheering me on when I was considering turning back, and Sara Wachter-Boettcher for her astute and practical advice from day one.

Special thanks to the editorial team at A Book Apart, especially Lisa Maria Martin and Katel LeDû, whose input and feedback made this book more awesome than it would've been on its own. And thank you to Scott Hudson, Dennis Kramer, Amanda Phingbodhipakkiya, Amy Lee, Rachel Nash, Jason Shen, Sam Cusano, Matias Duarte, Ryan Brownhill, Heather Daggett, Michal Staniszewski, Josh Murtack, Nicholas Jitkoff, and Nat Astor for taking the time to let me ask them so many questions about motion design.

I'm grateful to Ivana McConnell for covering Web Animation Weekly when book editing took up all my time, and to Justin Cone at Motionographer for seeing the need for a book like this within the motion design community.

To my husband, thank you for being a really supportive spouse. And I mean that in the "wraps a blanket around you and puts a hot cup of something in your hand so you can keep typing while he does your chores" sort of way.

And thank you to the countless others on Twitter and Facebook, to my friends and family, and to readers of my newsletter, who have all motivated me with their questions and their eagerness to know more.

RESOURCES

THE WORLD OF WEB animation is moving fast! I run the Web Animation Weekly newsletter to help folks like you keep up.

Additionally, the Animation at Work Slack community is full of wonderful, helpful people who love this space as much as I do. It's a great place to share ideas and get feedback from some of the brightest minds in this space.

If you're keen to dig into CSS Animations and Transitions and possibly the Web Animations API, here are some great starting points:

- My course on CSS Animations and Transitions comes packed with videos and code examples.
- Are you more of a reader, less into hands-on learning? Creating Web Animations by Kirupa Chinnathambi is a solid, accessible book written by someone who knows the topic very well.
- If you want to get started with the Web Animations API, I have heaps of resources on the topic.

The motion design industry has many good references for onboarding aspiring motion designers. Here are two of my favorite:

- Motion Graphics: Principles and Practices from the Ground Up by Ian Crook and Peter Beare is a course on the topic unto itself.
- Design for Motion by Austin Shaw features interviews with many prominent and accomplished motion designers alongside their work.

If you want to learn more about studio animation, there are two industry staples:

- *The Illusion of Life* by Ollie Johnston and Frank Thomas is a classic, almost a style guide for the Disney way of animation.
- *The Animator's Survival Kit* by Richard Williams is a starting point for people looking to get into studio animation, covering things like walk and run cycles and practical studio animation techniques.

However insightful these books, I personally feel they are only minimally applicable to designing with animation. If you're really drawn to studio animation, I encourage you to look at some lesser-known gems. My personal library contains:

- *Tezuka School of Animation, 1: Learning the Basics* from Tezuka Productions covers the basics of animation quickly and efficiently.
- *Chuck Amuck* is another great read from one of the more famous rivals of Disney animation.
- The *"Starting/Turning Point"* books contain a lifetime of essays by possibly the greatest animator alive today, Hayao Miyazaki. When I'm stuck for inspiration, a gentle read with a cup of tea from these books gets me on track again.
- *Starting Point, 1979-1996,* Hayao Miyazaki, VIZ Media LLC, 2014
- *Starting Point, 1997-2008,* Hayao Miyazaki, VIZ Media LLC, 2014
  If you'd like to master the art and science of storyboarding:
- For a more in-depth treatise on storyboarding for the web, I wrote a guide for *net Mag*.
- If you want to go even deeper, *Storyboard Design Course* by Giuseppe Christian is an excellent guide to storyboard techniques from a film perspective.

Lots of scientific research in the field of animation and interaction exists, some of it more applicable than others. I encourage you to keep an eye out for new and old research relevant to the field:

- *The Functional Art* by Alberto Cairo is my favorite book about data visualization, and it just so happens to have a fantastic multichapter section on the human visual system.
- *Vision and Art: the Biology of Seeing* by Margaret Livingstone is more about how images are processed by the brain and less about motion processing, but it's enjoyable and comprehensive.
- Animation Support in a User Interface Toolkit: Flexible, Robust, and Reusable Abstractions (PDF) by Scott E. Hudson and John T. Stasko is one of my favorite papers on the topic of interface animation.
- The ACM Digital Library contains a wealth of papers on all topics of human-computer interaction and computer animation.

REFERENCES: ANIMATION AT WORK

Shortened URLs are numbered sequentially; the related long URLs are listed below for reference.

Introduction

00-01 http://www.cc.gatech.edu/classes/AY2009/cs4470_fall/readings/animation.pdf

Chapter 1

01-01 https://smartech.gatech.edu/bitstream/handle/1853/3627/93-17.pdf

01-02 https://www.ncbi.nlm.nih.gov/pmc/articles/PMC3208769/

01-03 http://www.cracked.com/article_15239_the-5-most-annoying-banner-ads-internet.html

Chapter 2

02-01 https://web.nike.com/xp/sbdunk/index.html

02-02 https://www.fluevog.com

02-03 https://www.glossier.com

02-04 http://www.montereybayaquarium.org/animals-and-experiences

02-05 http://www.animalmade.com/

02-06 http://revisionisthistory.com/

02-07 https://www.polygon.com

Chapter 3

03-01 http://cubic-bezier.com/

03-02 http://easings.net/

03-03 https://www.nngroup.com/articles/response-times-3-important-limits/

03-04 https://research.googleblog.com/2009/06/speed-matters.html

03-05 https://www.doubleclickbygoogle.com/articles/mobile-speed-matters/

03-06 http://www.humanbenchmark.com/tests/reactiontime

03-07 https://en.wikipedia.org/wiki/Human_processor_model

03-08 http://alistapart.com/article/more-meaningful-typography

03-09 https://www.lightningdesignsystem.com/

Chapter 4

04-01 https://www.lightningdesignsystem.com/guidelines/motion/
04-02 goo.gl/PyBXI7
04-03 http://boords.com

Chapter 5

05-01 http://women.duluthtrading.com/
05-02 http://www.dailymail.co.uk/sciencetech/article-2542583/Scientists-record-fastest-time-human-image-takes-just-13-milliseconds.html
05-03 https://en.wikipedia.org/wiki/Time_perception
05-04 https://developer.mozilla.org/en-US/docs/Web/API/Web_Animations_API
05-05 https://www.w3.org/TR/UNDERSTANDING-WCAG20/seizure.html
05-06 http://vestibular.org/understanding-vestibular-disorder
05-07 https://github.com/w3c/csswg-drafts/issues/442
05-08 http://devtoolschallenger.com/

Resources

06-01 http://webanimationweekly.com/
06-02 http://slack.animationatwork.com/
06-03 http://rachelnabors.com/css-animations-course/
06-04 http://shop.oreilly.com/product/0636920050858.do
06-05 http://rachelnabors.com/waapi
06-06 https://www.bloomsbury.com/uk/motion-graphics-9781472569004/
06-07 http://www.routledgetextbooks.com/textbooks/9781138812093/
06-08 https://www.abebooks.com/book-search/title/the-illusion-of-life-disney-animation/
06-09 http://www.theanimatorssurvivalkit.com/
06-10 https://www.goodreads.com/book/show/969189.Tezuka_School_of_Animation_1
06-11 http://www.chuckjones.com/bugs-director-chuck-amuck/
06-12 https://www.goodreads.com/book/show/6342111-starting-point
06-13 https://www.goodreads.com/book/show/18223763-turning-point

06-14   http://www.creativebloq.com/web-design/create-storyboards-your-ani-mations-21619177

06-15   https://www.goodreads.com/book/show/4096346-the-storyboard-de-sign-course

06-16   http://www.thefunctionalart.com/

06-17   https://www.goodreads.com/book/show/56580.Vision_and_Art

06-18   https://smartech.gatech.edu/bitstream/handle/1853/3627/93-17.pdf

06-19   http://dl.acm.org/

Videos

Rachel Nabors began telling stories online as a teenager with her award-winning web comics. Her love of web technologies transformed into a career in front-end development, where she has worked with Mozilla, the W3C, and currently Microsoft to build the web forward. She tends the web animation community via the Animation at Work Slack and her web animation newsletter. When she isn't traveling the world, giving talks and kissing puppies, she can be found perched in Seattle, sipping a cup of fancy tea!

7

 A BOOK APART

WEBFONT HANDBOOK

BRAM STEIN

FOREWORD BY
INDRA KUPFERSCHMID

BRIEFS

Publisher: Jeffrey Zeldman
Designer: Jason Santa Maria
Executive Director: Katel LeDû
Managing Editor: Tina Lee
Editor: Caren Litherland
Technical Editor: Bianca Berning
Copyeditor: Katel LeDû
Proofreader: Caren Litherland
Book Producer: Ron Bilodeau

ISBN: 978-1-937557-64-5

A Book Apart
New York, New York
http://abookapart.com

TABLE OF CONTENTS: WEBFONT HANDBOOK

FOREWORD

FONTS ARE THE MOST important part of any website—of any visual design—because text is the most important part of the web.* Type shapes the written information we see before we read it, and helps us decide if we are even interested in reading it.

So imagine if we all had to wear the same handful of clothes. Loading in the morning would be much faster, but we'd all look very similar and would constantly confuse one another at a glance or from the back. (And this would be the case not only when wearing safe system clothes, but also when following trends and convenience, like using geometric sans serifs for everything.)

Choosing typefaces is the most exciting part of design* and I want to encourage you to pick from the whole embarrassment of high-quality riches. Look at letters and be more daring in your type choices and combinations—but also learn what are good and not-so-good, suitable and not-so-suitable fonts. There are things beyond aesthetics that are vital to know about when using fonts on the web, like rendering, glyph sets, and licensing options. In this book, Bram helps you take on these issues and avoid technical pitfalls. He'll get you up to speed on the more advanced font-loading tricks, OpenType features, and the latest developments in font technology.

Personally, though, I think hi-res hero images and bloated JavaScript are the pests of the web and we should stop using those and just go with type and all will be fine and fast and we'll never have to be stingy with subsetting or worry about how many kilobytes a font file is ever again and also because fonts are the best.*

—Indra Kupferschmid

---

*   subjective empirical research

INTRODUCTION

WEBFONTS MAKE THE WEB a more diverse, visually pleasing, and readable environment. In 2016, around 60% of the top thousand sites monitored by Alexa used webfonts. And they can be used for all text on a site—not just body text, but also headlines, tables, and captions. Great, right?

Well, yes and no. Webfonts also have some issues. Consider the *Mitt Romney Webfont Problem* (as described by Zach Leatherman). In early 2015, Mitt Romney announced that he would *not* run for president of the United States in the 2016 elections. Ironically, users on slow connections saw the opposite announcement: "Mitt Romney Is Officially Running for President" (**FIG 0**).

For these users, the primary webfont for the headline loaded and displayed most of the headline. The important word "not," though, was set in italic. It required a separate font file, and that file was slow to load. Oops.

And that's not the only problem with webfonts. You have to navigate a maze of font-licensing and hosting options, too. Once you've selected a font, you need to make sure it supports the languages your content is written in and renders legibly on all platforms and devices. Then there are the logistics and perception issues that come with loading an external resource for your most important content: the text.

When you buy an analog book, you don't need to download the markup, images, and fonts separately. The paper, text size, margins, and print quality have been chosen for you. What you see is what you get. On the web, you can never be sure what your content will look like. Your visitors may be using old browsers, old devices, or screen readers, or have slow network connections. They may have increased the default font size, disabled JavaScript, or have custom stylesheets. This is inherent to the web as a medium, and it affects developers, designers, and content strategists alike.

Mitt Romney Is Officially Running for President

By Betsy Woodruff

Republican anti-tax activist Grover Norquist is fond of saying that running for president is like getting malaria: Catch the fever just once, and

Mitt Romney Is Officially *Not* Running for President

By Betsy Woodruff

Republican anti-tax activist Grover Norquist is fond of saying that running for president is like getting malaria: Catch the fever just once, and

FIG 0: Slow-loading webfonts caused an erroneous headline to appear for some mobile users (left). The correct headline is shown on the right.

Think about that. Which matters most to you—conveying your message, or conveying your message in the correct font? In almost all cases, communicating your message matters most. The web is not—or at least shouldn't be—only for the privileged. Young, affluent people with perfect eyesight using modern devices with high-resolution screens on fast network connections constitute a small fraction of internet users. Don't forget about the rest.

So what's the solution? Should you avoid webfonts? No. Webfonts, if used well, are a valuable tool. This book will teach you how to select, use, and load webfonts so that they enhance—rather than undermine—your site's perceived and actual performance.

SELECTING
WEBFONTS

THROUGHOUT THIS BOOK, you'll see me use words like *character, typeface, style, font, glyph, family, foundry, script, subsetting,* and *rendering*. These terms come from the world of print typography, and they've retained their usefulness when discussing webfonts. So before we delve into choosing webfonts, let's pause for a moment to get our language straight. It'll be over soon, I promise.

Characters are used to digitally represent natural language. The letter *a* is a character, and so is 永. A character can be drawn in many ways but still have the same meaning. These drawings are called *glyphs*. For example, the character *a* has several alternate glyphs: *a*, ᴀ (small capital, not to be confused by the uppercase A), ᵃ, and ₐ.

A *typeface* is a set of glyphs that share a common design. Typefaces are designed by one or multiple *type designers*. Type designers can form a type *foundry*, which is just another name for a company that designs typefaces. A typeface can have multiple variations, commonly referred to as *styles*, such as italic, bold, and condensed.

A *font* is the delivery format for one or more typeface styles. For example, Elena is a typeface, but elena-regular.otf is a font. A font *family* is a collection of fonts with the same name and multiple styles. For example, Elena Regular and Elena Bold are two styles of the typeface Elena; elena-regular.otf and elena-bold.otf are two font files in the font family.

Each font has a set of languages and *scripts* it supports. A script, or writing system, is a way of visually conveying spoken language. Many languages share the same script; for example, English and Dutch both use the Latin script. *Subsetting* is the process of removing glyphs and features you don't need from a font. This results in a reduced font-file size. For example, if a font supports two different scripts but you only need one, you can remove the glyphs needed to support the other one and greatly reduce the file size of the font. The resulting file is called a *subset*.

When your operating system displays glyphs on the screen, it's referred to as text *rendering*. Because operating systems render typefaces in different ways, a font might look different from one operating system to the next. Some operating systems (like Windows) even offer multiple text-rendering engines, so text rendering can differ between browsers as well.

BEYOND AESTHETICS

Most books and articles that talk about choosing fonts focus on typeface design, or about how well one typeface pairs with another. But selecting good webfonts is about more than aesthetics. As boring as it may sound, comparing fonts based on licensing, hosting options, rendering quality, and language support is equally important.

Choosing fonts is also about more than file size. Fonts come in various formats and with different levels of language support. So unless fonts have exactly the same format and language support, they can't be compared on file size. We'll come back to file size in Chapter 3, which focuses on performance.

In the end, the choice of typeface is up to you. Good resources on selecting typefaces for web use abound; see the Resources section for specific examples. Once you've selected some typefaces you like, compare them based on their licensing and hosting options, language support, screen performance, and ability to set real content. Let's take a look at licensing first.

Licensing

When you "buy" a font, you're not actually buying the font file itself; you're buying a license to use the font in a specific way. That may sound cryptic, but it's quite simple. For example, when you buy an apple, you own that apple. When you eat it, or give it to someone else, it's gone. It's a consumable good.

Historically, you would buy metal or wood fonts—blocks of movable type—to use with a printing press. If you gave those fonts to someone else, they were, like the apples in my analogy, gone. That's not the case with digital fonts. Digital fonts are software, and are thus not consumed, but used. A license agreement (usually called the *end user license agreement*, or EULA) determines what you can and cannot do with the fonts you license.

Most EULAs place restrictions on how and where a font can be used. This makes sense; like everyone else, type designers should get paid fairly for their work. Many typefaces are the results of years of painstaking work. Accidental misuse (and, sadly, piracy) of fonts concerns professional type designers because it affects their livelihood. Therefore, commercial fonts often come with detailed license agreements.

Webfont licensing models can be divided into five categories: perpetual, limited, subscription, rental, and open-source. A *perpetual license* is purchased once and gives you the right to use the font forever, without any limitations on how long or how often you can use a font. This is a common license for desktop fonts—once purchased, you can use them in perpetuity. Sometimes perpetual licenses are also exclusive, meaning that the typeface can only be used by the entity that purchased the license. (This often happens when a corporation commissions a typeface for its own use.) Perpetual licenses, when available, are often the most expensive option for webfonts.

Webfonts sold by type foundries and resellers usually have *limited licenses* (**FIG 1.1**). These licenses place restrictions on where the font is used and how often it can be displayed. The restrictions are often divided into tiers: for a higher price, you can get more page views, or use the font on more domains. If you expect your site to become more popular, you may have to opt for a higher tier, or renegotiate the license once you reach the boundaries of the tier you originally chose. In most cases, the page-view numbers are based on an honor system, and are not actively monitored by the foundry (or reseller). It is up to you to upgrade your license once your site starts receiving more traffic. Most fonts sold with limited licenses are for *self-hosting*, which means that you need to place them on your own server.

By contrast, almost all webfont services use a *subscription* model (**FIG 1.2**). A recurring monthly or yearly fee gives you access to either a single font or a library of fonts, including hosting. Subscriptions normally place restrictions on usage, such as page views and the number of domains. These restrictions are automatically enforced by the webfont service; if you exceed your allowed number of page views, you will be prompted to upgrade to a higher tier. Popular subscription

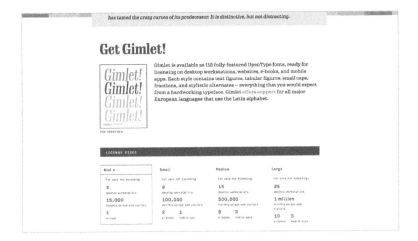

FIG 1.1: A great example of limited licenses by designer David Jonathan Ross. His Gimlet typeface can be purchased in four tiers: mini, small, medium, and large. It's unusual—and, in my opinion, laudable—to see desktop, ebook, and mobile application licenses in the same package as webfonts.

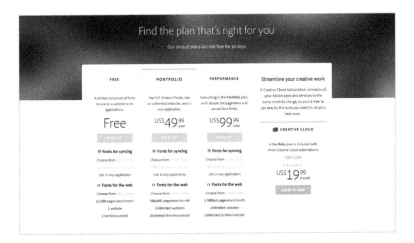

FIG 1.2: Different subscription plans at Adobe Typekit. Lower-tier plans impose more restrictions on the number of fonts, domains, and page views.

services include Adobe Typekit, Fonts.com (the Monotype Library Subscription), Type Network, and Cloud.typography. A new and interesting development is the so-called *font rental* model. A good example of a font rental service is Fontstand, which lets you use fonts for a fraction of their retail price. With Fontstand, you can rent a font for a period of thirty days, up to twelve months. After twelve months, Fontstand gives you a perpetual license. Each rented font also includes web hosting. Costs for the webfont service are calculated based on your usage. If you only need access to a font for a limited period (for mockups or other short-lived projects, say), this can be a great solution.

The fourth license model, open-source, is gaining in popularity. An open-source license gives you the latitude to modify a font as you wish (and often use it for free, although this is not always the case). Google Fonts is an example of a service that uses open-source licensing. Open-source and free fonts are sometimes dismissed as low-quality products that no "real" designer should use. And indeed, many open-source and free fonts are inferior: they are poorly drawn, or have limited language support, or render badly on some operating systems. One possible explanation for this is that open-source fonts don't generate a lot of income. It is difficult, if not impossible, for professional designers to make a living creating high-quality open-source typefaces.

Nevertheless, high-quality open-source and free fonts do exist. Many popular open-source typefaces, such as Source Sans Pro, Open Sans, and Fira, are sponsored by flush corporations like Adobe, Google, and Mozilla. They've been drawn by professional type designers, and include the same robust features—small caps, fractions, ligatures, extensive language support, and alternate figures—found in retail typefaces.

Which license you choose depends on the typeface you select, your budget, and your use-case. In most instances, the type foundry or reseller has selected a licensing model they prefer, which leaves you with little choice. If you're lucky, you can choose between multiple licensing options. Study your budget and user traffic. Are you expecting a huge amount of traffic and do you have a large budget? A perpetual license might be the best option in the long run. Are you expecting moderate traffic and have a smaller budget? Then a limited license might be appropriate. Do you redesign often, or experiment with many different fonts? Then a subscription or rental might be more appropriate.

The lines between the licensing models have become more and more blurred in recent years. For example, consider Google Docs: it's a web application that can export to PDF, Microsoft Word documents, and EPUB, and can also publish to the web. What kind of font license applies here? The font license for an application does not usually cover content created with the application, so a special license is most likely required. Perhaps we need a new hybrid (and, hopefully, simplified) licensing model that covers usage on desktop, ebooks, web, and mobile applications.

Regardless of which model you end up using, there are some licensing clauses you need to keep a close eye on. For example, the webfont license agreement from a popular type foundry contains the following clause:

> *You are not permitted to modify, adapt, translate, reformat, reverse engineer, decompile, disassemble, alter or attempt to discover the computer code of the webfonts or the designs embodied therein. The embedding or inclusion of webfonts, or the designs forming the webfonts, in software, hardware, digital documents, apps, applications, devices or in any other form is prohibited.*

Unfortunately, this common restriction is worrisome from a web developer's perspective. Not being able to subset a font or convert it to another format (if the fonts do not come in the font formats you need) will affect the file size of the font, and thus the speed at which the font can be downloaded. This can be particularly noticeable on slow network connections.

These clauses are often a form of quality control by the type designer. If there are a lot of "botched" versions of their font in the wild, it can reflect badly on them, and perhaps also complicate their customer support. For other type designers, though, such clauses translate into extra income: for a small fee, a type designer can create new subsets or perform conversions. If the font you're licensing doesn't come in the modern webfont formats—WOFF and WOFF2—pay attention to clauses like this. And don't hesitate to inquire directly with the type foundry or reseller about their policy on custom subsets. If they are unwilling to create a custom subset, or charge a high fee, it might be worth your while to explore other options. Fortunately, many foundries are more than happy to discuss these options if you ask them.

As you can see, licensing can get pretty complicated. So can hosting. That's why many web developers (and type designers) prefer to outsource this to a third party: a webfont service or reseller such as Adobe Typekit, Type Network, and FontShop. Let's look at hosting next.

Hosting options

People often ask me if they should host webfonts themselves, or if webfont services are better. The answer, as with most things in life, is: it depends. Self-hosting a font can sometimes be beneficial. If you can afford the initial up-front cost of a perpetual or limited webfont license, and have the technical expertise to use webfonts correctly, self-hosting is an attractive option.

With self-hosting, you have complete control over how fonts get loaded, which allows you to optimize your font-loading in a way that's not possible with third-party services. Furthermore, self-hosting makes your site more reliable: a third-party service could potentially be down for several hours, or even go out of business. This is not a hypothetical concern. The WebInk and Fontdeck webfont services shut their doors, and Typekit experienced a fairly significant outage in 2015. Because most browsers wait several seconds before showing fallback fonts, webfont services can be a single point of failure for your site unless you take extra care to load your webfonts asynchronously.

But a subscription or rental service might be more attractive if you like to experiment with different typefaces, don't have the requisite expertise to host your own fonts, or work for an agency that has multiple clients. Such services take care of

FIG 1.3: From Bézier curve to pixels. On the left is the outline of the glyph *a*. In the middle, that outline is superimposed on a pixel grid; any pixel whose center is inside the inline is turned on. On the right is the resulting rasterization.

hosting and licensing and usually give you access to their entire library for a fixed recurring fee. You don't have to worry about new browsers or webfont formats: the service takes care of this for you.

Another factor that will influence your decision is whether the typeface you want to use is available on a given webfont service. Some type designers prefer to sell directly to their customers instead of going through a reseller. If you wish to use fonts from these type designers, you might have no choice but to self-host, or to negotiate a custom agreement.

Rendering quality

Selecting a beautiful typeface is useless if it looks ugly on your visitors' screens. Rendering quality depends on several factors: the design of the font itself, hinting, and the rasterizer.

The glyphs inside a font are stored as mathematical Bézier curves. Storing glyph outlines as vector outlines instead of images allows them to scale to any resolution. To display them on screens, though, the outlines need to be turned into pixels at some point. This process is called *rasterization*. Operating systems perform rasterization by placing outlines on a pixel grid and coloring the pixels whose centers are inside the glyph (**FIG 1.3**).

FIG 1.4: Converting an outline to a low-resolution pixel grid. The resulting image has some odd characteristics: the stem of the *a* is much too thin and the bowl has opened.

On high-resolution screens, this results in a crisp pixel approximation of the outline. Lower-resolution screens, on the other hand, have fewer pixels with which to represent the outline. Simply coloring the pixels whose centers intersect with the outline produces unacceptable results (FIG 1.4).

Hinting

To address this issue on low-resolution screens, fonts often contain so-called *hinting instructions*. These instructions tell the rasterizer how to behave in certain situations. For example, a hinting instruction can slightly nudge the outline to the left or right to create a better pixel representation of the glyph outline. How these instructions are stored depends on the outline format of the font.

There are two competing outline formats: TrueType by Apple and Microsoft, and the *compact font format* (CFF) by Adobe. TrueType relies heavily on hinting instructions stored in the font to render correctly at different sizes, while CFF fonts rely more on the rasterizer (which depends on the operating system). This is a fundamental difference. The TrueType approach gives more control to the type designer, but requires extensive manual work; the CFF approach requires less work, but relies on the rasterizer to do the right thing.

One of the benefits of the CFF approach is that once the rasterizer gets smarter, all typefaces improve. This is not true

FIG 1.5: Antialiasing using grayscale values to represent the outline coverage of each pixel.

for TrueType fonts. Adding TrueType hints to one font does not benefit others; the hints are specific to a single font style. Another advantage of the CFF approach is the increasing resolution of screens. Higher screen resolutions result in more accurate pixel approximations of the outlines. This means that even without extensive hinting, text rendering will improve. Though this also applies to TrueType fonts, the initial large investment in adding hinting instructions will see diminishing returns as screen resolutions increase.

Antialiasing and gamma correction

In the examples we've seen so far, a pixel is either on or off, no matter how much of the glyph is present in each pixel. This poor approximation of mathematically perfect curves is called *aliasing*; *antialiasing* attempts to mitigate this.

The idea behind antialiasing is to figure out how much of the outline is present in each pixel and represent that with a grayscale value. In other words, if the outline covers 50% of a pixel, it uses a 50% black to color that pixel. If the outline covers the pixel completely, 100% black is used, and so on. This leads to an antialiased rendering that reduces the coarse, staircase-like appearance caused by the limited resolution of most displays (FIG 1.5).

The grayscale values in Fig 1.6 represent *coverage* of a pixel and not an actual color, even though the coverage is visualized as a color. The conversion from coverage to color may seem simple: 50% coverage equals gray (or whatever color your text is), and so on. But this ignores the fact that our eyes do not perceive color as linear: the same color at twice the numerical intensity isn't twice as bright.

For example, let's say you want to show a coverage of 50% black for a pixel. In a linear color space, this translates to a grayscale value of 128 (256 divided by 2). Our eyes, however, are non-linear and don't perceive a grayscale value of 128 as half the intensity of 256. Screens exploit our perception and also use a non-linear color space. A non-linear color space can store images more efficiently—why waste bits on values the human eye can't perceive? The conversion of linear colors to a non-linear color space is called *gamma correction*. The values used for gamma correction influence how antialiased text is perceived. Lower gamma values make the colors brighter, resulting in slimmer-looking text (FIG 1.6).

Different gamma values help explain why text can look thinner or heavier from one operating system to the next. Antialiasing and gamma correction can also make small text appear thinner on low-resolution screens. When a glyph is set at a small size, most of the pixels only receive partial coverage. To avoid the appearance of very thin text, some rasterizers artificially thicken the stems of glyphs. (This is one of the reasons text on macOS looks bolder than on other operating systems.) Antialiasing improves the quality of text rendering, but it's possible to do even better using something called *subpixel antialiasing*.

Subpixel antialiasing

Subpixel antialiasing makes use of the characteristics of screens to increase the resolution of rendered text. Each pixel in a screen is commonly made up of three oblong subpixels: red, green, and blue. (Not all screens have oblong subpixels; other configurations exist, but the same principles still apply.) Each of these subpixels can be controlled individually; subpixel antialiasing exploits that by applying the coverage calculation to each subpixel (FIG 1.7).

Gamma 1.0   Gamma 1.5   Gamma 2.2

Gamma 1.0   Gamma 1.5   Gamma 2.2

FIG 1.6: The same font set at different gamma levels. From left to right: gamma 1.0, gamma 1.5, and gamma 2.2. An optical illusion causes white text on a black background to appear heavier than black text on a white background.

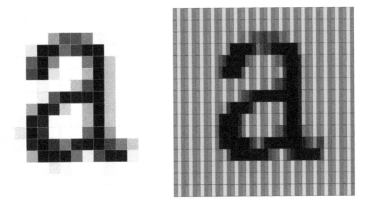

FIG 1.7: By targeting individual subpixels, subpixel antialiasing effectively increases the resolution of rendered text. The colors the naked eye perceives (left) are the result of setting individual coverage values for each subpixel (right); the three individual subpixels for red, green, and blue combine to form a single perceptible color. For example, combining 57% red, 85% green, and 100% blue produces a light blue.

The difference between these three antialiasing options becomes obvious at smaller text sizes. Without antialiasing, glyphs lose their distinctive outlines. Grayscale antialiasing makes glyphs blurry, but maintains their shape. Subpixel antialiasing renders sharp glyphs, but also introduces some color fringing at the glyphs' edges.

Operating systems

There are currently four major text-rendering engines: the *graphics device interface* (commonly known as GDI) and DirectWrite on Windows, CoreGraphics on macOS and iOS, and FreeType on Linux, Chrome OS, and Android (**FIG 1.8**). Although they vary in implementation, each rendering engine can perform grayscale antialiasing and subpixel antialiasing. In many operating systems, the choice of antialiasing method is user-selectable through a configuration setting or tool. On Windows, for example, subpixel antialiasing is called ClearType; on macOS, it's called LCD Font Smoothing.

Note, though, that it's not always possible for an operating system to use subpixel antialiasing. Operating systems on devices that support screen rotation, such as tablets and mobile phones, often disable subpixel antialiasing because the rotation means the physical subpixels are no longer arranged in a pattern expected by the rasterizer. The operating system can also decide to disable subpixel antialiasing when it doesn't recognize the type of screen. In this case, the OS can't be sure that the screen even has subpixels, or that they are arranged in the expected pattern. macOS, for example, disables subpixel antialiasing on external screens that aren't in its database of common screens.

Browsers

All browsers use the rendering engine from the operating system they run on. Chrome, for example, uses DirectWrite on Windows and CoreGraphics on macOS (though an exception is on the way: the Chrome team is considering using FreeType to render variable fonts on all operating systems). Windows is unique in that it offers two text rendering engines: GDI and DirectWrite. All modern browsers on Windows use DirectWrite, so most people won't have their text rendered with DirectWrite's inferior predecessor, GDI. However, some browsers, such as Firefox, use GDI on Windows when graphics hardware support is not available. Unfortunately, this means that using online browser-testing tools to test text rendering is not a good idea, because they use virtual machines. Although it is

WINDOWS	MACOS	IOS	ANDROID	LINUX	CHROME OS
GDI / DirectWrite	Core Graphics	Core Graphics	FreeType	Free Type	FreeType

FIG 1.8: Overview of the major text-rendering engines and platforms. Although Windows switched to using DirectWrite on Windows Vista SP2 and above, individual applications can still use GDI to render text.

technically possible to enable graphics hardware support on virtual machines, no online browser-testing tools offer this feature.

Even if the operating system can use subpixel antialiasing, browsers don't always use it. Many browsers have opted to disable subpixel antialiasing on HTML elements that are animated or use transparency. Browsers disable subpixel antialiasing for the same reason devices disable it: rotated or transformed subpixels no longer align with the screen. Grayscale antialiasing, on the other hand, works in any orientation, so it's an easier and cheaper option than performing subpixel antialiasing for all animated and transparent text. (**FIG 1.9**). Some browsers—Chrome on macOS, for example—also disable subpixel antialiasing on high-resolution screens. Still other browsers decided to only enable subpixel antialiasing on small text, because small changes in rendering are less visible at larger text sizes.

Subpixel antialiasing can also be disabled in CSS using the -webkit-font-smoothing and -moz-osx-font-smoothing properties. While these properties are supported by Chrome, Safari, Opera, and Firefox, they are not part of an official CSS specification (nor are they on a standardization track). Unfortunately, many CSS frameworks and libraries use the antialiased and grayscale values to make text appear lighter on macOS. Most developers don't realize this disables subpixel antialiasing and makes text appear blurrier, thereby hurting legibility. Don't use these properties. Changing someone else's preferred text rendering to be less legible is very inconsiderate. If you must use lighter text, use a font with a different weight.

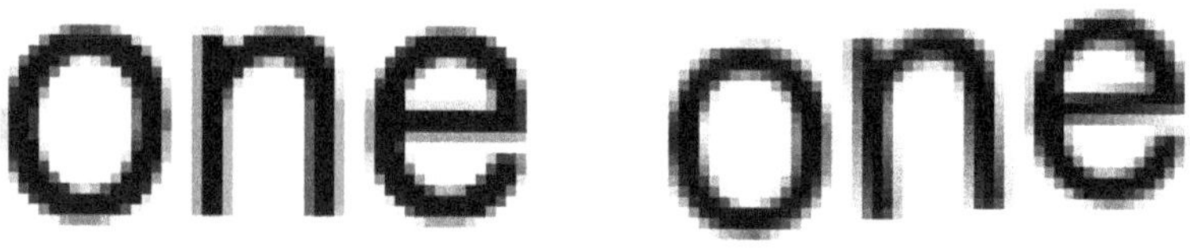

one one

FIG 1.9: The word "one" with subpixel antialiasing upright (left) and slightly rotated (right). Many browsers and operating systems disable subpixel antialiasing in cases where the text can be rotated (such as on tablets or HTML elements that can be transformed) or when the text is animated.

Alternatively, you can use Type Rendering Mix to apply weights based on the text-rendering engine.

There are many other cases where browsers disable subpixel antialiasing to provide a more consistent user experience. The rules browsers use to select the antialiasing method are constantly updated as new edge cases and problems are found. This makes it very hard to keep track of what is going on with your text rendering. What once used subpixel antialiasing may fall back to grayscale with the next browser update. The only way to know for sure how your text renders is to test it on actual devices.

Testing text rendering

It is likely that higher screen resolutions and smarter rasterizers will make poor text rendering a thing of the past. So, should you still pay attention to how a font renders? Definitely! Always check how well a font renders on all operating systems and devices that you target. Bad rendering is especially noticeable on thin weights. For example, a thin font that renders well on macOS may appear fragile on Windows (**FIG 1.10**).

A good way to test this is to set a representative piece of your content in the webfont and test it on actual devices and operating systems. As I mentioned in the previous section, virtual machines often have different rendering due to a lack of hardware acceleration, so using real devices and operating systems is a must.

The quick brown fox ju   The quick brown fox jur

The quick brown fox jumpe   The quick brown fox jumped

The quick brown fox jumped over t   The quick brown fox jumped over th

The quick brown fox jumped over the la   The quick brown fox jumped over the laz

The quick brown fox jumped over the lazy dog   The quick brown fox jumped over the lazy dog.

FIG 1.10: Jubilat Thin rendered on Windows 7 (left) and macOS (right). Note that macOS renders text "heavier" than Windows 7.

Most foundries and resellers offer specimen pages, but those are often designed to show off ideal situations. You want to see how a font behaves in the real world. For example, a specimen page may not be in the same language as your content. Perhaps a given font doesn't work well in your own language. The best way to test a font is to use it with your content and your design. Pay special attention to how it renders at different sizes and on different operating systems. It's also a good idea to set text with your preferred background color. A dark background can make a big difference in how text is rendered and perceived. Of course, testing with real content isn't always possible. You may not even have the content yet. The next best thing is to use Tim Brown's Web Font Specimen, a sample page that sets text at different sizes, colors, and backgrounds. It gives you a quick way to see how a font renders in different situations (**FIG 1.11**).

Sometimes, you get lucky. Designers occasionally make type-faces specifically for the screen: Hoefler & Co.'s ScreenSmart collection, Monotype's eText, and Font Bureau's Reading Edge Series are all good examples. The typefaces in these collections were designed with low-resolution screens in mind and should always render well, even on older operating systems. Of course, it pays to double-check the rendering on your target operating systems.

FIG 1.11: Tim Brown's Web Font Specimen in action. It compares a webfont against common "web-safe" fonts and shows how the font renders when set with different colors and backgrounds.

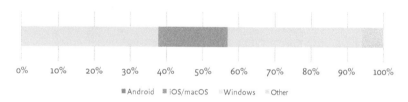

■ Android ■ iOS/macOS ▪ Windows ▪ Other

FIG 1.12: Worldwide operating system usage, according to StatCounter Global Stats (April 2017). Apple's devices represent a small fraction of global usage. Android and Windows dominate the market.

Always check your traffic statistics to find out which operating systems your visitors use. The operating system your designers and developers favor is probably not representative of your audience. In fact, the macOS and iOS operating systems used by most designers and developers are in the minority relative to worldwide operating system usage (**FIG 1.12**). You would do well to test rendering quality extensively on Android and Windows.

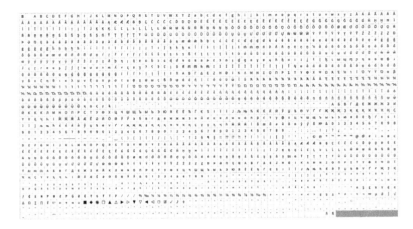

FIG 1.13: Source Sans Pro, designed by Paul D. Hunt, contains more than 2,000 glyphs.

Language support

A single font can't support all the languages and writing systems in the world. Even if type designers wanted to make such a font, they couldn't: OpenType fonts can only contain 65,536 glyphs. That's not enough for all characters in all languages and scripts. Instead, fonts are designed to address specific audiences, and therefore differ in language support. Many fonts support languages of the Latin writing system, while others focus on scripts such as Japanese and Arabic. It's up to the type designer (and the client, in the case of a custom font) to decide which languages and scripts are supported (**FIG 1.13**). Fonts often also include glyphs that are not related to any specific language or script, such as symbols, dingbats, and arrows.

Inside each font is a table that tells the operating system which Unicode characters are supported. The operating system needs this information to decide whether it can use the font to display a string of text. If no characters in the text are supported by the font, the browser will use a fallback font. If all characters are supported, the webfont is used. But what happens if there is a partial match? The missing characters are rendered in a fallback font, and the other characters in the webfont. This is visually very distracting (**FIG 1.14**).

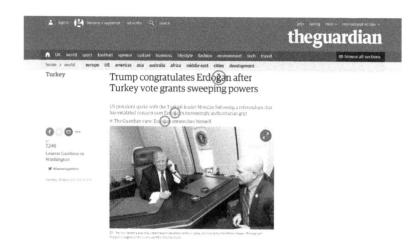

FIG 1.14: This text uses characters in both English and Turkish, but the webfont does not include Turkish characters. The missing characters (circled in red) are rendered in a fallback font.

To prevent situations like this, analyze your content to figure out what language and script support you need. You might be surprised. Even if you primarily write in English, you might find proper nouns, place-names, and loanwords that use accents and characters not found in English (like the word *résumé*). Your webfont needs to support these characters to keep them from resorting to fallback fonts.

OpenType features

In addition to glyphs, a font also contains *OpenType features*, which are special instructions that influence how a character or group of characters look and behave. Small caps, ligatures, and swashes are all examples of OpenType features. There are many different OpenType features—the OpenType specification currently standardizes more than 140 of them. Not every font contains all 140 features, though: it's up to typeface

العربية العربية

FIG 1.15: The word "Arabic" (language) in Arabic. Without enabling the required OpenType features for Arabic, the word renders incorrectly (left). When OpenType features are enabled, the word is shown correctly (right).

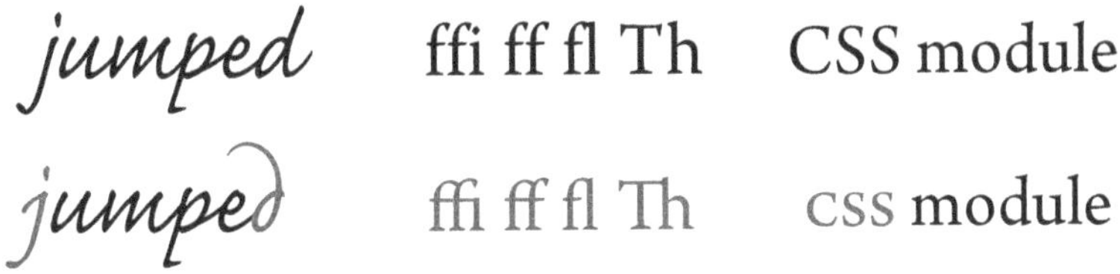

jumped ffi ff fl Th CSS module

jumped ffi ff fl Th css module

FIG 1.16: Some optional OpenType features. From left to right: contextual alternates, ligatures, and small capitals. Though optional, these features can improve the look of text.

designers to decide whether they want—or need—a feature. Some OpenType features—such as the contextual substitution of initial, medial, and final forms for Arabic—are specific to the writing system.

Broadly speaking, there are two types of OpenType features: required (**FIG 1.15**) and optional (**FIG 1.16**). Required OpenType features are necessary for text to render correctly; optional ones can be enabled by the user to access alternative glyphs and other special features.

Remember to look at which OpenType features are supported when you select a font. For instance, if your text contains a lot of abbreviations, it makes sense to find a font that has support for small capitals. Several uppercase characters in a row stand out; small capitals make abbreviations and acronyms blend into the rest of the text better. Similarly, if you're typesetting a lot of data in tables, tabular figures are a must. And so on. Decide on the OpenType features you need and then find a font that supports them.

Features for display text

Display typography is designed to attract attention. It invites readers in, encourages people to take action, and has a strong effect on brand awareness. In these situations, we welcome more exuberant OpenType features and pay close attention to the shapes of specific glyphs.

In the example above, use the OT features menu to enable and disable specific features. Toggle all relevant OpenType features on/off and study how the subtle differences add up.

ENABLE / DISABLE ALL FEATURES
As you change which features are enabled, the code sample below changes accordingly. Continue on CodePen to edit other aspects of the example, and you'll pick up right where you left off here.

FIG 1.17: The "Caring about OpenType Features" lesson on Typekit Practice shows several examples of OpenType features for various text settings.

The CSS specification requires that OpenType features necessary to show text properly are enabled by default, whereas optional features can be enabled by the user. The following features must be enabled by default: required ligatures ( ), ligatures ( ), contextual ligatures ( ), contextual alternates ( ), kerning ( ), localized forms ( ), and features required for the display of composed characters and marks (, , and). Other scripts and advanced typesetting, such as vertical text, require additional features to be enabled. Unfortunately, some browsers implement this part of the specification incorrectly and only enable some of the required features.

OpenType features can be enabled and disabled using the CSS font-feature-settings and font-variant properties. You can use these properties to, for example, access the stylistic alternates in a font and enable swashes. The following example uses both font-variant and the lower-level font-feature-settings (for browsers that do not support font-variant) to enable contextual alternates and swashes:

```
p {
    font-variant: contextual, swash(1);
    font-feature-settings: "calt" on, "swsh" 1;
}
```

Even though the font-feature-settings property has better browser support, you should prefer the font-variant property. The font-feature-settings property has a lot of issues: child elements don't inherit the OpenType features of their parent elements and the effects are not cumulative (in other words, you should always repeat all properties if you want to disable or enable a specific feature in a child element).

You can read more about using OpenType features in CSS in Tim Brown's "Caring about OpenType Features" lesson on Typekit Practice. The lesson includes many visual exercises for learning about OpenType features for body text, display text, and tabular data (FIG 1.17).

This chapter focused on selecting webfonts for non-aesthetic reasons—for example, what to look for in a license, how and why fonts render differently on some devices and operating systems, and their language and OpenType support. Now it's time to put our webfonts to use and load them in a browser. In the next chapter, we'll look at the @font-face syntax, font formats, how browsers load fonts, and some of the performance costs associated with loading webfonts.

USING WEBFONTS

NOW THAT YOU'VE SELECTED a font, let's put it on your website. Webfonts are defined in CSS through the @font-face rule. If you're a web developer, you've most likely written, copied and pasted, or at the very least seen an @font-face rule. For the sake of completeness, though, let's quickly run through a basic example:

```
@font-face {
    font-family: Elena;
    src: url(elena-regular.woff);
}
```

This creates a new webfont family that can be referenced through the font-family or font shorthand property. But something's missing here. When referencing a webfont in a font stack, always make sure to include at least one fallback font in case the webfont fails to load. Here, if Elena fails to load, the browser will fall back on the generic serif font family:

```
p {
    font-family: Elena, serif;
}
```

We'll talk more about fallback fonts and how they can be used to make your site appear to load faster in Chapter 3. For now, let's keep our fallback stack simple by including only the generic serif and sans-serif font families.

FONT FAMILIES

Creating a font family with multiple styles is accomplished by creating an @font-face rule for each style and using the same font-family name. The following @font-face rules create a family with a normal and bold style:

```
@font-face {
  font-family: Elena;
  src: url(elena-regular.woff);
  font-weight: normal;
}

@font-face {
  font-family: Elena;
  src: url(elena-bold.woff);
  font-weight: bold;
}
```

You can use this font family in your CSS by referencing the family name and weight in your selectors. This applies the regular style to paragraphs and the bold style to strong paragraphs:

```
p {
  font-family: Elena, serif;
}

p strong {
  font-weight: bold;
}
```

Besides font-weight, @font-face also accepts the font-style and font-stretch property descriptors, which define styles such as italic and condensed. All three property descriptors can be used to create a single font family with multiple styles. Theoretically, this lets you create a family containing 243 individual styles (nine font-weight values × three font-style values × nine font-stretch values). In practice, however, you're limited to twenty-seven values, since some browsers don't support font-stretch (FIG 2.1).

With luck, the remaining browsers will implement the font-stretch property soon, and you will be able to use all 243 font classifications.

IE 8	IE 9-11	EDGE	CHROME	FIREFOX	SAFARI	OPERA	ANDROID SYSTEM
No	Yes	Yes	Yes	Yes	No	Yes	No

FIG 2.1: Browser support for font-stretch at time of writing. (Check caniuse.com for current and version-specific browser support.)

FONT FORMATS

The src descriptor tells a browser where to get a font file. The previous examples used a single font format, but you'll often see URLs to multiple font formats combined with *format hints*, which are appended after the URL using the format("value") syntax. Format hints tell the browser what the format of the font file at a given URL is.

```
@font-face {
    font-family: Elena;
    src: url(elena-regular.woff2) format("woff2"),
         url(elena-regular.woff) format("woff");
}
```

If you list multiple formats, modern browsers will pick the first format they support based on the format hint. Therefore, it's important to list webfont formats in the order of best compression to least. Even though format hints are optional, always include them—they let the browser know about the format without needing to download the font. For example, if a browser does not support WOFF2, but does support WOFF, it can skip the WOFF2 font file based on the format hint.

Browsers support several webfont formats: OpenType (TrueType), EOT, WOFF, and WOFF2. Some browsers also support SVG fonts, but they're deprecated and should no longer be used (and should not be confused with the new OpenType-SVG format). EOT, WOFF, and WOFF2 are technically not font formats. They are compressed OpenType files with varying degrees of compression. WOFF2 offers the best compression, followed by WOFF and EOT (**FIG 2.2**).

In researching coverage for all browsers, you may have come across something called the bulletproof @font-face syntax by Fontspring. The bulletproof syntax uses EOT, WOFF2, WOFF, raw OpenType, and SVG font files for maximum browser coverage:

```
@font-face {
  font-family: elena;
  src: url(elena.eot?#iefix) format("embedded-
opentype"),
    url(elena.woff2) format("woff2"),
    url(elena.woff) format("woff"),
    url(elena.otf) format("opentype"),
    url(elena.svg#elena) format("svg");
}
```

The first URL line might look a little odd to you. Versions of Internet Explorer 8 and below do not support the syntax for multiple font formats, and treat the entire value of the src property as the URL. The bulletproof syntax tricks Internet Explorer 8 and below into thinking that the remaining URLs are part of the fragment identifier of the first URL. Because fragment identifiers are ignored when downloading files, Internet Explorer 8 and below simply use the first URL. Browsers other than Internet Explorer will skip the line because they do not support EOT. The rest of the entries are what you would expect: font formats listed in order of preference.

But is the bulletproof syntax still relevant? No. In fact, I think it's harmful. SVG fonts are deprecated and only supported by browsers that are no longer in use. Most websites support Internet Explorer 9 and up, yet the syntax lists EOT as the first preferred font format. Even though Internet Explorer 9 and up support WOFF, those versions will still download the EOT file, simply because it is listed first.

	WOFF2	WOFF	OPENTYPE	EOT
IE 8	No	No	No	Yes
IE 9-11	No	Yes	Yes	Yes
Edge	Yes	Yes	Yes	No
Chrome	Yes	Yes	Yes	No
Firefox	Yes	Yes	Yes	No
Safari	Yes	Yes	Yes	No
Opera	Yes	Yes	Yes	No
Android System	No	Yes	Yes	No

FIG 2.2: Browser support for font formats at the time of writing. Look for up-to-date and version-specific browser support for font formats at caniuse.com.

Because most websites no longer support old browsers, I highly recommend using a simplified syntax. This simplified syntax covers all modern browsers, as well as slightly older ones that are still in active use, such as Android 4.4 and earlier:

```
@font-face {
    font-family: Elena;
    src: url(elena.woff2) format("woff2"),
         url(elena.woff) format("woff"),
         url(elena.otf) format("opentype");
}
```

Even though older Android versions are still used, world-wide reliance on these browsers is rapidly dwindling. Soon you will probably be able to drop the raw OpenType format as well, and simplify the syntax even further:

```
@font-face {
  font-family: Elena;
  src: url(elena.woff2) format("woff2"),
       url(elena.woff) format("woff");
}
```

In this case, someone running an older browser will simply see your fallback fonts instead of the webfont. That's fine; they can still read the content in the fallback font. (More on fallback fonts later.)

There's another possible value for the `src` descriptor. The `local` function takes the name of a local font family. If the font happens to be installed on the system, the browser will use that instead, thereby avoiding an extra download.

```
@font-face {
  font-family: Elena;
  src: local("Elena"),
       url(elena-regular.woff2) format("woff2"),
       url(elena-regular.woff) format("woff");
}
```

While this may seem like a great optimization, nothing guarantees that the local font matches your webfont. You may get a different version of the font, a font with different language support, or even an entirely different font. For that reason, I usually recommend not using the `local` function unless you find these downsides acceptable.

FONT SYNTHESIS

What happens if you create a font family but (accidentally) use a style you didn't define? Bad things. Consider the following CSS that only defines a normal weight, but then tries to use the bold weight:

```
@font-face {
  font-family: Karmina, serif;
  src: url(karmina-regular.woff) format("woff");
  font-weight: normal;
}

h1 {
  font-family: Karmina, serif;
  font-weight: bold;
}
```

In this case, the browser recognizes the font family, but it doesn't have the correct style. Instead of rejecting the font family and using the fallback font, it tries to synthesize the style you asked for. It does this by taking the style it has and programmatically "bolding" it. The same thing occurs if you ask for italic but have only defined a regular style, and for small caps if the font does not contain real small-caps.

The resulting styles are often referred to as *faux bold* or *faux italic*, and they are highly undesirable. Type designers spend a lot of time designing italic and bold styles, which are of much higher quality than synthesized styles. The latter often suffer from spacing problems because they use the same spacing rules associated with the source they were generated from (**FIG 2.3**).

Synthesized font styles can be disabled in some browsers by setting the font-synthesis property to none. This will disable synthesized bold and italic and only show the desired weight:

```
p {
  font-synthesis: none;
}
```

It's also possible to disable only bold or italic by using weight or style as value. This disables synthesized bold on paragraphs and synthesized italics on h1 elements:

This is not italic. *This is italic.*

This is not bold. **This is bold.**

FIG 2.3: Synthesized italic and bold styles generated by the browser (left), and real bold and italic styles (right) of the same typeface. The real italic is redrawn; the faux italic is merely slanted. (Compare, for example, the synthesized lowercase *a* with the real one.) The bold may seem acceptable at first glance, but has spacing issues and unbalanced stroke contrasts resulting in an excess of black in some areas. This is especially noticeable in the connections between bowls, stems, and serifs.

```
p {
  font-synthesis: weight;
}

h1 {
  font-synthesis: style;
}
```

Currently, only Firefox and Safari support the `font-synthesis` property; other browsers will continue to show synthesized styles. Therefore, make sure you always define `@font-face` rules for the styles you use.

CONDITIONAL AND LAZY LOADING

Before it downloads a webfont, a browser requires *all* of the following conditions to be true:

- The *document object model* (DOM) node has text content. Some older browsers do not require this, but all modern ones do.
- The node's calculated style matches an `@font-face` rule in the document on the `font-family` name, and optionally the `font-weight`, `font-style`, and `font-stretch` values.

- The browser supports one of the font formats listed in the `src` descriptor.
- The node's text content has at least a partial match with the `unicode-range` descriptor (if the descriptor is present, and conditional loading is supported by the browser).

These conditions have several advantages: they enable *lazy loading* and *conditional loading*. Lazy loading allows a browser to download a webfont only if it is needed by some of the text on the page. (Some older browsers always load *all* fonts, but modern browsers only load the fonts needed to display the text on the page.)

You can load fonts conditionally using the `unicode-range` descriptor, which tells a browser which characters are included in a font. The browser uses that information to decide whether it should download a font or not. It does this by going through all of the text nodes in the DOM and checking to see if the node's characters are included in the `unicode-range` values. If some, or all, of the characters are included in the range, the browser will download the font. If there is no match, it can skip downloading the font.

You can use conditional loading to your benefit. Consider the following `@font-face` rule, which specifies Laura Worthington's Spumante font but only contains a single character: the ampersand (&). The `@font-face` rule uses a `unicode-range` descriptor to tell browsers that this font contains just a single character. In Unicode, the ampersand is encoded at `U+26` (hexadecimal).

```
@font-face {
  font-family: Spumante;
  src: url(spumante-ampersand.woff);
  unicode-range: U+26;
}
```

The `unicode-range` descriptor takes a comma-separated list of Unicode values, ranges, or wildcards. For example, the single `U+30-39` range covers all Latin digits, and the two comma-separated ranges `U+30-39` and `U+41-5A` cover both digits and

Latin uppercase letters A-Z. Wildcards, indicated by a question mark, are used to select all Unicode code points starting with the specified hexadecimal number. For example, U+2? selects the range U+20-2F.

By placing Spumante at the top of the font stack, the browser will use the ampersand from the webfont instead of the ones included in the other fonts in the stack (**FIG 2.4**):

```
h1 {
    font-family: Spumante, Acumin Pro, sans-serif;
}
```

You can use this trick to replace single characters in headlines. In our case, if the headline contains an ampersand, browsers will automatically download the Spumante font. If the headline does not contain any ampersands, the font will not be downloaded, saving an unnecessary download.

Conditional font-loading is even more useful than that, though. It's especially helpful when you need to support multiple languages or scripts on a site. A good example of this is the Minimore blogging platform, which features both English and Thai content (**FIG 2.5**).

The primary language of the Minimore site is Thai, but it also contains large sections in English. The font used on the site is divided into two separate font files: one for Latin-based languages and one for Thai (served by Google Fonts). The @font-face rules on the site use unicode-range to tell the browser which characters each font contains:

```
@font-face {
    font-family: Kanit;
    src: url(kanit-regular-thai.woff);
    unicode-range: U+0E01-0E5B, U+200B-206F, U+25CC;
}
```

Type & Typography
Type & Typography

FIG 2.4: Using unicode-range to download a font only when it is needed. The top phrase uses the default Acumin Pro ampersand, while the bottom example replaces it with the ampersand from Spumante.

FIG 2.5: Minimore, a blogging platform written in Thai and English. The site uses the Kanit font by type foundry Cadson Demak.

```
@font-face {
  font-family: Kanit;
  src: url(kanit-regular-latin.woff);
  unicode-range: U+0000-00FF, U+0131, U+0152-0153,
  U+02C6, U+02DA, U+02DC, U+2000-206F, U+2074,
  U+20AC, U+2212, U+2215;
}
```

Splitting them like this means that the two fonts are only downloaded when they are needed. On English pages, kanit-regular-latin.woff is downloaded; Thai pages get kanit-regular-thai.woff. Pages that combine both languages will download both font files. If the two fonts were combined, the resulting font would have to be downloaded on every page, even on those exclusively written in a single language.

The unicode-range property helps the browser make smart decisions about font-loading. Splitting font files by language also improves caching and performance. So why not use unicode-range everywhere?

Unfortunately, the property isn't fully supported by all browsers yet. Almost all browsers recognize the property and use it to select characters for rendering text, but fewer browsers use it to conditionally download webfonts (FIG 2.6).

For this reason, it's not always a good idea to include unicode-range for all @font-face rules. Instead of downloading only the languages and scripts needed to show the text on the page correctly, a browser with partial or no support for unicode-range will download all font files in the same family. So, by all means, use unicode-range—but use it only when you are fairly certain that a language subset will be needed. This avoids gratuitous downloads on browsers with only partial support, while still benefitting the majority of browsers that support conditional downloading.

PERFORMANCE COSTS

On slow network connections (and even on very fast connections), any remote resource takes time to download. A certain amount of time will always elapse between the moment a browser notices it needs a webfont and when the font is shown. In the next chapter, we'll focus on strategies for minimizing this time, but first we need to accept that webfonts come at a cost. Webfonts will never load as quickly as locally installed fonts. If that's not acceptable to you, then perhaps you should rethink using webfonts.

	CHARACTER SELECTION	CONDITIONAL LOADING
IE 8	No	No
IE 9-11	Yes	No
Edge	Yes	No
Chrome	Yes	Yes
Firefox	Yes	Yes
Safari	Yes	Yes
Opera	Yes	Yes
Android System	Yes	No

FIG 2.6: Support for unicode-range across browsers. Support for character selection means that the browser hides characters not included in the range. Full support means that the browser uses unicode-range to download fonts only when necessary, in addition to hiding the characters not included in the range.

What do browsers do in the time it takes to download a font? The answer depends on the browser. Most browsers hide text that uses a webfont while the font is being downloaded. Once the font has loaded, the page will be rendered again using the webfont. This is called a *Flash of Invisible Text*, or FOIT (**FIG 2.7**).

Note that the browser will not hide the entire page—just the parts that use the webfont. Images, videos, background colors, and text not using webfonts will be shown as soon as they load. In fact, even though it hides the text for which webfonts are being downloaded, the browser will lay out the page using a fallback font. It's important to understand that a FOIT happens only when the fonts are downloading. So even if you load a stylesheet containing @font-face rules asynchronously, the font-loading will still block rendering.

Not all browsers hide text while downloading webfonts. Some browsers will show the content using fallback fonts immediately, and replace the fallback font with the webfont

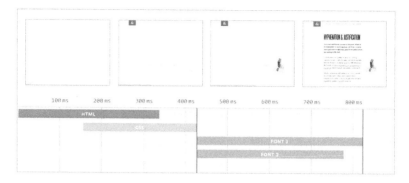

FIG 2.7: A Flash of Invisible Text (FOIT). Even though the content has loaded at around 400 milliseconds, the text remains hidden until the webfont finishes loading at 800 milliseconds.

when it loads. This is called a *Flash of Unstyled Text*, or FOUT (**FIG 2.8**). Browsers using FOUT show content earlier, but produce a slightly jarring effect when the fallback font is replaced with the webfont.

FOIT has a downside that FOUT does not have. What happens if the webfont takes a very long time to load? Well, your visitors will be staring at an empty space where the text should be until the connection timeout kicks in. This can take up to thirty seconds. Early on, browser makers rightly saw this as a problem and added a limit to the amount of time text can remain invisible.

Statistics gathered by Google Chrome have shown that most fonts load within three seconds, so browser makers adopted three seconds as a timeout gauge for hiding text. If a webfont takes more than three seconds to load in a browser using FOIT, the fallback font will be shown. The browser will continue to load the font in the background, and render the page again if the font eventually loads (**FIG 2.9**).

Chrome, Firefox, Safari, Opera and the default Android browser have all adopted FOIT as their default font-loading behavior. Only Internet Explorer and Edge use FOUT. What this comes down to is that font-loading behavior is inconsistent across browsers.

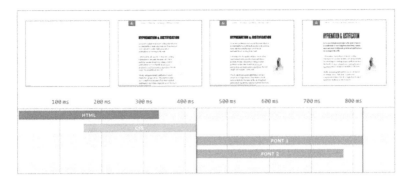

FIG 2.8: A Flash of Unstyled Text (FOUT). Content is shown as soon as it loads (400 milliseconds), and the page is rendered again once the webfont loads (800 milliseconds).

	FONT-LOADING	**TIMEOUT**
Internet Explorer	FOUT	n/a
Edge	FOUT	n/a
Chrome	FOIT	3 seconds
Firefox	FOIT	3 seconds
Safari	FOIT	3 seconds
Opera	FOIT	3 seconds
Android System	FOIT	3 seconds

FIG 2.9: FOUT and FOIT font-loading behavior in browsers. Safari adopted the three-second timeout in Safari 10; prior versions of Safari had no timeout value, which in some instances caused a very long flash of invisible text. Chrome recently reduced its three-second timeout to zero (essentially FOUT) for when a device is on a slow network connection, like 2G.

In Microsoft browsers, your site's visitors will immediately see fallback fonts, so you should style them accordingly. In other browsers, your text may be invisible for up to three seconds. If your site's visitors are unlucky, they'll have to wait three seconds for the invisible text to go away, then see fallback fonts for a couple seconds, followed by the actual webfont. Also, what happens if three seconds is too long for your customer base? A research study done by Google shows that more than 53% of mobile users abandon a website if it takes more than three seconds to load. Getting any content on the screen is more important than getting content on the screen in the right font.

What's missing here is *control*. Web developers need to be able to customize font-loading behavior and make tradeoffs based on the requirements of their customers versus their own wishes. Fortunately, this lack of control is addressed by a new @font-face descriptor currently being standardized. The font-display descriptor aims to make font-loading behavior configurable through CSS. We'll look at the font-display descriptor in Chapter 4, but note that it will take a while until font-display becomes available in all browsers. Until then, there are several good solutions for improving actual and perceived webfont performance that we can turn to right now.

OPTIMIZING
PERFORMANCE

PERFORMANCE BUDGETS ARE a good way to keep an eye on how efficient your websites and applications are. A performance budget includes limits on the number of requests, the number of bytes transferred, and the amount of time-to-first-render (the amount of time it takes to show something useful on the screen). For a great introduction to performance budgets, see Scott Jehl's *Responsible Responsive Design*.

Like every other resource, webfonts should be included in your performance budget from the outset. Sometimes, you'll discover that you just don't have the budget for webfonts. That's fine! Not every site needs webfonts. In fact, some high-profile websites don't use webfonts at all. It's hard to justify using webfonts when every millisecond of loading time counts toward your bottom line. Amazon refused to use webfonts for many years because page-load performance relates directly to their sales: faster pages sell more. (Encouraged by faster connections, they finally started using webfonts in early 2017.)

A webfont performance budget should focus on three things: the number of font requests, font-file size, and time-to-first-render. Reducing the number of requests can be accomplished by removing similar styles and relying on extensive caching (and, in the future, using variable fonts—but more on that in Chapter 4). Reducing font size is a combination of two factors: a font's character-set support and the font format. You can make fonts fit within your file-size budget by removing unnecessary characters and, as I explained in Chapter 2, by serving the right font format.

Sometimes performance isn't about actual performance, but about *perceived performance*—making your site *appear* faster. Because fonts block rendering in all browsers except Internet Explorer and Edge, you must pay special attention to improving the time-to-first-render. You can do this in two ways: by improving perceived performance by embracing FOUT, and by optimizing the moment webfonts start to load.

To keep examples simple, this chapter assumes that you're self-hosting webfonts. However, most of the optimizations covered here also work with webfont services (or are done automatically for you). If an optimization is not possible using a service, I'll call your attention to it.

REDUCING REQUESTS

There are two aspects to consider when reducing the number of font requests on a site: the first request and all requests to the same site after the first. On the first request, the browser needs to fetch all resources from a remote server, but on subsequent requests, some of the resources can be retrieved from the browser cache. Reducing the total number of font requests improves performance of the first request *and* subsequent requests, while caching only improves performance for repeat requests. Both are critical to improving the perceived and actual performance of your webfonts.

You can reduce the total number of requests by carefully planning your typographic choices. Each additional style comes with a cost; it adds complexity to your design system and counts toward your performance budget. Make sure you can justify that cost before adding a new style. Perhaps you can even repurpose an existing style. That isn't always possible, of course, but evaluating your typographic choices is a good place to start reducing the number of webfonts used on your site.

Another way to reduce the number of webfonts is to replace them with system fonts. Medium does this; it now uses system fonts in its user interface. The primary content still uses webfonts, but the system fonts ensure that the user interface is visible as soon as possible. It feels like a native experience. This change allowed Medium to reduce the number of webfonts it used while still providing a good and consistent reading experience on all platforms.

Unfortunately, using system fonts is harder than it should be. The recommended way of using them relies on a complex font stack. Most of the fonts in this stack are regular font-family names often used as system fonts. But the first two entries (`-apple-system` and `BlinkMacSystemFont`) are browser-specific ways of asking for the system default font. It only works in Safari on macOS and iOS, and in Chrome on macOS:

```
font-family: -apple-system, BlinkMacSystemFont,
  "Segoe UI", "Roboto", "Oxygen", "Ubuntu",
```

```
"Cantarell", "Fira Sans", "Droid Sans", "Helvetica
Neue", sans-serif;
```

In response to the rising popularity of system fonts, the W3C
has added a new generic font-family property for system fonts
to the CSS fonts module Level 4. The system-ui generic font
family will always map to the default user-interface font on all
platforms. There is no browser support for system-ui yet, but
once browsers start supporting it, you'll be able to reduce the
above font stack to a single item:

```
font-family: system-ui;
```

Using system fonts is a good way to reduce the number of
webfont requests, but there also a couple of common practices
that are too good to be true—indeed, they're counterproductive.

One such unhelpful optimization is inlining fonts in CSS
using base64 encoding. While inlining saves HTTP requests, it
also has many disadvantages: it disables progressive rendering
(where fonts render as soon as they download), affects caching,
and limits you to a single font format. Inlining also inflates the
file size enormously due to the inefficiencies of base64 encoding. A base64-encoded font is up to three times larger than a
regular font, though most of the size increase can be negated
by serving the CSS file with GZIP encoding.

A better way to achieve the performance benefits of inlining—reducing the number of HTTP requests—is to use HTTP/2.
HTTP/2's connection-multiplexing feature allows several
requests to use the same network connection. This reduces
the overhead of several individual requests significantly and
makes inlining obsolete. Best of all, HTTP/2 and browsers take
care of this automatically. If you have a server or *content delivery network* (CDN) that supports HTTP/2, all you need to do is
enable HTTP/2. Browser support for HTTP/2 (and its predecessor SPDY) is excellent, so there's no reason not to use HTTP/2.

Another technique that's becoming increasingly popular is
using the browser's local storage to store fonts. The basic idea
is to retrieve a stylesheet with inlined fonts on the first request
and then store the stylesheet in local storage. On subsequent

requests, the stylesheet is retrieved from local storage and inserted into the page. The benefit of this approach is that it only incurs a single network request on the very first visit; all subsequent visits can just fetch the fonts from local storage.

This technique has the same downsides as inlining fonts, but it has another drawback that is even more insidious. Imagine what would happen if every site started doing this. Every site you visit would deposit several hundred kilobytes of fonts in local storage. Unlike the browser cache, local storage is not automatically emptied. Your devices would soon run out of disk space. This is extremely rude behavior. Just because you visit a site once doesn't mean you need to carry around its webfonts forever. Don't do this. We'll look at an alternative solution using service workers later in this chapter.

CACHING

After reducing the number of total requests, we can move on to reducing repeat requests using the browser cache. If you're using a webfont service, you can skip to the section on reducing font size, because all webfont services use the browser cache correctly. Fortunately, if you're self-hosting, it's straightforward to set caching rules for fonts. All you need to do is set Cache-Control and ETag HTTP headers for fonts:

```
Cache-Control: public, max-age=31536000
ETag: "53749a2f29f940c418e605adcb972f728bb511bc"
```

In this example, we set a Cache-Control header of a year (60 seconds × 60 minutes × 24 hours × 365 days = 31536000). We also use make the resource public. This tells intermediate caches, such as proxies and CDNs, that the resource is public and may be cached. This header allows the browser to keep the font in its cache for at least a year. Of course, the browser may evict it from its cache earlier due to cache-size limits, or if users perform a manual purge (by emptying their browser cache).

The ETag header gives the resource a unique tag derived from the content of the resource. In this example, I have used a hash of the font file itself (so don't copy and paste this etag). If the resource changes, it will get a different tag. Using the tag, browsers can make conditional requests. If the tag the browser sends matches that of the remote resource, the server will respond with an HTTP 304 and it can skip sending the content.

These cache headers are great for fonts, because fonts don't change very often. If you do change your fonts, though, it's advisable to also give them a new URL. If you want to learn more about various content-caching strategies, Google's Web Fundamentals HTTP caching section is an excellent resource.

Using a CDN

Latency—the time it takes to transfer a resource from the source (server) to the destination (user)—is critical to webfont performance. The farther away the physical server and your visitor's device are, the longer something takes to transfer.

Let's say I'm trying to download a file from a server in San Francisco from my home in Copenhagen. Because of the physical distance between San Francisco and Copenhagen, it will take a while for the network packets to be sent halfway around the world. Whether that file is 100KB or 50KB, the distance doesn't change.

You can solve the latency problem by using a CDN. A CDN automatically distributes a copy of your content to servers all over the world. That way, visitors connect to the server closest to them, thereby reducing latency. A CDN is a worthwhile investment if performance and reducing latency are important to you.

REDUCING FONT SIZE

As I mentioned in Chapter 1, most fonts come with extensive language and script support. But if you don't need to support multiple languages and scripts, consider removing the glyphs you don't need. A big chunk of a font's file size is made up of the outline data of glyphs, so removing glyphs will significantly reduce a font's file size. You should also serve your fonts in the most efficient webfont formats: WOFF and WOFF2. Think of it like optimizing an image: you crop the parts of the image you don't need and select an appropriate compression format such as JPEG or PNG.

Remember, though (as we saw in the section on licensing): you can only subset if the font's license allows it. Most open-source fonts allow subsetting, so let's take Source Sans Pro as an example. The official release has a total of 1942 glyphs. The file size for the regular style is 230 KB (OpenType), 129 KB (WOFF), and 103 KB (WOFF2). That's not huge, but it's certainly not as small as it could be. If you use three weights of this font, you're looking at 690 KB (OpenType), 387 KB (WOFF), and 309 KB (WOFF2). That's much more than most images—and, unlike images, webfonts are render-blocking. We'll need to optimize this.

If your content is written exclusively in English, you could cut a significant portion of those glyphs and greatly reduce the file size. English consists of *a* to *z* lowercase and uppercase, figures, and some punctuation. The 133 characters shown in FIG 3.1 are a good approximation of basic English.

Creating a subset using these characters reduces the file size of our font files significantly (FIG 3.2). The OpenType file went from 230 KB to 19 KB. The WOFF file is now 13 KB, and the WOFF2 file 12 KB. That's amazing. Or is it?

Not quite. Subsetting removed diacritics, accents, and characters commonly used in other languages of the Latin writing system. If the content contains, for example, names from Germany and Portugal, any characters not in the default subset will fall back to some other font. The fallback font most likely won't match your webfont and will stick out like a sore thumb (FIG 3.3).

This doesn't mean that you should never subset. But it *is* a reason to be very careful when subsetting fonts. Try to find a balance between language support and file size. If you only use diacritics or characters from other languages sparingly, consider using unicode-range to let the browser automatically download subsets when necessary. For example, you could split the font into a Latin and Latin extended subset:

```
!  "  #  $  %  &  '  (  )  *  +  ,  -  .  /  0  1  2  3  4  5  6  7  8  9  :  ;  <
=  >  ?  @  A  B  C  D  E  F  G  H  I  J  K  L  M  N  O  P  Q  R  S  T  U  V  W  X  Y
Z  a  b  c  d  e  f  g  h  i  j  k  l  m  n  o  p  q  r  s  t  u  v  w  x  y  z     ¡
¢  £  ¤  ¥  ¦  §  ¨  ©  ª  «  ¬  ®  ¯  °  ±  ²  ³  ´  µ  ¶  •  ,  ¹  º  »  ¼  ½  ¾  ¿
'  ~  |  ‖  –  —  '  '  "  "  „  •  …  ‹  ›  €
```

FIG 3.1: A basic subset that covers most of the characters used in English.

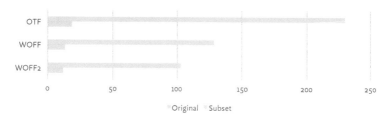

FIG 3.2: Original file size versus subset file size for OpenType, WOFF, and WOFF2 files.

Principles of Typeface Design with Frank Grießhammer & Tânia Raposo

This 8 week course is for anyone who has always wanted to design their own typeface, but is unsure where to start. Or for those who just love type, and wish they knew more about how it works. The participants will engage with the fundamental methods, tools

FIG 3.3: Heavy subsetting can sometimes produce unexpected results. Because they're not in the subset, the "ß" and "â" in this headline are rendered in a fallback font.

```
@font-face {
    font-family: Source Sans Pro;
    src: url(latin.woff) format("woff");
    unicode-range: U+0000-00FF, U+0131, U+0152-0153,
    U+02C6, U+02DA, U+02DC, U+2000-206F, U+2074,
    U+20AC, U+2212, U+2215, U+E0FF, U+EFFD, U+F000;
}
```

```
@font-face {
  font-family: Source Sans Pro;
  src: url(latin-extended.woff) format("woff");
  unicode-range: U+0100-024F, U+1E00-1EFF, U+20A0-
  20AB, U+20AD-20CF, U+2C60-2C7F, U+A720-A7FF;
}
```

On pages that use English, this will only download the first font file. On pages that need diacritics and other characters, the Latin extended font will be downloaded as well. Of course, the caveat that both files will be downloaded on browsers that do not support unicode-range still applies.

There's another problem with subsetting that's not immediately obvious: OpenType features do not work across subsets. For example, if you split Source Sans Pro into a Latin and Latin Extended subset, any OpenType feature that covers characters from both subsets will break. This isn't a theoretical issue; kerning data (the adjustment of spacing between letter pairs) is stored as an OpenType feature and will not work across the Latin and Latin Extended subsets.

If you're using a webfont service, you can skip the complexity around manually generating font formats and subsets. Most webfont services offer a user interface for basic subsetting (**FIG 3.4**). Such interfaces are usually limited to language-based subsetting and don't allow completely custom subsets. Nevertheless, they're very useful for reducing a font's file size.

If you're self-hosting, subsetting requires a bit of work. Depending on your skill level, you have two options: using Fontsquirrel's online Webfont Generator or using fonttools from the command line. I recommend the Webfont Generator if you're just starting out with subsetting, or if you only need to subset a handful of fonts. If you want to integrate subsetting into your build process, or automate it some other way, fonttools is the right choice.

The Webfont Generator gives you a lot of subsetting options. You can subset based on character type, language, or Unicode table, or create a completely custom subset (**FIG 3.5**). Once you've generated a subset, the Webfont Generator gives you a ZIP file containing the subset in all webfont formats.

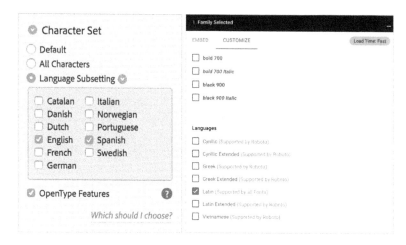

FIG 3.4: Subsetting options in Adobe Typekit (left) and Google Fonts (right). Many other webfont services offer similar or more advanced subsetting options. By selecting and deselecting the various subsetting options, you can immediately see the effect on file size.

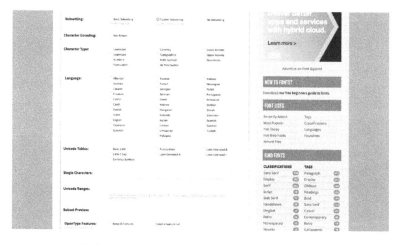

FIG 3.5: Fontsquirrel's options allow subsetting by character type, language, Unicode table, or individual characters.

If you prefer to use a command-line tool, fonttools is an excellent choice. You can install fonttools using Python's pip package manager:

```
$ pip install fonttools
```

This installs a whole set of font-manipulation tools (which are beyond the scope of this book, but worth exploring if you're interested). The one we're going to use is called pyftsubset, which is fonttools' subsetting utility. To use it, call it from the command line with the input font and one or more options. In this example, we'll use pyftsubset to create a WOFF subset with only the characters *abcdefg*. This is just an example. A real subset might include other characters, such as *é, ø*, and *æ*.

```
$ pyftsubset font.otf --text="abcdefg" --flavor=woff
```

This creates a subset called font.subset.woff. Because we used the `--flavor=WOFF` option, the tool outputs the subset as a WOFF file. You can also use `--flavor=WOFF2` to create a WOFF2 file (or a raw OpenType font if you leave out the `--flavor` option). The pyftsubset utility has dozens of other options, but I recommend using its default settings until you've become more experienced with subsetting.

It can be cumbersome to manually figure out which characters you need. Luckily, the Filament Group has created a tool called glyphhanger that extracts the characters used on a website and generates a list of Unicode characters you can pass to pyftsubset. You can install glyphhanger using Node's package manager, npm:

```
$ npm install glyphhanger -g
```

Once installed, run glyphhanger by giving it a URL to a website. The site can either be a local file, a local development server, or a remote site. The glyphhanger tool will grab all the content on the site and generate a list of Unicode characters.

```
$ glyphhanger --unicodes http://www.example.com/

> U+a,U+20,U+2e,U+44,U+45,U+4d,U+54,U+59,U+61,U+62,
U+63,U+64,U+65,U+66,U+67,U+68,U+69,U+6b,U+6c,U+6d,
U+6e,U+6f,U+70,U+72,U+73,U+74,U+75,U+76,U+77,U+78,
U+79
```

Copy and paste the list of Unicode characters and pass them to pyftsubset with the --unicodes option.

```
$ pyftsubset font.ttf --unicodes=U+20a,U+20,U+2e,
U+44,U+45,U+4d,U+54,U+59,U+61,U+62,U+63,U+64,U+65,
U+66,U+67,U+68,U+69,U+6b,U+6c,U+6d,U+6e,U+6f,
U+70,U+72,U+73,U+74,U+75,U+76,U+77,U+78,U+79"
--flavor=woff
```

This creates what I've come to call a *perfect subset* for www. example.com. The subset only contains the characters that are used on the page. All of the caveats about careful subsetting still apply, of course. A perfect subset doesn't anticipate characters you might want to use in the future. However, using glyph-hanger is a good way to generate a base list (which you can then manually adjust later, if necessary) of all of the characters used on your site.

When serving these font files, you'll also need to pay attention to server-side compression. WOFF and WOFF2 are compressed font formats, but raw OpenType (TrueType) files are not. Compression is optional for EOT files, and most webfont generators do not generate compressed EOT files. So if you use raw OpenType or EOT fonts, remember to enable GZIP compression on your server.

EMBRACING FOUT

Most of the performance costs of webfonts are surmountable, but let's reflect on the role webfonts play. Are they *really* required to show your content? As I asked in the Introduction, what matters most to you? That people read your content as soon as possible, or that people read your content in your preferred font? I suspect that many of your visitors would prefer the former over the latter.

We need to start thinking of webfonts as progressive enhancement instead of expecting webfonts to be a resource that is always available. The baseline experience of your site has always been, and will always be, just plain HTML and CSS. Webfonts enhance that experience. In fact, there's no guarantee that visitors to your site will see webfonts at all. The Opera Mini browser is used by hundreds of millions of people, and it does not support webfonts. Without you doing a thing, those users are already excluded from using the webfonts you specify.

That means there are two possibilities you should design for: when webfonts are *not* available, and when webfonts *are* available. For that reason, I believe FOUT should be the default behavior in all browsers. Because it's not a given that webfonts will always be available, we should design for that scenario from the start. Pretending the problem does not exist by hiding the text isn't helpful; in fact, it tangibly hurts people.

The easiest way to embrace FOUT on all browsers is to load your fonts asynchronously using the font-loading API. The font-loading API is a new addition to CSS. It provides a JavaScript API that can manipulate the @font-face rules on the page. You can query the descriptors of each @font-face rule, explicitly load fonts, get notified when they load, and programmatically create new @font-face rules.

Let's use the font-loading API to load the Abelard font asynchronously. We start off by using the font-family name in our CSS font selectors, and then loading the font through the font-loading API. By using the API, we won't need to manually write an @font-face rule.

```
p {
  font-family: Abelard, Georgia, serif;
}
```

You can create a new @font-face rule by creating a new FontFace instance and passing it a family name as the first parameter, and a list of URLs as the second parameter. The second parameter has the same syntax as the src descriptor. By using the same syntax, the FontFace constructor can carry out the same font-format selection as normal @font-face rules.

```
var abelard = new FontFace('Abelard', 'url(abelard.woff2) format("woff2"), url(abelard.woff) format("woff")');
```

To keep the examples in this chapter simple, I'll leave out multiple formats from now on—but you should always include them, because not all browsers support the same webfont formats. Offering multiple formats lets the browser chose the most optimal format it supports.

The FontFace constructor takes a third optional argument: an object with descriptors. These are the same descriptors you can use in @font-face rules: weight, style, stretch, unicodeRange, featureSettings, and variant.

```
var abelard = new FontFace('Abelard',
  'url(abelard.woff2)', {
    weight: 'bold',
    style: 'normal',
    unicodeRange: 'U+0000-00FF, U+0131, U+0152-0153'
  });
```

Once you have a FontFace instance, call the load method to load the font. The load method returns a *promise* that is resolved when the font has successfully loaded and rejected when it fails to load.

```
abelard.load().then(function () {
  console.log('Abelard has loaded.');
}).catch(function () {
  console.log('Abelard failed to load.');
});
```

However, loading a font via the load method does not automatically make the font visible on the page. You still need to explicitly add the font to the document by adding the FontFace instance to the document.fonts set. The global document.fonts property contains a set of all the webfonts used in the document.

```
var abelard = new FontFace('Abelard', '...');

abelard.load().then(function () {
  document.fonts.add(font);
});
```

The two-stage loading process may seem odd at first, but it's quite handy. It allows you to make sure the font is available before using it. You can avail yourself of this to prevent the browser from hiding text while the font is loading, or to perform some action after the font loads. It is also what makes the font-loading asynchronous. The document (and by extension the *CSS Object Model*, or CSSOM) isn't aware of the webfont until it has finished loading and will use one of the fallback fonts (Georgia, or the generic serif). Once the webfont has finished loading, it will be added to the document. At that point, the browser will rerender the document and use the font right away.

```
// mysite.css
p {
  font-family: Abelard, Georgia, serif;
}
```

```
// mysite.html
<script>
  var abelard = new FontFace('Abelard',
  'url(abelard.woff)');

  abelard.load().then(function () {
    document.fonts.add(abelard);
  });
</script>
```

To load multiple fonts, create multiple FontFace instances and load each one individually. This will load the fonts in parallel and independently of one another.

```
var abelard = new FontFace('Abelard',
  'url(abelard.woff)');
var bligh = new FontFace('Bligh',
  'url(bligh.woff)');

abelard.load().then(function () {
  console.log('abelard has loaded.');
});

bligh.load().then(function () {
  console.log('bligh has loaded.');
});
```

Sometimes it's helpful to group font-loading calls together, as when loading related fonts, for example, or to avoid excessive reflows. Because the load method returns a promise, we can use the Promise.all method to wait until all fonts have loaded before adding the fonts to the document. If one of the fonts fails to load, the promise returned by Promise.all will be rejected. This side effect can be used to avoid an inconsistent experience when one font fails to load but others don't.

```
var abelard = new FontFace('Abelard',
  'url(abelard.woff)');
var bligh = new FontFace('Bligh',
  'url(bligh.woff)');

Promise.all([
  abelard.load(),
  bligh.load()
]).then(function () {
  document.fonts.add(abelard);
  document.fonts.add(bligh);
});
```

The CSS font-loading API is a great improvement. It gives you precise control over font-loading and font events, something that was previously very complex. Unfortunately, the API does not yet have widespread browser support. The latest versions of Chrome, Firefox, Safari, and Opera support the API, but Microsoft Edge and slightly older browser versions do not (FIG 3.6). Until we have reliable browser support for this API, we'll need to resort to JavaScript libraries that perform similar tasks. Two libraries fit the bill: Adobe Typekit's Web Font Loader and my own Font Face Observer.

The difference between these two libraries is the level of abstraction they provide. Web Font Loader provides a high-level interface for loading fonts from several webfont services and self-hosted fonts. Font Face Observer aims to be a very minimal implementation of the core functionality of the CSS font-loading API. We'll use Font Face Observer for the remainder of this chapter, but the examples can also be implemented using Web Font Loader.

Let's start by including Font Face Observer on your page. To avoid blocking rendering, we load the JavaScript file asynchronously. Then, in the onload handler of our script, we load the fonts using Font Face Observer's API:

INTERNET EXPLORER	EDGE	CHROME	FIREFOX	SAFARI	OPERA	ANDROID SYSTEM
No	No	Yes	Yes	Yes	Yes	No

FIG 3.6: Support for the CSS font-loading API. Check caniuse.com for up-to-date browser support information.

```
<head>
  ...
  <script>
    var script = document.createElement('script');
    script.src = '/path/to/fontfaceobserver.js';
    script.async = true;

    script.onload = function () {
      // your font loading code goes here
    };
    document.head.appendChild(script);
  </script>
</head>
```

Font Face Observer's API is almost identical to the CSS font-loading API. The major difference is that Font Face Observer does not take a list of URLs as input. Instead, it expects you to write your own `@font-face` rules in CSS. This allows you to use Font Face Observer even if you don't have direct access to fonts (for example, if you're using a webfont service). Let's write an `@font-face` rule and use the webfont in a selector for paragraphs:

```
@font-face {
  font-family: Abelard;
  src: url(abelard.woff2) format("woff2"),
       url(abelard.woff) format("woff");
}
```

```
p {
    font-family: Abelard, Georgia, serif;
}
```

Then, we create a new FontFaceObserver instance and call its load method. Font Face Observer also accepts a second (optional) argument with descriptors such as weight and style. The load method returns a promise that is resolved when the font loads and rejected when it fails to load, just like the native font-loading API.

```
var abelard = new FontFaceObserver('Abelard');

abelard.load().then(function () {
    console.log('Abelard has loaded.');
}).catch(function () {
    console.log('Abelard failed to load.');
});
```

You may have noticed that this does not actually load the font asynchronously. Unlike the font-loading API, the @font-face rule is already in the document, so the browser will eventually load the font because it is used in the font stack for the paragraph selector. Let's fix that.

Remember, as discussed in the section on lazy loading in Chapter 2, that the browser doesn't download a font if it isn't used. You can exploit this behavior to load fonts asynchronously—by telling the browser about your webfont only after you've loaded it. Do this by adding a class to the HTML element when the font has loaded. If the font loads, set the fonts-loaded class on the HTML element:

```
var abelard = new FontFaceObserver('Abelard');
var html = document.documentElement;

abelard.load().then(function () {
    html.classList.add('fonts-loaded');
});
```

Then, change the CSS selector to use the webfont only when the fonts-loaded class is present. When the page initially loads, the fonts-loaded class is not set (because the JavaScript hasn't executed yet), so all paragraphs will use the fallback font stack. When the JavaScript loads, the font-loading will start in the background. Once the font loads, the fonts-loaded class will be set, triggering the second selector. Because the second selector includes the webfont, the browser will try to download it. However, it will quickly discover that it has already loaded the font and will use it to rerender the page (almost) immediately.

```
p {
    font-family: Georgia, serif;
}

.fonts-loaded p {
    font-family: Abelard, Georgia, serif;
}
```

This little trick results in consistent font-loading behavior across all browsers. Your visitors will see the fallback fonts first, followed by the webfont when it loads. It's a little more work to separate your font stacks into two groups (default behavior on one hand, loaded webfonts on the other), but this separation will come in handy later.

Remember that most browsers have a three-second timeout on font-loading. Personally, I consider this too long. If visitors have already started reading your content, swapping in webfonts can be very distracting. Using a one-second timeout seems better to me. With a helper function, you can set our own timeouts for font-loading.

```
function timeout(time) {
    return new Promise(function (resolve, reject) {
        setTimeout(reject, time);
    });
}
```

This helper function creates a promise that is rejected when a certain amount of time has expired. You can create timers by calling the function with the number of milliseconds you want it to wait for. Because both `load` and `timeout` return a promise, you can use the `Promise.race` function, which "races" two promises against each other, to limit the amount of time it takes for the fonts to load. The first promise to get resolved (or rejected) wins the race.

```
var abelard = new FontFaceObserver('Abelard');
var html = document.documentElement;

Promise.race([
  abelard.load(),
  timeout(1000)
]).then(function () {
  html.classList.add('fonts-loaded');
});
```

If the font fails to load, or if the timeout fires before the font loads, the top-level promise is rejected and the `fonts-loaded` class is not set. If that happens, your visitors will continue to see fallback fonts. Note that this does not cancel the font download. The font will continue loading in the background and will be available from cache on the next request.

After all this, you may be wondering if it's a good idea to load webfonts through JavaScript. What if the JavaScript fails to load, or the user has JavaScript disabled? That's the beauty of treating webfonts like progressive enhancement. If the fonts take too long to load, or don't load at all, your visitors will simply see the default behavior: fallback fonts.

MINIMIZING FOUT

The thing I try to avoid most in my designs is not FOUT, but a jarring shift in the layout when a webfont finishes loading. This shift is usually due to sizing discrepancies between your layout in systems fonts and your chosen webfont.
— Jason Santa Maria, On Web Typography

Most opposition to using FOUT is based on the distracting effect that happens when the fallback font is replaced with a webfont. This happens because each font has its own metrics. Let's take a quick detour and talk about some of the metrics inside a font. Each glyph in a font is drawn within a virtual square, often referred to as the *em box* (**FIG 3.7**).

In theory, a type designer can place a glyph anywhere inside the em box, but in practice, almost all glyphs are aligned to the *baseline* of the font. The baseline is where the bottom of most glyphs rest. Some characters (like *p* or *q*, for example) extend below the baseline, but the main body of the glyph is still placed on the baseline.

Another useful metric is called the *x-height*. The x-height is the vertical space between the baseline and top of lowercase glyphs. It's derived from the height of a lowercase *x* (hence the name). The parts of the glyphs that extend below the baseline are called *descenders*; the parts that extend above the x-height are called *ascenders*. The *cap height* is the height of the capital glyphs.

With that out of the way, let's return to the original question: why does text reflow when you replace one font with another? Two separate factors are at play: the x-height and the width of each glyph. If you compare two glyphs from different typefaces using the same font size (and thus em box), the difference in width and x-height becomes visible (**FIG 3.8**). Larger-bodied fonts take up more space in their em box than smaller-bodied ones. While the individual differences in width and x-height are small for individual glyphs, these metric differences add up over an entire paragraph and cause a reflow of text.

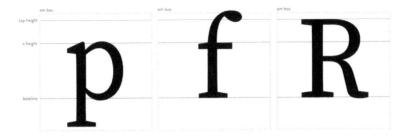

FIG 3.7: The glyphs for p, f, and R in Source Serif Pro shown inside their em box. In some cases, it is possible for a glyph to extend beyond the em box; see the f in the middle.

You can minimize reflow by selecting a fallback font based on how similar its x-height and width are to your webfont (**FIG 3.9**). But that can be misleading: just because a font is drawn at a different size doesn't mean it's not a good match.

You shouldn't use x-height to compare fonts without also adjusting the font size. By adjusting the font size, it is often possible to find that fonts have very similar metrics, resulting in less reflow (**FIG 3.10**).

You can either exactly measure the difference in x-height between your webfont and the fallback font, or visually adjust the size until it looks right to you (**FIG 3.11**). Note, though, that the eye is arguably almost always better. As Tobias Frere-Jones has written, "we read with our eyes, not with rulers, so the eye should win every time."

The font-size-adjust property is the official CSS way of doing the same thing automatically. It allows you to specify a font's x-height as a multiplier of the font size:

```
p {
    font-size: 1.2rem;
    font-size-adjust: 0.5;
}
```

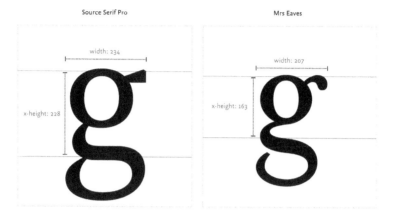

FIG 3.8: Source Serif Pro (left) and Mrs Eaves (right) are set at the same font size (em box), but are drawn at different sizes. Source Serif Pro is wider and has a larger x-height than Mrs Eaves.

Geogrotesque	Gill Sans	Arial

In olden times when wishing still helped one, there lived a king whose daughters were all beautiful, but the youngest was so beautiful that the sun itself, which has seen so much, was astonished whenever it shone in her face.

In olden times when wishing still helped one, there lived a king whose daughters were all beautiful, but the youngest was so beautiful that the sun itself, which has seen so much, was astonished whenever it shone in her face.

In olden times when wishing still helped one, there lived a king whose daughters were all beautiful, but the youngest was so beautiful that the sun itself, which has seen so much, was astonished whenever it shone in her face.

FIG 3.9: On the left, a webfont with two potential fallback fonts (center and right) set at the same font size. Gill Sans' x-height is smaller than the webfont's, while Arial's x-height is larger. At first glance, Gill Sans appears to be a closer match to the webfont —but first impressions aren't always correct.

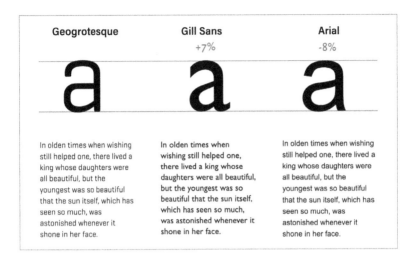

FIG 3.10: The same webfont and fallback fonts. The fallback fonts' sizes have been adjusted to match the x-height of the webfont. Now Arial turns out to be a much better fallback candidate.

FIG 3.11: Monica Dinculescu's Font style matcher lets you visually match a fallback font with a Google Webfont.

In this example, we ask the browser always to keep the font's x-height at half the font size. By using font-size-adjust, the browser will automatically scale the font size so that the x-height of the webfont and fallback font match. This would be a great way to minimize the reflow of text; unfortunately, though, at the time of writing, font-size-adjust is only supported by Firefox (although Chrome is working on an implementation.) Look for up-to-date browser support for font-size-adjust on caniuse.com.

We can achieve a similar effect by using the fonts-loaded class that we added to the HTML element. By manually changing the font size (and thus the x-height) when the webfont loads, we make the webfont more closely match the fallback font:

```
p {
    font-family: Arial, sans-serif;
    font-size: 1.2rem;
}

.fonts-loaded p {
    font-family: Georgia serif, Arial, sans-serif;
    font-size: 1.20rem; /* 1.2rem x 1.00 */
}
```

But there's another problem with fallback fonts. They aren't always available or reliable. Fallback fonts consist of three categories: system fonts, application-installed fonts, and user-installed fonts. System fonts come with the operating system you are using; every operating system has its own set of preinstalled system fonts. Georgia, Times New Roman, Arial, and Verdana are system fonts on Windows, for example. Android has only three system fonts: Roboto, Noto Serif, and Droid Mono.

Sometimes fonts come bundled with applications. Microsoft Office for Mac, for instance, bundles several fonts that are system fonts on Windows. You can't rely on application-installed fonts to be available, though, because not everyone has the same applications installed.

Finally, there are user-installed fonts—fonts that users download and manually install. Many font services also offer "sync" subscriptions that install fonts from a library on the system. These fonts may be installed for as long as the user's subscription is valid.

To make matters even more complicated, it's possible to install custom fonts in place of system fonts. On some devices, a system font may be replaced with a more recent version of the font (for example, one with better language support or improved rendering). Users can also replace system fonts with fonts they prefer or consider more legible.

Basically, there is no such thing as a web-safe font.

As a result, fallback fonts have varying degrees of support across operating systems and devices. A good site for checking which fonts are available where is Zach Leatherman's Font Family Reunion. Typing in a font family name shows you where a font is available, where it is not, and where its name is aliased to another font (**FIG 3.12**).

This will help you find fallback fonts fairly reliably, but until all browsers support font-size-adjust, selecting fallback fonts will remain a manual and error-prone process.

Luckily, there's another trick we can use to minimize FOUT. After the first request, the browser will have the font files in cache. Retrieving fonts from cache is very fast, so there is no need to wait for the JavaScript to explicitly load the font if we know it is already in the cache.

For this to work, we need a location to keep track of the state of the browser cache. Using local storage is not a good idea, because it sticks around for much longer than most resources in the cache. Almost all browsers support *session storage*, which is like local storage except that it is purged automatically at the end of the browsing session (i.e., when the browser window is closed).

Using session storage to remember that fonts have loaded successfully gives us a good (albeit imperfect) approximation of the state of the browser cache. If we check the cache state and discover that the font we're trying to load is most likely in the browser cache, we can immediately start using it. This may result in a very brief flash of invisible text, but because the font is cached, this creates a more visually pleasing experience than a very brief flash of fallback fonts.

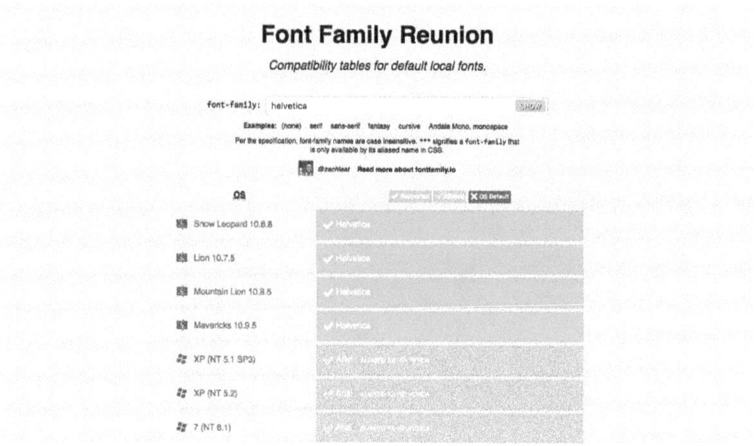

FIG 3.12: Results for Helvetica on Zach Leatherman's Font Family Reunion. Helvetica is available on macOS, but is aliased to Arial on Windows, Roboto on Android, and Liberation Sans on Linux.

The code is placed in the head of our page. On each execution of the JavaScript, session storage is checked for the `fonts-loaded` flag. If it is set, we know the fonts have been loaded earlier in the same session, and the `fonts-loaded` class is immediately set on the HTML element. If the `fonts-loaded` flag is not set, we load Font Face Observer and use it to load the webfont. Once the webfont has loaded, the code sets the `fonts-loaded` class and set the `fonts-loaded` flag in session storage:

```
var html = document.documentElement;

if (sessionStorage.fontsLoaded) {
  html.classList.add("fonts-loaded");
} else {
  var script = document.createElement("script");
  script.src = "/path/to/fontfaceobserver.js";
  script.async = true;
```

```
script.onload = function () {
  var abelard = new FontFaceObserver('Abelard');

  abelard.load().then(function () {
    html.classList.add('fonts-loaded');
    sessionStorage.fontsLoaded = true;
  });
};
document.head.appendChild(script);
}
```

The result of this trick is that on requests with an empty cache, the fonts will be loaded asynchronously. All browsers will see an initial flash of fallback fonts, followed by the webfonts. On the next request to the page (or another page on the same site), the fonts will be loaded from browser cache and be shown almost immediately if the browser session is still active (i.e., if the browser window has not been closed).

So far, I've primarily discussed optimizing font-loading by making fewer requests, caching, and loading fonts asynchronously. These optimizations assume a stable network connection. That's not always a given, though. Wouldn't it be nice to be able to use webfonts even if the network is unreliable or entirely unavailable? That's the problem offline-first webfonts attempt to solve.

OFFLINE-FIRST WEBFONTS

The basic idea behind offline-first is simple: webfonts are cached on your first visit to a page, and remain available even if the browser is offline. This is possible through the magic of *service workers*. A service worker is a script that sits between your site and the browser's cache and network stack. For our purposes, you can think of service workers as a programmable browser cache that is available even if there is no network connection.

Implementing offline support for webfonts starts by registering a service worker. The following code first checks to see if the browser supports the service worker API, and then registers the service worker once the page has loaded. Waiting for the page to load ensures that the service worker does not affect other critical assets on the page's first load.

```
<script>
if ('serviceworker' in navigator) {
  window.addEventListener('load', function () {
    navigator.serviceworker.register('/service-worker-v1.js');
  });
}
</script>
```

Next up is the service worker script itself (service-worker-v1. js). The service worker listens to two high-level events: install and fetch. The install event fires when the browser registers the service worker for the first time. You can use this event to set up a new custom cache for your site. I've called mine my-site-v1. It's a good idea to include a version number in your service worker file and cache name so you can switch to a different cache when you update your service worker.

Once the cache is open, add all assets you want cached. In this case, I've added two font files. You may notice that I've only cached font files in the WOFF2 format. That's on purpose. At the time of writing, all the browsers that support service workers also support WOFF2. Service workers can cache other assets, too, so you probably want to add your other assets to the cache.

```
self.addEventListener('install', function (event) {
  event.waitUntil(
    caches.open('my-site-v1').then(function (cache)
    {
      return cache.addAll([
        '/path/to/font-regular.woff2',
        '/path/to/font-bold.woff2'
      ]);
    })
  );
});
```

Next, set up a listener for `fetch` events, which fires each time the browser tries to fetch a resource. Instead of going directly to the network, the code first checks to see if the resource is in the custom cache. If the resource is cached, it returns the resource immediately. If the resource is not cached, it makes a network request and returns the result.

```
self.addEventListener('fetch', function (event) {
  event.respondWith(
    caches.match(event.request).then(function
(response) {
      return response || fetch(event.request);
    })
  );
});
```

That's all you need for a basic offline-first webfont implementation. There are two benefits to loading webfonts this way: the obvious advantage is that webfonts are available offline. The less obvious benefit is that by using service workers, you might get a higher cache-hit ratio on your webfonts. Unlike a regular cache, service-worker caches are only evicted once the browser runs out of cache (disk) space.

The beauty of this implementation is that it's completely orthogonal to your regular font-loading implementation. You don't need to make any changes to your client-side font-loading code. Service workers enhance the offline experience and work exclusively in the background (apart from the couple of lines that register the service worker).

Congratulations! This wraps up the longest and toughest chapter of this book. You learned about several aspects of performance:

- How to reduce the number of webfont requests by making economical typographical choices;
- The benefits of caching and the importance of using a CDN to reduce latency;
- How to reduce the file size of a webfont by removing characters, glyphs, and features you don't need;
- How to improve your perceived performance by loading fonts asynchronously;
- How to embrace FOUT and minimize its effects;
- How to make sure fonts are available offline.

In the next chapter, we'll look at some new and upcoming features that will make it easier and more efficient to load webfonts.

LOOKING AHEAD

WEBFONTS HAVE COME a long way since they first appeared on the scene in 2009. They are everywhere now. As with any web technology, webfont development continues at a steady clip. A handful of upcoming features and technologies will completely change how you load and use webfonts: the font-display descriptor, preload instructions, color fonts, and variable fonts. All of these features are at various stages of standardization and implementation. During this process, the specifications will likely change. Given the importance of these features for webfonts and web performance, however, I've decided to include them in this book. Many of the features have at least one implementation (even if experimental), which is a good first step toward becoming a recommended standard that is implemented in all browsers.

font-display

The font-display descriptor is meant to let web developers customize font-loading behavior. Instead of the browser deciding whether to use FOUT or FOIT, the font-display descriptor returns control to the developer. It takes five values: auto, block, swap, fallback, and optional. The descriptor goes inside an @font-face rule and defines the loading behavior for that font only.

```
@font-face {
  font-family: Abelard;
  src: url(abelard-regular.woff);
  font-display: block;
}
```

The initial value for the font-display descriptor is auto, which is defined as the default browser behavior. For most browsers, this is likely to be block or swap, because they are closest to existing FOIT and FOUT implementations (FIG 4.1).
The block value blocks the rendering of webfonts until either the webfont loads, or three seconds have passed since loading started (FIG 4.2). If the font loads, it will be rendered

auto	DEFAULT BROWSER BEHAVIOR (INITIAL VALUE).
block	Block rendering while downloading the webfont for up to three seconds. After three seconds the fallback font will be shown. If the webfont loads afterwards, show the webfont.
swap	Show the fallback font right away and the webfont when it loads.
fallback	Show the webfont if it is available within 100ms. If it is not available, show the fallback font. If the webfont takes longer than three seconds to load, continue showing the fallback font.
optional	Show the webfont if it is available within 100ms, otherwise show the fallback font indefinitely.

FIG 4.1: Overview of the font display values and how they affect font display behavior. The font display property does not affect font-loading itself, but only how the browser behaves while fonts are loading.

immediately. The block value is useful when the text needs to be shown using the webfont. Take a type designer's website showcasing typefaces, for example. Showing fallback fonts would not be a good experience in this case.

If more than three seconds have passed, a fallback font will be shown. Font-loading continues even after the fallback font has been shown. If the webfont eventually loads, it will replace the fallback font. This behavior is similar to a flash of invisible text, or FOIT (**FIG 4.3**).

Unlike block, swap does not block rendering and shows the fallback font immediately. Once the webfont loads, the fallback font is replaced. The swap value is a good default for font-loading: it shows content early and assumes webfonts load in a timely manner.

There is no timeout associated with swap, so, as with block, the webfont will be shown whenever it loads, even if that takes a long time. This can prove very distracting for readers. If the font takes ten seconds to load (which isn't unthinkable for a large font on a slow network connection), replacing it creates

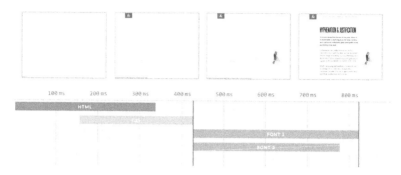

FIG 4.2: Even though the content has already loaded,   blocks the rendering of text while the font is loading.

FIG 4.3: Using   to show a fallback font while the webfont is loading. When the font loads, the fallback font is replaced.

a jarring experience. And because the fallback font likely has different metrics from the webfont, replacing it makes the text appear to shift around.

The fallback value attempts to solve this problem. If the font is available in cache or can be retrieved within 100 milliseconds, it will be shown immediately (**FIG 4.4**). This avoids the reflow that happens when a fallback font is replaced by a webfont. And it's especially helpful when most of your customer base is on slower connections, and you consider webfonts important—but not critical—to the user experience.

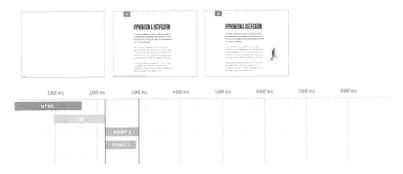

FIG 4.4: Using *fallback*, the font is shown immediately if it loads within 100 milliseconds (from the point the webfonts start loading).

If the font is not in cache, or takes longer than 100 milliseconds, the fallback font will be shown. If the font loads within three seconds, it will be displayed when it loads. But if the font takes more than three seconds to load, the fallback font will continue to show. The assumption here is that replacing the fallback font within three seconds is less disruptive than replacing it later (FIG 4.5).

Depending on your target audience, a higher or lower timeout figure may be more appropriate. For people on fast network connections, three seconds may be too long; for those on slow connections, three seconds may be too short. Unfortunately, it is not yet possible to configure the timeout values. Future iterations of the *font-display* descriptor will, I hope, make it possible to configure timeouts for each value.

The last value is *optional*, which only shows a webfont if it can be loaded within 100 milliseconds. Even though a webfont won't appear if it takes longer than 100 milliseconds to load, the browser will continue to download the font (albeit with a lower priority). This means that, most likely, the very first request with an empty cache will not display the font, but subsequent requests will show the font immediately. Using *optional* is a good choice when you consider a webfont truly optional, for example when it is used decoratively.

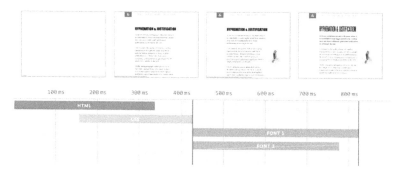

FIG 4.5: The   value in action. Once the content has loaded, fallback fonts are shown immediately. If the webfont loads within the timeout, it replaces the fallback font.

Even though the font-display descriptor is still a draft specification, it's already implemented in Chrome and Opera, and in Firefox behind a configuration option. That means you can start experimenting with it today.

PRELOAD

When web browsers encounter an @font-face rule, they don't immediately download the font (except versions of Internet Explorer 8 and below, which always download all fonts). Instead, they wait until they know that the font is used on the page. This seems like a great optimization. Why download something you don't need?

Let's dig into this a bit further. The following three @font-face rules define three styles of the same font family: a regular style, a bold, and an italic. If a page uses only the regular style, the browser will only download the regular font file. If another page uses regular and bold, both files will be downloaded (or retrieved from cache). And so on. This is, as we recall from Chapter 2, lazy loading: fonts are only downloaded when they are used on the page (**FIG 4.6**).

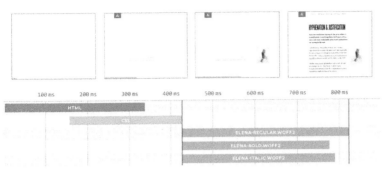

FIG 4.6: Webfont lazy loading. The fonts do not start loading until the HTML and CSS have fully loaded at 400 milliseconds.

```
@font-face {
    font-family: Elena;
    src: url(elena-regular.woff2) format("woff2"),
        url(elena-regular.woff) format("woff");
}

@font-face {
    font-family: Elena;
    src: url(elena-bold.woff2) format("woff2"),
        url(elena-bold.woff) format("woff");
    font-weight: bold;
}

@font-face {
    font-family: Elena;
    src: url(elena-italic.woff2) format("woff2"),
        url(elena-italic.woff) format("woff");
    font-style: italic;
}
```

However, this also means that the browser needs to know about the contents of the page; that information is stored in the text nodes of the DOM. Additionally, the browser needs to know which fonts are used for each text node. Style information is stored in the CSSOM. Only by cross-referencing the DOM and CSSOM can the browser figure out which fonts are used on the page.

In other words, the browser needs a fully constructed DOM and CSSOM before it can start downloading webfonts. Unfortunately, the DOM and CSSOM often depend on loading resources like external stylesheets over the network. Thus, webfonts won't start loading until quite late in the page-load process.

This is a bit silly. Web developers know—or should know— whether a font is used on the page. After all, they're the ones who include the `@font-face` rules in the first place. Alas, the browser needs to figure this out by itself. For some resources, like images, this is fine, but as we saw in Chapter 3, webfonts are a render-blocking resource. We shouldn't have to wait for the browser to figure this out. We need a way to tell the browser that webfonts are critical and should be loaded as soon as possible.

Luckily, a new specification does exactly that. It's called `preload`, and it lets web developers specify which resources should be preloaded by the browser. At the time of writing, browser support for preload is limited to Chrome and Opera, but it will likely soon find its way into other browsers.

Preload can be used in two different ways: as a `link` element or as an HTTP header. The `link` element contains a reference to the resource that should be preloaded. It also has a new attribute, `as`, which tells the browser what type of resource it is and how it should be prioritized. For example, if the browser knows that webfonts are render-blocking, it can prioritize them before other (preloaded) resources. The `type` attribute tells the browser what media type (sometimes also called MIME type) the resource has. It can use this to select the most optimal format, or to skip downloading a resource if it doesn't support that format. The `crossorigin` attribute is required because, in most browsers, fonts are subject to *cross-origin resource sharing* (CORS), which defines the rules around requesting resources like fonts from other domains.

```
<head>
  ...
  <link rel="preload" href="elena-regular.woff2"
  as="font" type="font/woff2" crossorigin>
  ...
</head>
```

Alternatively, it's also possible to set an HTTP Link header on either the HTML or CSS file. The syntax is slightly different, but it conveys the same meaning as the HTML link element.

```
Link: <elena-regular.woff2>; rel=preload; as=font;
  type="font/woff2"; crossorigin
```

The performance improvement of using preload is nothing short of amazing when looking at a network timeline (FIG 4.7). The regular style loads much earlier than the other styles. In fact, using preload in combination with subsetting and caching can either eliminate FOUT entirely or, at the very least, significantly reduce it.

Preload should only be used for your most critical webfonts—for example, fonts used to render body text or headlines. Preloading every font on your site defeats the point of prioritizing one font over another: if everything is important, nothing is.

Another interesting side effect of using preload only for the regular style is that the browser will generate synthesized italic and bold styles while the real ones are still loading. (Revisit the section on font synthesis in Chapter 2 for why, and when, the browser synthesizes styles.) Even though synthesized styles are generally considered undesirable, they approach the style of the specified webfont better than a fallback font ever could. This means that when the other styles eventually load, the switch from synthesized style to the real one will be barely noticeable.

Because browsers that don't support preload will ignore preload instructions, it's safe to start including them on your site. Once other browsers start supporting the preload specification, you'll get a nice performance improvement without having to do anything. Preload works best with self-hosted fonts, but can also work with webfont services whose font files are publicly accessible and have stable URLs.

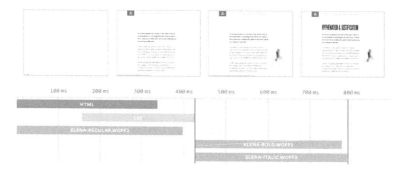

FIG 4.7: By preloading elena-regular.woff, the browser can render the main body text much earlier than the default lazy loading. (In this case, it even finishes before the HTML and CSS are fully loaded.)

COLOR FONTS

Until recently, all type has been a single color. Type could *have* a color, but it would be a single solid color, without gradients or transparency. This has worked well for years (centuries, even)—but the prevalence of emoji has forced font technology to adopt a more colorful stance. Without color, displaying emoji would be incredibly difficult—and much less fun. (FIG 4.8).

Apple, Google, and Microsoft have long had their own their own proprietary OpenType color-font extensions, which were only supported in their own ecosystems. There is also a fourth color-font extension that resulted from a collaboration between Adobe and Mozilla.

All four color-font extensions have been adopted by the OpenType standard. Thus, there are now four competing color-font extensions in the OpenType specification (FIG 4.9).

Two of the formats (by Apple and Google) are image-based; they embed images inside the font. This works well for font sizes that match the original resolution of the images, but as soon as the text size is increased or decreased, the images become blurry. The Microsoft format is based on layering outlines and giving each layer a color. While this approach allows

FIG 4.8: Emoji, often colorful, are difficult to represent with a single color. These emoji are part of the EmojiOne package, which is also available as an OpenType SVG font.

SBIX	Apple	PNG/JPEG/TIFF stored in the font.
CBDT/CBLC	Google	PNG stored in the font.
COLR/CPAL	Microsoft	Overlapping layers with color palettes.
SVG	Adobe & Mozilla	SVG stored in the font.

FIG 4.9: Overview of color-font extensions in OpenType, and what makes them unique.

for multiple colors, it has a couple of drawbacks: it doesn't support gradients and transparency, and it is difficult to decompose drawings into layers.

The SVG OpenType extension embeds SVG files inside a font. This means that the full power of SVG is available: colors, gradients, transparency, and even animation. (Implementations are not required to support animation, though, so don't get your hopes up for crazy animated fonts). Because SVG is vector-based, it will scale as well as a regular font.

FIG 4.10: Bixa Color by Novo Typo, the first commercially available OpenType SVG font.

Even though the color-font extensions have limited browser support, there are already several commercially available color fonts: Bixa Color by Novo Typo (**FIG 4.10**), Bungee by David Jonathan Ross, and Trajan Color by Adobe. Based on these font releases, it appears that type designers favor the SVG OpenType extension over the others. Be sure to keep an eye on these developments.

VARIABLE FONTS

At the ATypI conference in Warsaw in 2016, a significant addition to the OpenType specification was announced: OpenType variations, also called variable fonts. Unlike a regular font, a variable font can contain the entire design space of a typeface. A *design space* consists, theoretically, of all the possible styles of a typeface, and is defined by one or multiple axes along which the design varies.

For example, consider a typeface that has thin, light, regular, semibold, bold, and black weights. Instead of storing those weights as individual font files, a variable font contains the outline data for a single weight plus instructions for deriving the other weights. All other styles are *interpolated* at runtime. This allows the operating system to generate any style based on a single outline, creating near-infinite possibilities for weights (**FIG 4.11**).

One important limitation of variable-font technology is that interpolation only works between outlines that have the same number of Bézier control points. It's not possible for new control points to appear during the interpolation. However, control points can be added by using variation alternates or feature variations, at the cost of storing an additional outline. This limitation will affect styles that differ significantly from the default, like italics, which will most likely continue to be a separate (variable) font.

Weight is not the only axis in a variable font. There are four other registered axes: width (**FIG 4.12**), optical size, italic, and slant. Type designers can also define their own axes, leading to infinitely flexible typography. This is not only very exciting for typeface designers, but also for web developers.

Variable fonts will bring many benefits to web development. In the short term, we'll likely see performance improvements. The extent of these performance gains will depend on the fonts you use and the design of your site. Take a very simple variable font with a weight axis, for example. If you only use a single weight of this variable font, you won't see any performance benefit. In fact, because the variable font contains the outlines and interpolation instructions, you may even see a slight increase in file size. If you use two or more weights, however, you'll start seeing benefits, since all other weights will be interpolated based on the same outline data.

The performance results become more difficult to anticipate when a variable font has more than two axes. What's certain, however, is that variable fonts will make it possible to start using more styles for the same performance cost. Over the long term, we'll start seeing more and more type that adapts to its container, creating exciting new opportunities for truly responsive design and richer web typography.

Browser vendors and the W3C are currently working on changing the CSS font specification to support OpenType vari-

FIG 4.11: Instances of the weight axis of a lowercase *e* in Amstelvar (by David Berlow of Font Bureau). The default weight is highlighted in red and the interpolated weights are shown in black.

FIG 4.12: Instances of the width axis in Amstelvar. Interpolation gives designers access to any width instance along the entire axis. The default width is highlighted in red, and the interpolated widths are shown in black.

ations. The proposal doesn't just define new properties for variable fonts; it also modifies existing CSS properties; the font-weight, font-style, and font-stretch properties will be modified to accept a numerical value in addition to their current values. For example, font-weight will be changed so that it accepts any value from 1 to 999. These values will map to the standardized weight axis in a variable font.

```
p {
    font-family: Amstelvar, serif;
    font-weight: 652;
}
```

The font-style and font-stretch properties are extended in a similar manner and map to the width and slant axis within a variable font.

The CSS draft for variable fonts also introduces two new properties: font-optical-sizing and font-variation-settings. When enabled, the font-optical-sizing property lets the browser automatically select an appropriate optical size based on the font size and screen pixel density. Optical sizes are size-specific versions of the same glyph, often made to improve legibility and readability in running text (where finer design details get lost), or to show off more finesse when set large.

The font-variation-settings property is a low-level way to access and manipulate standard and custom variable font axes. The syntax is similar to font-feature-settings: the property takes one or multiple axes names with a value. In the following example, I set the standard weight axis to 541 (equivalent to font-weight: 541) and the custom x-height axis to 672.

```
p {
    /* Set the x-height axis to 672, and the weight
    axis to 541 */
    font-variation-settings: "xhgt" 672, "wght" 541;
}
```

This amazing flexibility means variable fonts will also make great fallback fonts, because they can be tweaked to have similar metrics to webfonts. I'm hopeful that once the major operating systems support variable fonts, we'll also start seeing variable system fonts.

And with that, we've reached the end of this chapter. As you can see, there are many exciting—and, most important, useful—new developments in web typography. Keep an eye on these technologies. They will change the way you use and think about webfonts.

CONCLUSION

I hope this book has shown that webfonts are, more than anything else, an enhancement—a useful, beautiful tool for improving the design and readability of your site. But webfonts are *optional*. If you treat them as an enhancement, most problems associated with them go away.

You just need to keep a couple of simple ground rules in mind. Don't rely on browser defaults—hiding text from your visitors while webfonts are loading results in a terrible user experience. Always load your fonts asynchronously so they don't block a page from rendering. In the worst case, your fonts will fail to load and your visitors will see fallback fonts. That's fine. That's how the web is supposed to work. And fallback fonts are not "unstyled" text, so don't forget to style them.

Always optimize your webfonts if the license allows it. Using the right font format and subsetting will significantly reduce a font's file size and make it load faster. Analyze the font styles used on your site, and be considerate about the number of styles you want to use so that you can reduce the number of downloads. Don't forget about caching. The quickest request is from the browser cache.

The future of webfont-loading performance looks bright. By combining `font-display` and preload instructions, you'll be able to solve most webfont-loading issues easily. In addition, you'll soon be able to start dropping support for older webfont formats. EOT is only necessary for Internet Explorer 8 and below, and raw OpenType files are only necessary for Android versions prior to 4.4. If usage of those browsers continues to decline, you'll be able to serve only WOFF and WOFF2 in the future.

This massively simplifies loading webfonts. Just put `@font-face` rules in your CSS with the `font-display` descriptor set to `fallback`. This will give you a good loading experience; if the webfont is cached, it will be used immediately. If the font is not cached, your visitors will see fallback fonts until the webfonts load:

```
@font-face {
  font-family: Abelard;
  src: url(path/to/abelard-regular.woff2)
  format("woff2"),
      url(path/to/abelard-regular.woff)
  format("woff");
  font-display: fallback;
}

@font-face {
  font-family: Abelard;
  src: url(path/to/abelard-italic.woff2)
  format("woff2"),
      url(path/to/abelard-italic.woff)
  format("woff");
  font-style: italic;
  font-display: fallback;
}
```

Then, in the head of your HTML files, put a preload directive for the regular weight. This will guarantee that the regular weight is loaded as soon as possible:

```
<link rel="preload" href="abelard-regular.woff2"
  as="font" type="font/woff2" crossorigin>
```

That's all there is to it. With native font-display and preload support, you won't need to modify your font stacks or use JavaScript to load fonts. Of course, we're not quite there yet, so until then, use the asynchronous font-loading strategy described in this book.

Web design and development differ from other disciplines insofar as their environment is relatively uncontrolled. You can never really know in what context people will consume your content. It could land anywhere—big screens, small screens, old browsers, slow network connections. You need to design and account for all of those possibilities.

By harnessing techniques from this book, you'll be able to use webfonts in the best possible way: as *progressive enhancement*. Treat fallback fonts as a baseline experience and enhance that with webfonts. Remember: your site doesn't need to look identical in each circumstance, as long as it is *accessible*. People who visit your site will thank you.

RESOURCES

While writing this brief, I referenced many articles, books, and tools created by a wonderful and diverse community of web designers, developers, and type designers. I've tried to catalog some of my favorite websites, articles, tools, and books here. This list is by no means exhaustive, but it should provide a good starting point for your own research. I've also created a companion site, webfonthandbook.com, where a version of this list will evolve to keep pace with current developments.

- A Comprehensive Guide to Font Loading Strategies: The title says it all. This is an excellent in-depth guide on font-loading strategies.
- Alphabettes: A showcase for work, commentary, criticism, and research on lettering, typography, and type design.
- CSS Fonts Specification: The CSS specification for fonts. Don't be afraid to read specifications; they are excellent resources.
- Fonts in Use: A source of inspiration for designing with type and a showcase for how fonts are used in the wild.
- The Raster Tragedy at Low Resolution Revisited: A must-read resource if you're interested in type rendering, antialiasing, or gamma correction.
- Typekit Practice: A collection of lessons, exercises, and references on typography.
- Typographica: An excellent resource for learning about high-quality typefaces for your projects.
- Web Font Anti-Patterns: An ongoing series on webfont-loading antipatterns: find out how *not* to load webfonts.
- Web Font Loading Patterns: An overview of font-loading best practices: how to prioritize one webfont over another, group loading, use timeouts, and more.
- Web Fundamentals: A guide by Google on how to build an excellent web experience. It covers performance, architecture, offline loading, security, and design.

Tools

Throughout this book, I've introduced several tools that will help you use or create webfonts. It's impossible to cover all the great tools I use, but I've tried to list some of the best here. All of these tools are either open-source or free to use.

- AxisPraxis: A playground for trying out variable fonts.
- ChromaCheck: A tool that detects your browser's support for color fonts.
- Font Face Observer: A fast and simple webfont-loading JavaScript library. Font Face Observer is more low-level than the Web Font Loader, but also much more powerful. *Disclaimer: I wrote Font Face Observer, so I may be a little very biased.*
- Font Family Reunion: Compatibility tables showing the availability of common locally installed fonts on various operating systems. Very useful when creating reliable font fallback stacks.
- Font style matcher: A tool for matching fallback and webfonts using font size, letter spacing, and word spacing.
- FontSquirrel Webfont Generator: An online tool to easily create font subsets. It will also generate all webfont formats for you.
- FontTools: A great collection of tools for manipulating and creating fonts. You need to be comfortable with the command line to use FontTools.
- GlyphHanger: A utility to automatically create subsets based on the content of your site.
- Homebrew Webfont Tools: If you're on macOS, you can use this Homebrew repository to easily install common webfont tools.
- Size Calculator: A tool for calculating the viewing distance, physical size, and perceived size of type.
- The State of Web Type: Up-to-date data on browser support for type and typographic features in CSS. Much like CanIUse, but with a more in-depth focus on type and typography.

- Type Rendering Mix: A JavaScript library that detects your browser's text-rendering engine and antialiasing settings, so you can apply custom styles.
- WebPagetest: A service to test and visualize your site's performance. Very helpful in finding and resolving performance issues.
- Web Font Loader: A JavaScript library you can use to customize font-loading. It has plugins to load fonts from Google Fonts, Typekit, and Fonts.com, as well as self-hosted fonts.
- Web Font Specimen: A specimen page for testing how a typeface behaves in various settings. Useful when you're comparing typefaces and testing how they render on various operating systems and devices.

Further Reading

There are many great books on type and typography. These, however, have a special place in my heart. I recommend you buy and read them.

- Tim Brown, *Combining Typefaces*
- Donald E. Knuth, *Digital Typography*
- Cyrus Highsmith, *Inside Paragraphs*
- Jason Santa Maria, *On Web Typography*
- Robert Bringhurst, *The Elements of Typographic Style*
- Richard Rutter, *Web Typography*

ACKNOWLEDGEMENTS

This book would not exist without help from the A Book Apart team: Caren Litherland, Katel LeDû, and Tina Lee. Thanks for challenging and encouraging me, and for making my thoughts sound coherent. I couldn't have written this book without you. To Bianca Berning: thank you for being my tech editor. Your feedback has made this book better than I ever imagined it could be. To Indra Kupferschmid: thank you for writing the foreword—I'm honored.

A very special thanks to Tim Brown, without whom this book would not exist. Thank you for your encouragement, advice, and years of friendship.

Thanks to everyone who provided invaluable feedback on early drafts: Allen Tan, Ben Mitchell, Christopher Slye, Dave Arnold, Elliot Jay Stocks, Frank Grießhammer, Indra Kupferschmid, Jake Giltsoff, Liz Galle, Marko Iskander, Myles C. Maxfield, Persa Zula, Robin Rendle, Roel Nieskens, Wenting Zhang, and Zach Leatherman.

Finally, many thanks to my wife for her patience during the evenings and weekends I was working on this book instead of spending time with our family. A big hug to my son Alex; you're (literally) the reason I get up every morning. I love you both.

REFERENCES:
WEBFONT HANDBOOK

Shortened URLs are numbered sequentially; the related long
URLs are listed below for reference.

Introduction

00-01 https://www.zachleat.com/web/mitt-romney-webfont-problem/

Chapter 1

01-01 https://processtypefoundry.com/fonts/elena/
01-02 https://typekit.com/
01-03 https://www.fonts.com/
01-04 http://www.typenetwork.com/
01-05 https://www.typography.com/
01-06 https://fontstand.com/
01-07 https://fonts.google.com/
01-08 https://github.com/adobe-fonts/source-sans-pro
01-09 https://fonts.google.com/specimen/Open+Sans
01-10 https://github.com/mozilla/Fira
01-11 https://blog.typekit.com/2015/08/11/well-that-was-just-awful-details-on-yesterdays-font-serving-outage/
01-12 http://typerendering.com/
01-13 https://www.html5rocks.com/en/tutorials/internals/antialiasing-101/
01-14 http://webfontspecimen.com/
01-15 https://statcounter.com/
01-16 http://practicaltypography.com/small-caps.html
01-17 http://caniuse.com/#feat=font-variant-alternates
01-18 https://practice.typekit.com/lesson/caring-about-opentype-features/

Chapter 2

02-01 https://developer.mozilla.org/en-US/docs/Web/CSS/font-weight
02-02 https://developer.mozilla.org/en-US/docs/Web/CSS/font-style

02-03 https://developer.mozilla.org/en-US/docs/Web/CSS/font-stretch

02-04 https://helpx.adobe.com/typekit/using/ot-svg-color-fonts.html

02-05 http://blog.fontspring.com/2011/02/the-new-bulletproof-font-face-syntax/

02-06 http://minimore.com/

02-07 https://www.doubleclickbygoogle.com/articles/mobile-speed-matters/

Chapter 3

03-01 https://abookapart.com/products/responsible-responsive-design

03-02 https://medium.design/system-shock-6b1dc6d6596f

03-03 https://drafts.csswg.org/css-fonts-4/#extended-generics

03-04 http://www.guypo.com/why-inlining-everything-is-not-the-answer/

03-05 http://bramstein.com/writing/web-font-anti-patterns-inlining.html#base64-encoding-and-decoding

03-06 https://httpstatuses.com/304

03-07 https://developers.google.com/web/fundamentals/performance/optimizing-content-efficiency/http-caching

03-08 https://github.com/adobe-fonts/source-sans-pro

03-09 https://www.fontsquirrel.com/tools/webfont-generator

03-10 https://github.com/fonttools/fonttools

03-11 https://github.com/filamentgroup/glyphhanger

03-12 https://drafts.csswg.org/css-font-loading/

03-13 https://github.com/typekit/webfontloader

03-14 https://fontfaceobserver.com/

03-15 http://caniuse.com/#feat=font-loading

03-16 https://frerejones.com/blog/typeface-mechanics-001

03-17 https://meowni.ca/font-style-matcher/

03-18 http://caniuse.com/#search=font-size-adjust

03-19 http://input.fontbureau.com/systemfont/

03-20 http://fontfamily.io/

03-21 https://developers.google.com/web/fundamentals/instant-and-offline/service-worker/registration

Chapter 4

04-01 http://tabatkins.github.io/specs/css-font-display/

04-02 https://w3c.github.io/preload/

04-03 http://caniuse.com/#feat=link-rel-preload

04-04 https://www.emojione.com/

04-05 http://stateofwebtype.com/#color%2520fonts

04-06 https://bixacolor.com/

04-07 https://djr.com/bungee/

04-08 https://typekit.com/fonts/trajan-color

04-09 https://www.youtube.com/watch?v=6kizDePhcFU&feature=youtu.be

04-10 https://medium.com/@tiro/https-medium-com-tiro-introducing-open-type-variable-fonts-12ba6cd2369

04-11 http://fontbureau.typenetwork.com/

04-12 https://www.microsoft.com/typography/otspec/fvar.htm#VAT

04-13 https://drafts.csswg.org/css-fonts-4/#extended-generics

Resources

05-01 http://webfonthandbook.com

05-02 https://www.zachleat.com/web/comprehensive-webfonts/

05-03 http://www.alphabettes.org

05-04 https://www.w3.org/TR/css-fonts-3/

05-05 https://fontsinuse.com/

05-06 http://www.rastertragedy.com/

05-07 https://practice.typekit.net

05-08 https://typographica.org/

05-09 http://bramstein.com/writing/web-font-anti-patterns.html

05-10 http://bramstein.com/writing/web-font-loading-patterns.html

05-11 https://developers.google.com/web/fundamentals/

05-12 http://www.axis-praxis.org/

05-13 https://github.com/roeln/chromacheck

05-14 https://fontfaceobserver.com/

05-15 http://fontfamily.io/

05-16 https://meowni.ca/font-style-matcher/

05-17 https://www.fontsquirrel.com/tools/webfont-generator

05-18 https://github.com/fonttools/fonttools

05-19 https://github.com/filamentgroup/glyphhanger

05-20 https://github.com/bramstein/homebrew-webfonttools

05-21 https://sizecalc.com/

05-22 http://stateofwebtype.com/#color%2520fonts

05-23 http://typerendering.com/

05-24 https://www.webpagetest.org/

05-25 https://github.com/typekit/webfontloader

05-26 http://webfontspecimen.com/

INDEX:
WEBFONT HANDBOOK

ABOUT THE AUTHOR

Bram Stein is a developer and product manager. He cares a lot about typography and is happiest working at the intersection between design and technology. In his spare time, he maintains Font Face Observer, Type Inspector, and several other tools for improving web typography.

Bram writes for several magazines and is a contributing author to *Smashing Book 5*. He also speaks about typography and web performance at conferences around the world.

Printed in the USA
CPSIA information can be obtained
at www.ICGtesting.com
LVHW060239290124
768939LV00031B/3